booksonline

Read this book online today:

With SAP PRESS BooksOnline we offer you online access to knowledge from the leading SAP experts. Whether you use it as a beneficial supplement or as an alternative to the printed book, with SAP PRESS BooksOnline you can:

• Access your book anywhere, at any time. All you need is an Internet connection.
• Perform full text searches on your book and on the entire SAP PRESS library.
• Build your own personalized SAP library.

The SAP PRESS customer advantage:

Register this book today at *www.sap-press.com* and obtain exclusive free trial access to its online version. If you like it (and we think you will), you can choose to purchase permanent, unrestricted access to the online edition at a very special price!

Here's how to get started:

1. Visit *www.sap-press.com*.
2. Click on the link for SAP PRESS BooksOnline and login (or create an account).
3. Enter your free trial license key, shown below in the corner of the page.
4. Try out your online book with full, unrestricted access for a limited time!

Your personal free trial **license key**
for this online book is:

jan9-spv3-8ywm-xg27

Integrating SAP® ERP Financials

 PRESS

SAP PRESS is a joint initiative of SAP and Galileo Press. The know-how offered by SAP specialists combined with the expertise of the Galileo Press publishing house offers the reader expert books in the field. SAP PRESS features first-hand information and expert advice, and provides useful skills for professional decision-making.

SAP PRESS offers a variety of books on technical and business related topics for the SAP user. For further information, please visit our website: *www.sap-press.com*.

Vincenzo Sopracolle
Quick Reference Guide: Financial Accounting with SAP
2010, app. 650 pp.
978-1-59229-313-1

Naeem Arif, Sheikh Muhammad Tauseef
SAP ERP Financials: Configuration and Design
2008, app. 450 pp.
978-1-59229-136-6

Shivesh Sharma
Optimize Your SAP ERP Financials Implementation
2008, app. 700 pp.
978-1-59229-160-1

Manish Patel
Discover SAP ERP Financials
2008, app. 550 pp.
978-1-59229-184-7

Naeem Arif and Sheikh Muhammad Tauseef

Integrating SAP® ERP Financials

Configuration and Design

Galileo Press

Bonn • Boston

Galileo Press is named after the Italian physicist, mathematician and philosopher Galileo Galilei (1564–1642). He is known as one of the founders of modern science and an advocate of our contemporary, heliocentric worldview. His words *Eppur se muove* (And yet it moves) have become legendary. The Galileo Press logo depicts Jupiter orbited by the four Galilean moons, which were discovered by Galileo in 1610.

Editor Kelly Grace Harris
Copyeditor Julie McNamee
Cover Design Graham Geary
Photo Credit iStockphoto.com/seraficus
Layout Design Vera Brauner
Production Manager Kelly O'Callaghan
Production Editor Graham Geary
Typesetting Publishers' Design and Production Services, Inc.
Printed and bound in Canada

ISBN 978-1-59229-300-1

© 2011 by Galileo Press Inc., Boston (MA)

1st Edition 2011

Library of Congress Cataloging-in-Publication Data
Arif, Naeem.
    Integrating SAP ERP financials : configuration and design / Naeem Arif, Sheikh Tauseef. — 1st ed.
        p. cm.
    ISBN-13: 978-1-59229-300-1
    ISBN-10: 1-59229-300-X
    1. SAP ERP. 2. Accounting—Computer programs. 3. Accounting—Data processing. 4. Investments.
I. Tauseef, Sheikh. II. Title.
    HF5679.A75 2010
    657.0285'53—dc22
    2010035941

Contents at a Glance

Dear Reader,

If your company is moving or has recently moved to ECC 6.0 and you're using or planning to use SAP General Ledger, you need to understand how the integration works. In their second book, Naeem Arif and Sheikh Muhammad Tauseef will help you navigate these complicated waters by offering a clear, concise manual on integration with SAP ERP Financials. The book focuses on the end-to-end processes used in business scenarios (sales order to cash receipt, procure to pay, etc.), and explains the key integration points in each.

Although this is Naeem's and Tauseef's second book with SAP PRESS, it was my first opportunity to work with them personally, and it was a pleasure to witness their dedication to the manuscript and their continued efforts to make sure they covered all their bases. I'm confident that you will find this second book an excellent complement to their first, *SAP ERP Financials: Configuration and Design*.

We always look forward to praise, but are also interested in constructive feedback that will help us improve our books. We encourage you to visit our website at *www.sap-press.com* and share your feedback about this work.

Thank you for purchasing a book from SAP PRESS!

Kelly Grace Harris
Editor, SAP PRESS

Galileo Press
100 Grossman Drive, Suite 205
Braintree, MA 02184

kelly.harris@galileo-press.com
www.sap-press.com

Contents

4   Integrating the Purchase-Order-to-Payment Process   139

5 Integrating SAP ERP HCM with SAP ERP Financials 211

6 Integrating Asset Accounting, Investment Management, and Project Systems ... 257

Preface

Welcome to *Integrating SAP ERP Financials*, our second book, which builds on the information presented in our first book, *SAP ERP Financials: Configuration and Design* (also published by SAP PRESS). In the SAP world, after consultants understand the configuration and design of their primary component, they often branch out to look at the connection points, or integration points, with other components. This book is designed to explain these integration points by discussing how SAP ERP Financials links to other components. We also consider, from a business point of view, how you can maximize the business processes associated with these components. If you are familiar with our first book, this book will enable you to build on your knowledge and take your understanding to another level.

Similar to our first book, this book takes a process-based view and looks at both the configuration and design steps to provide real examples of how each activity should be configured on an SAP ERP 6.0 system.

Why This Book?

In 2008, I (Naeem Arif) was first invited by SAP to present at the SAP Financials (Europe) conferences. The topic I was asked to speak about was entitled "An In-Depth Guide to SAP System Integration Points to Ensure Financial Process Optimization." I set off with great excitement, knowing this was a topic that none of the other presenters had really wanted — people always knew a little bit here and a little bit there, but no one had attempted to cover it all. Excitement quickly turned into a mass of questions, which in turn became a long list of topics that could be included. Panic set in: Where do we draw the line with SAP when the whole system is a nothing short of an Aladdin's cove of integration points?

I called Tauseef, and we decided to sit down and discuss our experiences and so agree what the audience would want to hear. Several meetings later, we arrived at the conclusion that, for such an important subject area, few information sources are readily available. No courses taught SAP integration; instead, consultants became component experts and then naturally evolved into integration consultants (as opposed to being trained as such). Tauseef and I had spent so much time helping our Logistics and HCM colleagues that we had amassed a great wealth of knowledge on a number of topics, which we had taken for granted. In reality, this level of knowledge and understanding was sparse in the marketplace; people had a good understanding of specific areas, but not a wide understanding across the core SAP ERP components. As we put together a long list and then shortened it to include in the SAP Financials presentation, the idea emerged that we should scope a manuscript for all the relevant topics we had discussed. Following the good feedback from the 2008 and 2009 conferences, we tailored the contents of this book based on the questions the audiences asked. The more we thought about it, the more we realized that this important topic does not get as much coverage as it deserves.

After contacting SAP PRESS, they were very excited about what we had to offer and were keen to work with us again. We decided right at the start to scope based on what the reader would want to read, focusing on the common problems and gaps in knowledge that we would expect them to have. Using this approach, we agreed on an adventurous range of topics that we felt would best suit the reader. In reading this book, we hope you will feel that this approach has been beneficial to you and that you gain a good understanding of the integration points in the processes listed, as well as a good understanding of how the configurations in SD, MM, and HR impact financial processes. This is what we set out to explain and what we have delivered.

If you enjoyed reading *SAP ERP Financials: Configuration and Design*, this second book should complete your journey of expanding your understanding beyond just SAP ERP Financials. By understanding the topic of integration, you will be able to improve the quality of any SAP ERP implementation and support a wider range of components and processes. We are extremely pleased with the content we have managed to squeeze into this book, and we hope you will benefit greatly by it.

Objectives

No two SAP solutions are the same, so it is always difficult to explain to someone how a specific solution should be provided. When reading this book, you should look at the examples given and then apply them to your own situation to best decide how to satisfy your business requirements. SAP has evolved so much over the past 18 years that there is a solution for the majority of business processes across the globe. For this reason, never believe that SAP cannot satisfy a business process — some custom development may be necessary, but it can almost always be done.

Although not everyone has read our previous book, this book builds on where *SAP ERP Financials: Configuration and Design* left off. Having understood the configuration and design of the SAP ERP Financials component, we now take you outside this component and look at the various touchpoints with the other components. In this book, we look at the following key processes:

▸ Sales order to cash

▸ Purchase order to payment

▸ Payroll

▸ Asset Accounting (AA) with Investment Management

For each process, we review the configuration and design. To achieve this, we explain the configuration and design on the non-Financials components as well. After finishing each chapter, you'll understand the configuration of parts of Sales and Distribution (SD), Materials Management (MM), Payroll, and Investment Management. Because of the comprehensive coverage of these areas, you'll understand and be able to speak about each of these processes confidently.

Figure 1 shows the links between various components to see how each connects to the SAP General Ledger. This concept of links serves as the basis for this book, and we will cover each area in detail as we move through the text.

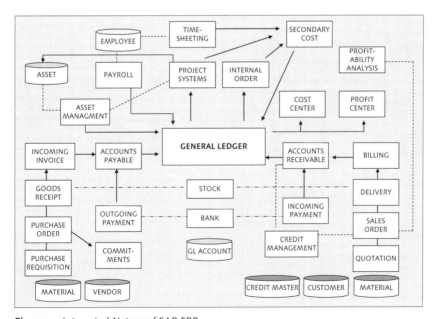

Figure 1 Integrated Nature of SAP ERP

Prerequisites

We have written this book from basic SAP principles and explain each step clearly, so that you can use the content no matter what your level of knowledge of SAP principles. We cater to a variety of SAP users in both Finance and Logistics, including payroll consultants, integration managers, process consultants, test managers, and even project managers.

This book is written as an end-to-end read, but you can pick those chapters and areas that interest you most. Understand, however, that from an SAP point of view, simply trying to learn from a book or a course will only take you so far. To have a fully effective learning experience, you must be able to look at the screens and apply your learning with some practical exercises. Although there are no exercises or activities for you to perform in this book, we assume that you will cement your learning by recreating the configuration steps using the SAP software.

Approach

The approach we take in this book is to look at the user's perspective, using a process point of view. This is because people who work in an organization are more likely to know what their business function is than the SAP ERP subcomponents that they access.

Looking back at Figure 1, we represent a typical organization's business processes in terms of the main documents produced in each stage. If you start in the bottom-right corner, you see the process of a customer making a sales order following through to the receipt of the incoming payment. On the left side, you start with an outgoing purchase order and end this business by making the outgoing payment. In the middle are the finance elements, and toward the top right, you see the controlling objects, which are important to these processes.

We'll use this diagram as a guide through the book as we talk about each of these objects and how they play their part in integrating SAP ERP Financials.

Acknowledgments

Naeem Arif

I have once again called upon the patience of my family to allow me to spend the many, many hours away from them. Thank you all for supporting me through this opportunity. I have great respect for my parents, who have molded me into the person I am today, and I hope we have many more years together. Thanks to my wife for putting up with me on this again; I promise not to start any new projects now that this is done. My children are my inspiration, and I hope this book inspires them to excel in whatever field they choose in life — always aim for the top, and don't accept less than the best.

I have to thank others as well. I don't think I could have completed this book if I were working with anyone other than Tauseef; he is a great guy and a good friend. I always wish him and his family the best in all they do. This book has proven that international projects can be successfully completed!

I have to thank all of my colleagues at SB for giving me ideas that may have found their way into this book over the past few years. I don't have the space to mention the entire SAP team, but Dawn, Brian, Masayood, Kamran, Hussain, and Boon Sin have all helped me proofread sections of this book. Thank you for your ideas, time, and support.

It was a pleasure to work with SAP PRESS again. Kelly Harris did a great job in keeping us on track and supporting us, even though I am sure there were some long dark nights!

Tauseef Sheikh Muhammad

After receiving a very good response from our first book, Naeem and I were looking to write a book that would not only give real value to readers but also provide information on a topic that is not covered in great detail in already-available SAP books. Integration came up again and again as a key topic, and, considering its complexity as well as the fact that there is not enough material on the subject, we decided that writing a book on the topic would be a valuable help to readers.

I want to thank my parents, who always remember me in their prayers, support me in every endeavor, and have made me who I am today. I would also like to thank my brother Hafeez, my sisters, and especially my wife, Asima, and children, Rayyan and Zayna, who are my inspiration in everything I do and every choice I make in life. A special thanks to Naeem, who is a great friend and the only reason I can call myself an SAP author today. If it were not for him, I would have never even thought of writing a book. And at the end, working with SAP PRESS has again been a wonderful experience; I would like to thank Kelly Harris for her patience and support during the entire duration of the project.

"Everything that has a beginning has an end."
—The Oracle, The Matrix Revolutions

1   Introduction

In this chapter, we offer a brief introduction to the topic of integration as a whole.

1.1   What Is Integration?

If you asked different people for their definitions of integration, you would get a range of answers. Integration (from the Latin *integer*, meaning whole or entire) generally means combining parts so that they work together or form a whole. This seems reasonable, but what does that mean in terms of IT systems? For our purposes, *integration* is the seamless interaction of technology, processes, and thinking.

With any system, you can't have a fully integrated solution until you've integrated those three key components of technology, processes, and thinking. These components should supplement each other; they should not be the cause of conflict. If all three components aren't completely integrated, the resulting end product may be ineffective.

When designing a solution, you should consider the impacts of each component when looking at the setup, use of master data, and transaction processing. A simple example here is the use of the reference field in financial documents. If you know the reference field is widely available to search on, you should ensure that this field is used appropriately so that documents can be found easily. Designing a process without this field makes the task of searching for documents more difficult. As a result, users must resort to a nonstandard search option, instead of using the standard reporting tools. We spend a bit of time looking at this issue in the next section.

1.2   Configuring SAP ERP for an Integrated Solution

In Section 1.1, What Is Integration?, we looked at an example that demonstrated how changing the way we use the system could lead to a nonstandard solution. That example shows a breakdown in process and demonstrates a common issue where people assume that merely purchasing SAP ERP will solve all of their problems with integration.

When you load SAP ERP, you get a fully integrated solution. The system has a number of organizational objects and master data set up already, and you can chose to use these as they are. However, after you start to configure your own company code, number ranges, chart of accounts, and so on, the new configurations will deviate from the standard solution. Therefore, you need to ensure that you link these configuration steps together to maintain integration.

SAP ERP can be completely integrated as long as you think about the configuration and design in detail and test them thoroughly. For each activity, you need to ensure that you clearly understand how information will be passed from one transaction to another. You also need to ensure that the fields on master data objects are used in a consistent manner. SAP ERP master data is usually extensive, so it's important to ensure that each object is correctly set up for use and maintained.

1.3   Four Approaches to Good Integration

The best advice we can give for good integration is to use SAP ERP in the way it was designed. However, you will always find yourself using fields or transactions that are slightly different from your original SAP ERP software to satisfy your unique business processes. When you consider a solution, try to consider the complete end-to-end process to be sure of where you are starting and where you want to finish. For this purpose, design lead should be consistently present throughout the design of the entire process.

Second, process maps, flow charts, and swim lanes are good ways to graphically represent this process. A process design document explains the SAP ERP screens and transactions, as well as the inputs and outputs of the system (interfaces). It's also important not to forget the reporting requirements. Often reporting requirements are critical and overlooked until the end, when you realize that the standard SAP ERP reports can't be used based on the fields you've selected in your process.

The final two guidelines for a good approach to integration are prototyping and integrated testing. You should always prototype the solution you are proposing in detail to ensure it will accomplish what you want it to do. More importantly, you should test your outcome as an integrated solution with a common design lead present throughout to ensure the flow of data and information is consistent and constant.

We cannot emphasize how important the testing of the solution is; this is the only real way to identify issues and resolve them quickly.

1.4 SAP Navigation Basics

We end our introduction by offering a basic explanation of SAP navigation for those readers who may be new to this area.

SAP screens are structured to ensure consistency. Figure 1.1 shows the main areas of a standard screen, and the following list describes the screen elements in more detail.

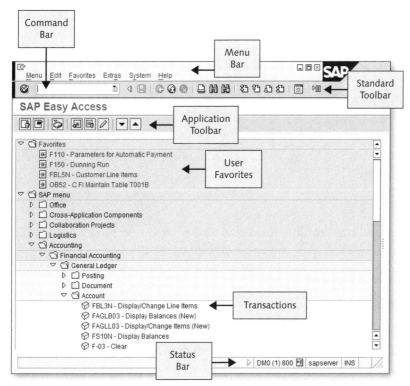

Figure 1.1 Standard Screen

▶ **Menu bar**

The menu bar is the top line of any main window in the SAP system. The menus shown here depend on which application you are currently working in.

▶ **Command field**

You have an option to start an application by directly entering its transaction code in the command field, which is hidden as default.

▶ **Standard toolbar**

The buttons in the standard toolbar are shown on every SAP screen. The buttons that cannot be used in a specific application are deactivated. You can view the flag with the name or function of the button if you place the cursor over it for a few seconds.

▶ **Title bar**

The title bar names the function in which you are currently working.

▶ **Application toolbar**

The application toolbar shows the buttons available in the application in which you are currently working.

▶ **Checkboxes**

The checkboxes allow you to select several options from a group of fields.

▶ **Radio buttons**

Radio buttons are also options available for selection, but you can only select one option in this case.

▶ **Tab**

The tabs allow you to group similar types of fields in different subscreens to improve clarity.

▶ **Status bar**

The status bar displays information on the current system status, such as warnings and errors. You can also change the display variant to show, for example, the transaction code of the transaction you are currently in.

Several options are available to navigate in SAP systems:

▶ Using transaction codes in the command field

▶ Selecting items from menus in the menu bar

▶ Selecting items from the favorites list or from the user or SAP menus

From the SAP Easy Access screen, you can call any transaction using Transaction XXX without any prefix (where XXX is the transaction code in question). The following prefixes are used with the transaction name to execute commands:

▶ **/n:** Cancels the current transaction in which you are working.

▶ **/nXXX:** Calls Transaction xxxx directly from another transaction.

▶ **/oXXX:** Calls Transaction xxxx in a new session directly from another transaction.

▶ **/nend:** Ends the logon session with a confirmation dialog box.

▶ **/nex:** Ends the logon session without a confirmation dialog box.

▶ **/i:** Deletes the session you are currently using.

▶ **/o:** Displays an overview of your sessions.

1.5   Accessing the Customizing or Configuration Areas

When logging on, you are always taken to the same initial screen that you saw in Figure 1.2. This takes you into the application side, or user side, of the system where you process system transactions, maintain master data, and run reports.

The other side of the system that you need to access as an SAP consultant is the configuration side. Customization (commonly referred to as configuration) is the process by which you make settings in SAP ERP tables to set up the way you want your system to work. This is the main reason SAP ERP is such a powerful system — you can customize it to meet your own specific business requirements.

SAP provides an Implementation Guide (IMG) that structures these activities and makes it easier to complete. You can access the IMG via two routes:

▶ Go through the application menu: SAP Easy Access Menu • Tools • Customizing • IMG • Execute Project.

▶ Enter Transaction SPRO directly into the command bar.

1.6   Summary

As we get ready to delve into the content of the book remember that even the most experienced SAP consultants do not know the entire system. There is a lot of complex material in this book, and you shouldn't expect to learn everything after a single read-through. It will take time to read, understand, and practice implementing the full content.

Best of luck!

This chapter provides a basic explanation of the enterprise structure in SAP ERP, discussing how each component interrelates with the others and provides a basis for integration. The enterprise structure must be completed before we can apply the concepts of integration discussed in later chapters.

2 SAP Enterprise Structure

This chapter introduces the common organizational objects and master data that are consistently used throughout this book. You may be aware of some of these, but it's important to review these now to get a high-level understanding of what they are and where they fit in. We'll revisit some of these concepts in more detail later in the book.

In this chapter, we explain the basic configuration steps required to define your SAP ERP enterprise structure. An *enterprise structure* is a set of key building blocks that are required for further configuration. You must design and finalize decisions about the enterprise structure early in the project; later design changes can result in serious issues and significant increases in costs.

This chapter provides information about the following:

► Definitions and basic configuration steps related to enterprise structure elements

► Explanation of key SAP ERP Financials and Controlling (CO) master data

Although we assume that you have a basic understanding of SAP ERP, we think it's essential to mention organizational elements before moving on to more complex integration concepts. There may be some duplication in later chapters, as these concepts are briefly explained first in this chapter, and then also explained in more detail in their relevant chapters, but this chapter provides only a preview of the detail that is to come.

2.1 Enterprise Structure Elements: Definition and Basic Configuration

In this section, we explain the definition and basic configuration of the following relevant enterprise structure elements that are discussed throughout this book:

► Company code

► Controlling area

► Credit control area

► Chart of accounts

► Chart of depreciation

► Sales organization

► Purchase organization

► Personnel area

2.1.1 Company Code

The company code is an independent legal accounting entity for which a complete set of financial statements can be prepared to meet the statutory requirements of a given country. This organizational unit is used to structure the business organization from a financial accounting perspective. Defining a company code is a very important and mandatory step that significantly affects later configuration because a lot of other objects are assigned against the company code in SAP ERP.

Complete balance sheets and profit and loss (P&L) reports are produced at the company code level, so it's usually defined at the legal entity level. Some of the key considerations when making a decision about defining your company codes are listed here:

► Do you have separate legal entities?

► Do you operate in many different countries and thus are required to produce multiple financial statements based on local requirements?

► Is your organization large enough for you to report on discrete business units?

For the purpose of this book, we have decided to create one company code, for which we will need to define a four-digit alphanumeric naming convention. When creating your own company codes, you should adopt a convention that makes sense for your individual organization; if you have many company codes, for example, you may want to define criteria that will make it easy to identify each entity. Many large organizations agree on a naming convention at the beginning of their SAP ERP project for all of the possible company codes that would be implemented in the initial and rollout stages.

To define a company code, use the following menu path in IMG: SPRO • ENTERPRISE STRUCTURE • DEFINITION • FINANCIAL ACCOUNTING • EDIT, COPY, DELETE, CHECK COMPANY CODE (Transaction OX02). SAP ERP provides a number of country-specific templates that you can use to copy from and create your own company code. When you copy an SAP-delivered template or a user-created company code, the system asks if you want to copy dependent objects at the same time; this allows you to copy all of the associated entries simultaneously. However, if you're confident that you won't need these entries for your new company code, you can ignore the message and instead use the EDIT function to manually configure all of the customizing tables for your new company code. Note that you can create your new company code using either the COPY function or the EDIT function. In the former, you use an SAP-delivered template or a user-created company code as a template; in the latter, you use the NEW ENTRIES button (as explained next) to create your company code from scratch.

> **Note**
>
> When you copy all dependent objects, the system copies everything in the language of the template country.

Create your own company code by clicking the NEW ENTRIES button. Figure 2.1 shows some of the SAP-delivered country templates for reference.

The configuration screen for creating a new company code is very simple, as the company code is merely a placeholder, an ID against which configuration can be made.

Figure 2.2 shows the basic settings for defining a new company code. You are required to enter the city, country, currency, and language for your company code in this screen.

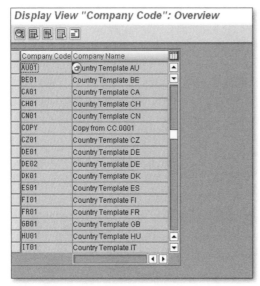

Figure 2.1 SAP-Delivered Company Code Country Templates

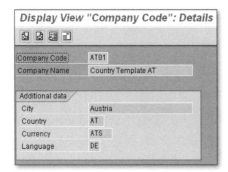

Figure 2.2 Basic Settings for Creating a New Company Code

After creating a company code, you must configure the address information for it. The address information that is entered can be used for creating output (e.g., customer statements), which you may want to send out to third parties. Click the ADDRESS icon on the screen, as shown in Figure 2.2, and the system takes you to the address screen for your company code, as shown in Figure 2.3.

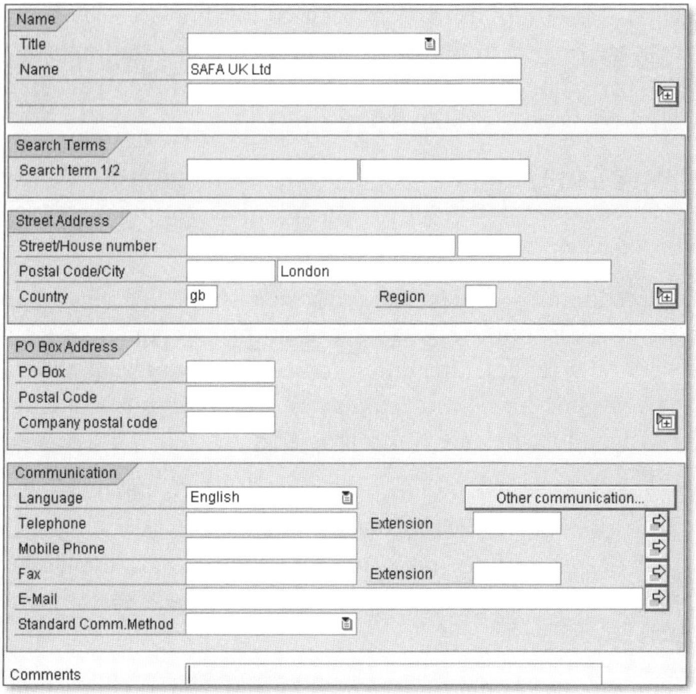

Figure 2.3 Address Details for a Company Code

You have now defined your company code in SAP ERP.

> **Note**
>
> For the purposes of this book, it is not necessary to explain further configuration steps (fiscal year variant, posting period variant, etc.) that are also assigned to company codes.

2.1.2 Controlling Area

The controlling area is an object that sits solely within the Controlling (CO) component. It structures the internal accounting operations — such as cost and revenue — of an organization, and also defines how you can allocate costs and revenues to account assignment objects (e.g., cost center, profit center, etc.). Controlling areas enable you to produce management reporting and help you in analysis and decision making. International organizations may set their controlling areas by international boundaries because this often represents boundaries for legal reporting requirements as well. Many companies use cost center and profit center hierarchies to reflect their departmental reporting analysis.

Company codes must be assigned to controlling areas. A controlling area can have one or many company codes assigned to it, but a company code cannot be assigned to more than one controlling area.

Our discussions in this section only explain the purpose and basic configuration of the controlling area; in the rest of the book, we look at the components within controlling areas that are relevant for integration (cost centers, internal orders, etc.). For the purposes of this book, we have defined one controlling area, and our company code will be assigned to this one controlling area.

To define the controlling area, use the following menu path in IMG: SPRO • ENTERPRISE STRUCTURE • DEFINITION • CONTROLLING • MAINTAIN CONTROLLING AREA. In the resulting screen, select MAINTAIN CONTROLLING AREA, which shows you a list of all of the existing predelivered controlling areas. You may choose to copy one of these, or, alternatively, create your own.

To create a new controlling area, click the NEW ENTRIES button, and provide a four-digit code for your controlling area. This code may be the same as your company code or something completely different. After entering the information shown in the following list, the screen should look like Figure 2.4.

▶ CONTROLLING AREA
Enter the four-digit alpha-numeric value that represents your controlling area.

▶ NAME
Enter the description of your controlling area.

▶ PERSON RESPONSIBLE
Enter the name of the person who is in charge of this controlling area. This information is not used anywhere else, so you can simply enter "Director of Finance," or whatever is appropriate.

▶ ASSIGNMENT CONTROL
Enter the relationship between the controlling area and the company code. There are two options in this case:

  ▶ CONTROLLING AREA SAME AS COMPANY CODE: Use this option when there is a one-to-one relationship between company code and controlling area.

> ▸ Cross-Company-Code Cost Accounting: Use this option when two or more company codes are assigned to one controlling area. This allows cross-company cost accounting within this controlling area.

▸ Currency Type
Define the currency that should be used throughout your controlling area in this field. If, in the Assignment Control field, you selected option 1, Controlling Area Same as Company Code, the system automatically provides the company code currency in this field. If you selected option 2, Cross-Company-Code Cost Accounting, you have the following six choices:

> ▸ Company code currency (10): You can use this currency only when all of the company codes use the same currency.

> ▸ Any currency (20): You can select any currency in this field; this gives the maximum flexibility when choosing a controlling area currency.

> ▸ Group currency (30): You maintain this currency at the client level, and it can be used to reconcile the SAP ERP Financials and CO components.

> ▸ Hard currency (40): This currency is used in countries where the inflation rate is very high, and makes sense where the assigned company codes are from the same country.

> ▸ Index-based currency (50): This currency is used to support external reporting requirements in countries where inflation is very high and unstable.

> ▸ Global currency (60): You can use this currency if you have defined global companies in your configuration. You also need to ensure that all of the companies assigned to your controlling area belong to the same company and also use the same currency.

▸ Currency
Define the default currency for your controlling area. The selection made in the Currency Type field will influence the choices that are available to you in this field.

▸ Chart of Accts
Enter the chart of accounts that should be used by your controlling area. All of the company codes assigned to your controlling area must use the same chart of accounts that has been assigned to the controlling area.

▸ Fiscal Year Variant
Specify the fiscal year variant. Just like chart of accounts, this variant must be the same for the assigned company codes and the controlling area.

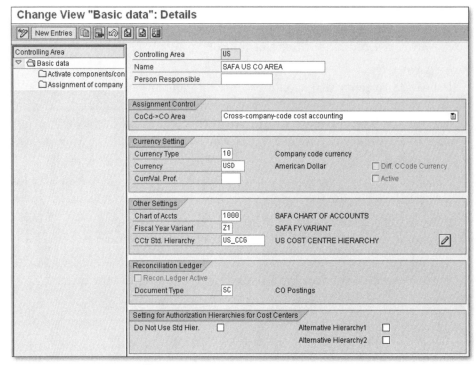

Figure 2.4 Maintain Controlling Area Basic Settings

Before we move on to the next sections in this chapter, we need to briefly discuss the concept of real and statistical postings. When you make income and expense entries in SAP ERP Financials, they give rise to real and statistical postings in the CO component.

You can further process real postings and use them for cost allocations within the CO component by using distributions and assessments. One rule of thumb is that only one real posting takes place in this component, and all other postings for that transaction become statistical.

Statistical postings are only used for information purposes, and there are no restrictions on making statistical postings in the system.

The most important point is that the account assignment object — that is, cost center, internal order, and so on — must make the determination about whether a posting is statistical or real; no other criteria can make this determination. Let's explore this concept further by giving some examples.

In Scenario 1, shown in Table 2.1, the real posting is determined by the cost center, and the statistical posting is received by the profit center.

Posting in SAP ERP Financials	Posting in CO	
	Real	**Statistical**
1) Expense general ledger account 2) Cost center	Cost center	Profit center as derived from cost center master record

Table 2.1 Scenario 1: Only Cost Center Assignment

In Scenario 2, shown in Table 2.2, an internal order has determined the real posting, and both cost center and profit center have received the statistical postings. This means that if the order is real, the cost center will automatically take the statistical posting, and for the profit center, postings are always statistical.

Posting in SAP ERP Financials	Posting in CO	
	Real	**Statistical**
1) Expense general ledger account 2) Cost center 3) Internal order (real)	Internal order	Cost center, profit center as derived from cost center master record

Table 2.2 Scenario 2: Real Internal Order and Cost Center Assignment

In Scenario 3, shown in Table 2.3, the internal order has again determined the posting by taking the statistical posting, as it is a statistical order, and the cost center has taken the real posting.

Posting in SAP ERP Financials	Posting in CO	
	Real	**Statistical**
1) Expense general ledger account 2) Cost center 3) Internal order (statistical)	Cost center	Internal order, profit center as derived from cost center master record

Table 2.3 Scenario 3: Cost Center and Statistical Internal Order Assignment

Next, we'll look into defining the credit control area.

2.1.3   Credit Control Area

The credit control area is used to define an overall credit limit for a defined group of customers. It allows control for the processing of transactions with customers and also represents a basic control for restricting your credit exposure. The limit you set at this level influences all of the customers that fall within this credit control area. Most organizations define one credit control area per company code. A prerequisite for creating a credit control area is defining the fiscal year variant.

In our scenario, we use some simple settings to support our credit control activities. We define our credit control area (as shown in Figure 2.5) by using the following menu path in IMG: SPRO • ENTERPRISE STRUCTURE • DEFINITION • FINANCIAL ACCOUNTING • DEFINE CREDIT CONTROL AREA.

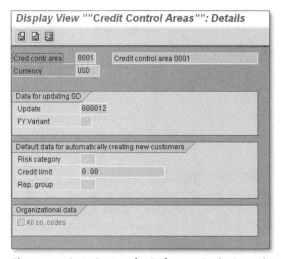

Figure 2.5 Basic Settings for Defining a Credit Control Area

The following list includes the entries for important fields when defining your credit control area:

▶ UPDATE
This controls which items are included within the calculation of open items, that is, credit exposure. Many organizations use "000012" to include the value of open sales orders in their credit exposure calculation.

▶ FY VARIANT
Enter your fiscal year variant.

▶ DEFAULT DATA FOR AUTOMATICALLY CREATING NEW CUSTOMERS
The settings made here are applied as a default to all new customers when they are created.

After you've created your credit control area, it needs to be assigned to your company code. This is very important from an integration point of view because data within this credit control area is linked to the company code through this assignment. We discuss this assignment and other related settings as part of Chapter 3, Integrating the Sales-Order-to-Cash-Receipt Process.

2.1.4 Business Area

Business areas are used to provide departmental reporting analysis; they were most relevant before Profit Center Accounting (PCA) was offered as part of SAP ERP solutions. Organizations can use business areas to track postings relating to different parts of the business and thus obtain additional analysis. Although the functionality has been overshadowed by the development of profit centers, internal orders, and profitability analysis, business areas remain in the system, and some organizations use them to satisfy minor business requirements.

Business areas can be used for both balance sheet and P&L analysis. However, an organization cannot assign bank, equity, or tax information to business areas directly, so you can't create legally required financial statements or tax reports using business areas alone.

Further discussion of business areas is outside the scope of this book.

2.1.5 Chart of Accounts

The chart of accounts is a structured list of the general ledger accounts that should be used to report ledger postings. You should define the chart of accounts based on your reporting requirements to provide you with the appropriate level of financial information needed to manage your business. General ledger accounts are defined at the chart of accounts level and then extended into the company codes they are used in. The same chart of accounts can be assigned to multiple company codes at the same time.

The configuration of the chart of accounts outlines the control information, such as the length of the code. Organizations usually adopt a numeric structure to their general ledger codes, and there is flexibility in the code length based on the size of your account code list. The SAP ERP implementation is sometimes a good time to review your coding structure and decide on the correct combination of general ledger accounts, cost centers, profit centers, and other account assignment elements. You can define your chart of accounts using the following IMG path: SPRO • FINANCIAL ACCOUNTING (NEW) – GENERAL LEDGER ACCOUNTING (NEW) • MASTER DATA • G/L ACCOUNTS • PREPARATIONS • EDIT CHART OF ACCOUNTS LIST (Transaction OB13).

Figure 2.6 shows an example of a system-delivered chart of accounts.

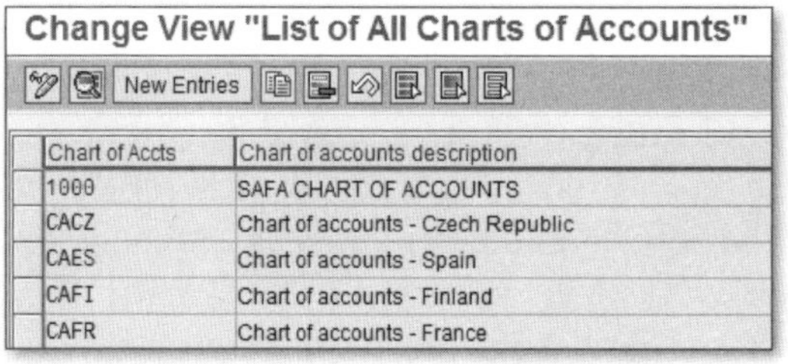
Change View "List of All Charts of Accounts"

New Entries

Chart of Accts	Chart of accounts description
1000	SAFA CHART OF ACCOUNTS
CACZ	Chart of accounts - Czech Republic
CAES	Chart of accounts - Spain
CAFI	Chart of accounts - Finland
CAFR	Chart of accounts - France

Figure 2.6 SAP-Delivered Chart of Accounts

If you want to create a new chart of accounts, click the NEW ENTRIES button, enter the relevant details, and save. The settings for our chart of accounts are shown in Figure 2.7.

After defining your chart of accounts, assign it to your company code using the following IMG path: SPRO • FINANCIAL ACCOUNTING (NEW) – GENERAL LEDGER ACCOUNTING (NEW) • MASTER DATA • G/L ACCOUNTS • PREPARATIONS • ASSIGN COMPANY CODE TO CHART OF ACCOUNTS (Transaction OB62).

Remember the difference between the roles of the general ledger account and the account assignment objects (cost center, profit center, internal order, etc.). A general ledger account records the type of income or expenditure, whereas the account assignment object provides departmental or business unit analysis.

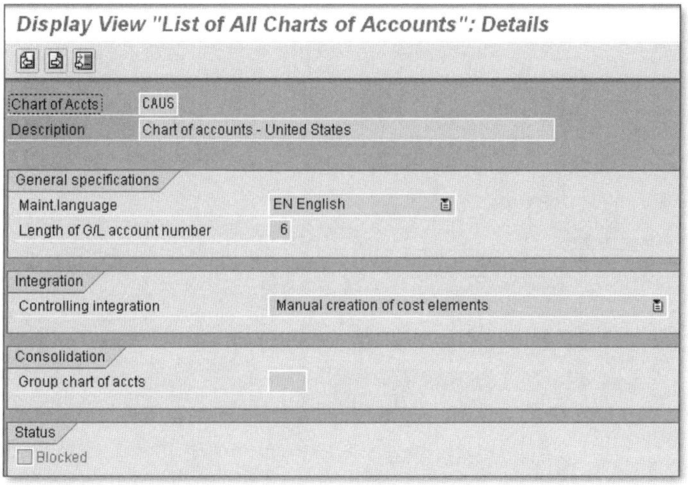

Figure 2.7 Chart of Accounts Basic Settings

2.1.6 Chart of Depreciation

You can define the chart of depreciation as the organizational element that is used to manage various legal requirements for the depreciation and valuation of assets. A chart of depreciation is basically a directory of depreciation areas arranged according to your business and legal requirements. Like company codes, these are usually country-specific but do not need to be aligned with any other organizational units. A chart of depreciation can be used for all of the company codes in a given country.

To create your chart of depreciation, copy a reference chart of depreciation, including all of the depreciation areas from that reference chart of depreciation. You can use the chart of depreciation to manage all different types of valuation rules for your assets in a specific country or economic region. If you do not need any depreciation area that is copied from the reference chart of depreciation, you always have the option to delete it.

The IMG path for this configuration step is SPRO • FINANCIAL ACCOUNTING (NEW) • ASSET ACCOUNTING • ORGANIZATIONAL STRUCTURES • COPY REFERENCE CHART OF DEPRECIATION/DEPRECIATION AREAS. A screen with activities, including COPY REFERENCE CHART OF DEPRECIATION, appears, as shown in Figure 2.8.

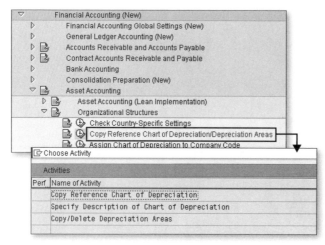

Figure 2.8 Copy Reference Chart of Depreciation

To copy a chart of depreciation, double-click the COPY REFERENCE CHART OF DEPRE-CIATION activity. In the next screen, click the COPY icon, as shown in Figure 2.9.

The COPY dialog box appears next. Specify the chart of depreciation to copy from and the chart of depreciation to copy to (the latter is a number you assign). Click the checkmark icon.

Figure 2.9 Copy Chart of Depreciation

The system returns a message related to the transport of number ranges and addresses. Click the checkmark icon on the message, and maintain the number ranges and addresses manually in the system.

After you have copied the chart of depreciation, go back into the activity screen shown in Figure 2.8, and double-click SPECIFY DESCRIPTION OF CHART OF DEPRECIA-TION. Change the name of your chart of depreciation, as shown in Figure 2.10.

Go back to the activity screen shown in Figure 2.8, and select the activity COPY/DELETE DEPRECIATION AREAS. Behind each chart, you can find the valid depreciation areas for that chart, as shown in Figure 2.11. As explained earlier, delete the depreciation areas that are not needed from your new chart of depreciation, or add new depreciation areas by copying them.

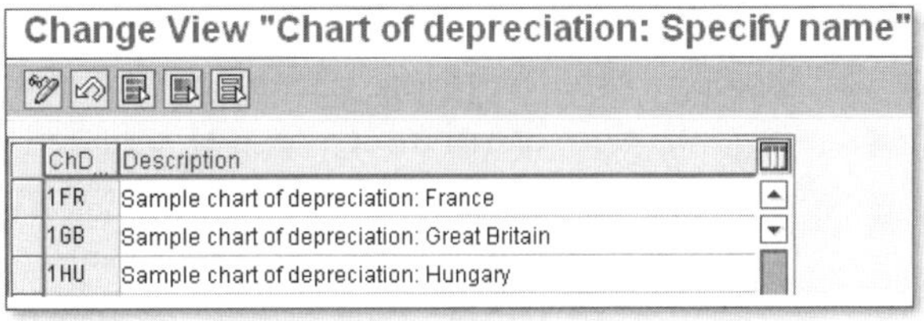

Change View "Chart of depreciation: Specify name"

ChD	Description	
1FR	Sample chart of depreciation: France	▲
1GB	Sample chart of depreciation: Great Britain	▼
1HU	Sample chart of depreciation: Hungary	

Figure 2.10   Chart of Depreciation – Specify Name

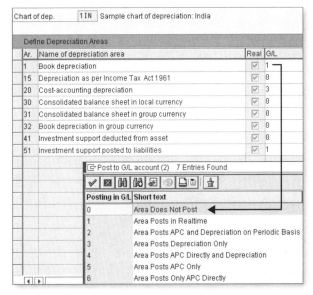

Figure 2.11   Depreciation Areas for Your Chart of Depreciation

After you've defined your chart of depreciation, you must assign it to your company code. (We cover the assignment to a company code and other detailed configuration steps in Chapter 6, Integrating Asset Accounting, Investment Management, and Project Systems.)

2.1.7   Sales Organization

The sales organization is the highest organizational object in the Sales and Distribution (SD) component. You define your rules for the sales and distribution of goods and services in your organization at the sales organization level, which also helps you decide how many sales organizations you need.

Within a sales organization, you can define controls around processes and master data; for example, you can set up your customer master record differently for each sales area level (a combination of sales organization, distribution channel, and division — explained in detail in Chapter 3), which may relate to different customer regions. A company code may have many sales organizations assigned to it, for example, to represent the different sales regions or service areas in your company code. A sales organization can only be assigned to a single company code, though, so whatever master data or controls you set up for your sales organization must be set up for each sales organization separately.

You can configure your sales organization by using the following menu path: SPRO • ENTERPRISE STRUCTURE • DEFINITION • SALES AND DISTRIBUTION • DEFINE, COPY, DELETE, CHECK SALES ORGANIZATION. This takes you to the screen shown in Figure 2.12.

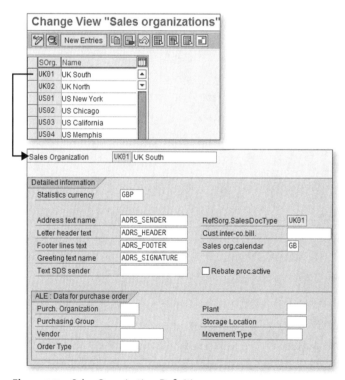

Figure 2.12 Sales Organization Definition

After you define the sales organization, you assign the sales organization to the company code. In Figure 2.13, you can see that you can assign many sales organizations to the same company code.

SOrg.	Name	CoCd	Company Name	Status
UK01	UK South	UK	SAFA UK	
UK02	UK North	UK	SAFA UK	
US01	US New York	US	SAFA US	
US02	US Chicago	US	SAFA US	
US03	US California	US	SAFA US	
US04	US Memphis	US	SAFA US	

Figure 2.13 Assigning the Sales Organization to the Company Code

2.1.8 Purchasing Organizations

A purchasing organization is an important element in the procurement process and is comprised of a collection of purchasing activities that relate to all or part of an organization. These purchases can relate to many companies within an organization (centralized purchasing), or just one company (Decentralized purchasing). Decentralized purchasing is most suited for companies that have a presence in many countries around the world.

In this section, we discuss the creation of purchasing organizations. Their assignment to either company code or plants is explained in Chapter 4, Integrating the Purchase-Order-to-Payment Process. The menu path for creating a purchasing organization is SPRO • ENTERPRISE STRUCTURE • DEFINITION • MATERIAL MANAGEMENT • MAINTAIN PURCHASING ORGANIZATION.

Figure 2.14 shows the main screen for creating a purchasing organization in SAP ERP. Click the NEW ENTRIES button, and enter the four-character purchasing organization number, together with the long description for the purchasing organization in the NEW ENTRIES screen.

Purch. Organization	Purch. Org. Descr.	
0001	Einkaufsorg. 0001	
0005	IDES Deutschland	
0006	IDES USA	
0007	IDES Deutschland	
0008	SAFA UK	

Figure 2.14 Creating a Purchasing Organization

Depending on your company's requirements, you can have different types of purchasing organizations set up in the SAP ERP system. These types determine the next step in setting up purchasing organizations, which is to assign your newly created purchasing organization to one company code, multiple company codes, or a plant.

2.1.9 Personnel Area and Subareas

From a financial point of view, the company code is at the top of the enterprise structure, which is usually set up to represent legal entities in line with statutory law. Similarly, an organization must also comply with HR laws, which are the rules governing the way people are employed and paid. The personnel area is the highest object on the HR side, and it is used to represent HR rules and regulations. The personnel area serves as a placeholder against which you can assign various rules and configuration objects and run different reports.

Within the personnel area, we can find other ways of segregating our employees; for example, the personnel subarea can be used to group together different types of groups of employees, perhaps separated by region or by salaried versus hourly workers.

Personnel areas are set up in the following area of the IMG: SPRO • ENTERPRISE STRUCTURE • DEFINITION • HUMAN RESOURCES MANAGEMENT • PERSONNEL AREAS. The initial screen is shown in Figure 2.15.

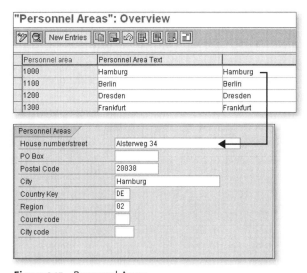

Figure 2.15 Personnel Areas

In Figure 2.15, you can see that behind each personnel area, you also need to enter some basic address information. Personnel areas need to be assigned to a company code and can only be assigned to one company code, although you may want to assign multiple personnel areas to the same company code. (The assignment of personnel areas to a company code is explained in detail in Chapter 5, Integrating SAP ERP HCM with SAP ERP Financials.)

2.2 Key Master Data Objects

In this section, we explain the key Financial Accounting (FI) and Controlling (CO) master data objects and explain their importance from an integration point of view. These master data objects are used throughout this book as part of the end-to-end processes, such as purchase-to-pay and order-to-cash. The key master data objects we cover in this section are as follows:

- General ledger account
- Cost center
- Cost element
- Profit center
- Internal order
- Segment

In this section, we don't look at how the master data objects are created but rather at the important fields within these master data objects. If you understand the importance of the fields within a specific master record, you will be able to create it more accurately and efficiently.

2.2.1 General Ledger Account

The chart of accounts, as we've already discussed, is the structure of the general ledger accounts to be used throughout the system, and the general ledger is the tool used for capturing the company's financial transactions at the lowest level possible. The general ledger account structure should be designed to reflect external financial reporting, and no intelligence should be built in for any form of departmental or cost center reporting because you can get information on these dimensions from the CO component. A chart of accounts can be used by many company codes, and each general ledger account holds separate values for each company code.

General ledger accounts are extremely important because they act a bridge between FI and other components, as they are a major part of integration. Depending on the business scenarios you are implementing in a project, you will likely be required to create specific general ledger accounts throughout the life of a project.

A general ledger account has two segments:

▶ **Chart of accounts segment**
Contains data that is common to all of the company codes using this chart of accounts, for example, name, description, whether the account is a balance sheet account or a P&L account, and so on. This also means that this section of the general ledger account master data is common for all of the company codes assigned to this chart of accounts.

▶ **Company code segment**
Contains data that is unique to the company code's specific requirements, for example, the currency, tax code, settings for open item management, line item display, and so on. For the company codes assigned to this chart of accounts, you can make changes to this section of the general ledger master data, according to your specific requirements.

Access SAP menu • accounting • financial accounting • general ledger • master records • G/L accounts • individual processing • centrally or execute Transaction FS00, and you will see the screen shown in Figure 2.16, which shows some of the important fields on the Type/Description tab of the general ledger master data.

Following are the two most important fields on this record:

▶ Account Group
Account groups help you group accounts of the same type (material, reconciliation, P&L statements, etc.) together and also control the number ranges and the field status (screen layout) of the company code segment.

▶ Group Account Number
Many companies use group charts of accounts for reporting financial statements of the group entities for consolidation purposes. The group chart of accounts is mapped to your operational chart of accounts (i.e., the chart of accounts that is used to directly post entries in the system). Note that when you define your operational chart of accounts and assign a group chart of accounts to it, this field becomes a mandatory field, and you will be required to enter the group account number in this field to save the general ledger master data.

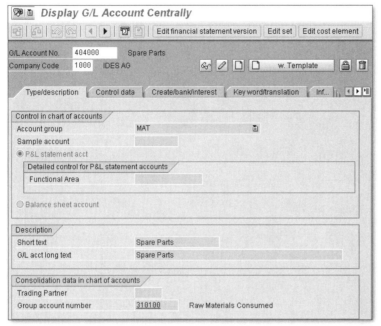

Figure 2.16 General Ledger Master Record – Type/Description Tab

In the same screen, you can clearly see the link to the cost element for all of the P&L accounts, and you can create, change, or display the relevant cost element from this screen.

Figure 2.17 shows the CONTROL DATA tab in the general ledger master record. Some of the most important fields are described in the following list.

▶ RECON. ACCOUNT FOR ACCT TYPE
The reconciliation account connects subledgers to the general ledger in real time. The details of the financial transactions are maintained in the subledger and at the reconciliation account level. The following subledgers are connected to the general ledger via reconciliation accounts:

▶ Accounts receivable

▶ Accounts payable

▶ Assets

▶ Contract accounts receivables

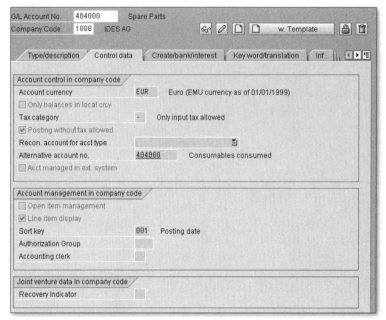

Figure 2.17 General Ledger Master Record – Control Data Tab

▶ OPEN ITEM MANAGEMENT
If this indicator is set in the master record, the items belonging to a specific general ledger account are either open items or cleared items. When open item management is activated, the balance of an account is always the balance of the open items in that account. You should always manage the general ledger accounts with open item management if you want to check whether an offsetting posting has already taken place for a business transaction. The accounts with open item management must have line item display activated (explained next). We recommend that you use open item management for the following accounts:

  ▶ Bank clearing accounts

  ▶ Clearing accounts for goods receipt/invoice receipt

  ▶ Salary clearing accounts

▶ LINE ITEM DISPLAY
Line items are posted to a specific account. In contrast to a document item, a line item only contains information relevant from a specific account point of view. You can display the following line items in a general ledger account:

  ▶ **Open items:** Items that are still open and need to be cleared.

▶ **Cleared items:** Items that have already been cleared.

▶ **Noted items:** Information notes that are not meant to be part of the general ledger and do not update the transaction figures, but only serve as a reminder for payments due or to be made as down payment requests.

▶ **Parked items:** Items that are parked and not yet posted to the account.

> **Note**
>
> The line item display takes up additional database space, so you should only use it if there is no other way of looking at the line items.

Figure 2.18 shows the CREATE/BANK/INTEREST tab. The most important fields are explained in the following list.

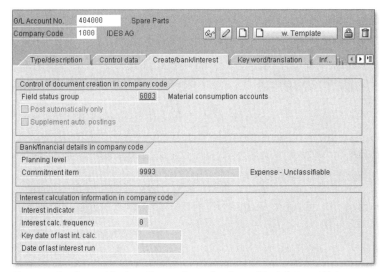

Figure 2.18 General Ledger Master Record – Create/Bank/Interest Tab

▶ FIELD STATUS GROUP

The purpose of the field status group is to hide fields that are not required; for example, an asset account does not require information about interest calculations, whereas a bank may require this information. You can set certain fields as mandatory for certain accounts to ensure that input errors are avoided and important information is not missed during the process.

Certain fields are grouped together, and their field status is valid for the entire group, for example, INTEREST INDICATOR and KEY DATE OF LAST INT. CALC. The

ACCOUNT CURRENCY and FIELD STATUS GROUP fields are always required fields. This status cannot be changed in the system.

▶ POST AUTOMATICALLY ONLY
You can set this flag if you want a specific general ledger account to receive automatic postings only; that is, no manual postings should be made to it. A good example would be the tax payable accounts or GR/IR (goods receipt/ invoice receipt) accounts.

2.2.2 Cost Elements

Cost elements describe the origin of costs, and are defined as either primary or secondary. Primary cost elements represent costs that are incurred from outside of your company, while secondary cost elements typically represent activities incurred within your company. The chart of accounts contains all of the general ledger accounts belonging to FI.

Cost and revenue accounts in FI have an identical twin in the CO component in the form of revenue and cost elements. This ensures that postings from the former are transferred to the latter in real time. This also means that when you create a general ledger account in FI, you must create a primary cost element for it in the CO component so that expenses can be reconciled in both components. You must create the primary cost elements as general ledger accounts in FI before you can create them in the CO component, and you can create secondary cost elements only in the CO component (they are not represented by a general ledger account in FI). Use secondary cost elements to record the internal flow of values for activities such as assessments in Cost Center Accounting (CCA) and settlements in internal orders.

Primary Cost Elements

Primary cost elements are the CO version of P&L accounts. Whenever a posting is made to a general ledger P&L account with an equivalent cost element, the posting is mirrored in that cost element and, therefore, in CO. This keeps the general ledger and the CCA ledger in sync. You can configure your system so that every time a new P&L account is created, an equivalent cost element is automatically created with the same account number. As part of that configuration, the system recognizes whether the new account is an expense account or a revenue account through the general ledger account ranges. The key implication of this is that the P&L reports that are based on CO data are going to match up to the balances in the general ledger accounts.

Secondary Cost Elements

Unlike primary cost elements, which have a corresponding P&L account in the general ledger, secondary cost elements are purely used within the CO component, and do not have a corresponding general ledger P&L account. After you've created a primary cost element for a general ledger account, it's important to assign an object to it (such as a cost center or internal order), so that, when the information flows to the CO component from FI, you know exactly where the cost originated. Also, when creating cost elements, you must assign a cost element category that actually determines the type of transactions for which you can use that cost element. One example would be category 01, primary cost elements, which is used for expense postings.

Figure 2.19 shows the master data screens for a cost element, which you can access by using the following menu path: SAP MENU • ACCOUNTING • CONTROLLING • COST ELEMENT ACCOUNTING • MASTER DATA • COST ELEMENT • INDIVIDUAL PROCESSING • DISPLAY (Transaction KA03). Some of the most important fields are explained in the following list.

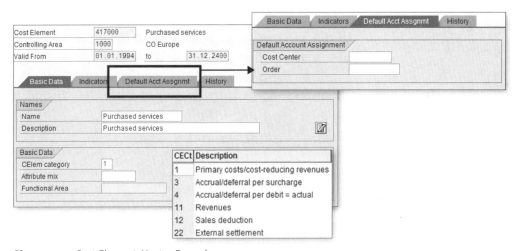

Figure 2.19 Cost Element Master Record

► CELEM CATEGORY
   When you create a cost element, you have to assign a cost element category to it. This assignment helps in determining the transaction for which you can use the specific cost element.

▶ DEFAULT ACCT ASSGNMT

The default account assignment setting ensures that postings made to this cost element are posted to the default cost center or the internal order maintained in these fields if they are not entered at the time of initial postings.

2.2.3 Cost Center

In SAP ERP, the cost center is the location where costs are actually incurred. You can set up cost centers based on your functional requirements, allocation criteria, the type of activities or services provided, your geographical locations, and areas of responsibility. Use the menu path SAP MENU • ACCOUNTING • CONTROLLING • COST CENTER ACCOUNTING • MASTER DATA • COST CENTER • INDIVIDUAL PROCESSING • DISPLAY (Transaction KS03) to display some important fields on the cost center master record, as shown in Figure 2.20.

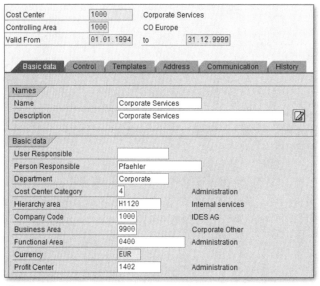

Figure 2.20 Cost Center Master Record

The USER RESPONSIBLE and PERSON RESPONSIBLE fields can be linked to the workflow within SAP ERP for approval purposes. COST CENTER CATEGORY provides default control indicators to cost centers at the time of creation and at the time of assigning functional areas and reporting. You can also see that this is the place where you assign the company code, business area, functional area, and profit center, which means that when a posting is made to this cost center, it will, for example, automatically post to the business area or the profit center maintained in these fields.

Note that the cost centers cannot be created within the CO component unless you have completed the standard hierarchy, which is a structure to which all cost centers within the controlling area must be assigned. How you define your structure is generally up to you. We recommend that you define the structure so that it reflects the internal areas of responsibility and the controlling and decision-making structures within your organization. These are usually the same as the internal functional areas depicted in your company's organization chart. Figure 2.21 shows an example cost center hierarchy.

▽ H1	** Standard Hierarchy CA1000
▷ H1000	Company 1000 - Germany
▽ H2000	Company 2000 - UK
▽ H2010	Corporate
▽ H2110	Executive Board
2-1110	Executive Board
▽ H2120	Internal services
2-1000	Corporate Services
2-1200	Cafeteria
2-1210	Telephone
2-1220	Motor Pool
2-1230	Power
▷ H2200	Administration & Financials
▷ H2300	Marketing and Sales
▷ H2400	Technical Area
▷ H2100	IDES Portugal
▷ H23-1000	IDES Spain
▷ H2700	Company 1000 - Germany
▷ H9999	IDES Additional area
▷ H9500	Training
▷ H9800	H9800

Figure 2.21 Example Cost Center Hierarchy

2.2.4 Profit Center

A profit center represents an organizational subunit that operates practically independently on the market, bears responsibility for its own costs and revenues, and can be expanded to become an investment center. This is called a company within the company concept. Profit Center Accounting (PCA) supports a division of the enterprise in areas of responsibility for profits. The essential difference between profit centers and business areas is that profit centers are used for internal control, while business areas are more geared toward an external viewpoint. Profit centers differ from cost centers in that cost centers merely represent the units in which capacity costs arise, whereas the person in charge of the profit centers is responsible for its balance of costs and revenues.

Many companies choose to use profit centers for group reporting rather than the company code. A company code represents a statutory entity that may have multiple profit centers. Note that in SAP General Ledger (informally known as the New General Ledger), PCA is now part of the general ledger rather then CO. This means that business users don't have to wait for month-end to prepare their financial statements because they will now be available at any time through FI with information updated on a real-time basis.

Use the menu path SAP MENU • ACCOUNTING • FINANCIAL ACCOUNTING • GENERAL LEDGER • MASTER RECORDS • PROFIT CENTER • INDIVIDUAL PROCESSING • DISPLAY or Transaction KE53 to view some of the important fields on a profit center master record, as shown in Figure 2.22.

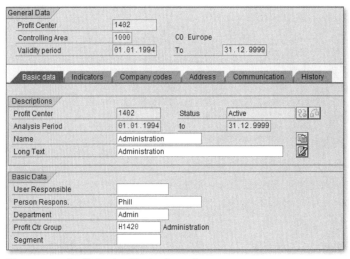

Figure 2.22 Profit Center Master Record

In SAP General Ledger, SAP has now added another dimension of a segment (explained later in this chapter) to the profit center master record, which enables financial statements to be prepared at the segment level. You are required to enter the segment in the profit center master record if you have selected the segment scenario in the SAP General Ledger configuration.

To conclude our discussion of profit centers, let's briefly discuss the concept of profit center determination, as users sometimes struggle to understand how a certain profit center was determined at the time of postings. As you've already seen with cost center creation, you assign a profit center in its master data, which means that when any entry is made in the cost center, profit center information is automatically updated. This also ensures that if you are reviewing the postings in PCA, you can tell which cost object was used at the time of the original entry, that is, the cost center. Also, all of the entries come from postings from other objects, and they are only mirrored in PCA.

Table 2.4 shows the rules for profit center determination.

Scenario/Rule	Description
Substitution rule exists in SAP ERP Financials or in the CO component	If you have set a substitution rule in SAP ERP Financials or the CO component to determine the profit center, this will have the highest priority at the time of profit center determination.
Entry using cost or revenue element	If the data is transferred using a cost or revenue element, the profit center is always determined from the master records of cost centers or internal orders assigned to them at the time of entry.
Entry using balance sheet accounts or P&L accounts	If at the time of entry to a balance sheet account or P&L account, no profit center was mentioned, and you have configured a setting in the configuration step "Choose additional balance sheet and profit and loss accounts," the system determines the profit center using this setting.
No profit center mentioned in the posting document	The system posts to the dummy profit center when it cannot determine the profit center from the posting document.

Table 2.4 Rules for Profit Center Determination

2.2.5 Internal Order

Internal orders can be used to represent individual tasks or projects that you want to report on, in addition to the other account assignment objects such as cost centers. Internal orders can support task-oriented planning, monitoring, and allocation of costs. They can be real (in which case, they collect costs while the task or project is going on) or statistical (in which case, they can exist for long periods of time to provide an additional reporting dimension).

One of the most important concepts in internal order accounting is the order type. You always create an internal order with reference to an order type. Order types pass on certain settings to the internal orders that are created with reference to that order type. They are also created at the client level and are available to any controlling area within that client. In general, there are four types of orders:

▶ **Overhead cost order**
These monitor costs related to internal activities settled to cost centers.

▶ **Investment orders**
These monitor costs related to internal activities settled to fixed assets.

▶ **Accrual orders**
These offset postings for accrued costs calculated in the CO component.

▶ **Orders with revenues**
These capture revenue that is not part of the core business of the company's operations.

Figure 2.23 shows some of the internal order fields in its master record. Just as cost centers were linked to a company code, business area, and a profit center, internal orders are linked to the same objects, as well as other objects, as shown in Figure 2.23.

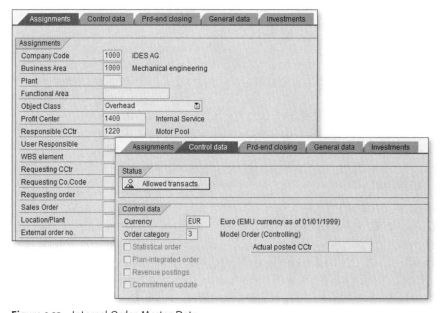

Figure 2.23 Internal Order Master Data

Information about the user responsible, currency, and order category can also be entered in this screen. As explained earlier, an internal order can be real or statistical. If the STATISTICAL ORDER field is flagged, this order becomes a statistical order, and it can accept postings but cannot settle it to any other object.

2.2.6 Segment

You can define a segment as a division within a company, for which you can create financial statements to meet external reporting requirements. The U.S. GAAP and IFRS accounting principles require companies to prepare and report financial statements on the basis of segments. As part of SAP General Ledger, you can now define segments in your system for this purpose. As explained earlier, you enter a segment in the master record of a profit center, which means that the segment is only released as a combination with the profit center. If no segment is specified manually during posting (only possible for transactions in FI), the segment is determined from the master record of the profit center. This profit center can be assigned manually or derived as explained in Section 2.2.4, Profit Center.

If you want to apply different rules to derive the segment during posting, you can define your own rules for this. The document splitting procedure is the prerequisite for creating financial statements at any time for the segment dimension. Another prerequisite for this is to set up a zero balance setting for the segment characteristic in the SAP General Ledger configuration.

> **Note**
>
> To understand more about SAP General Ledger and its functionality, refer to our first book, *SAP ERP Financials: Configuration and Design*.

Note that if you are using segment reporting, make sure that you change the field status group to add the SEGMENT field (as shown in Figure 2.24). Otherwise, the field will not appear and will result in issues during data entry.

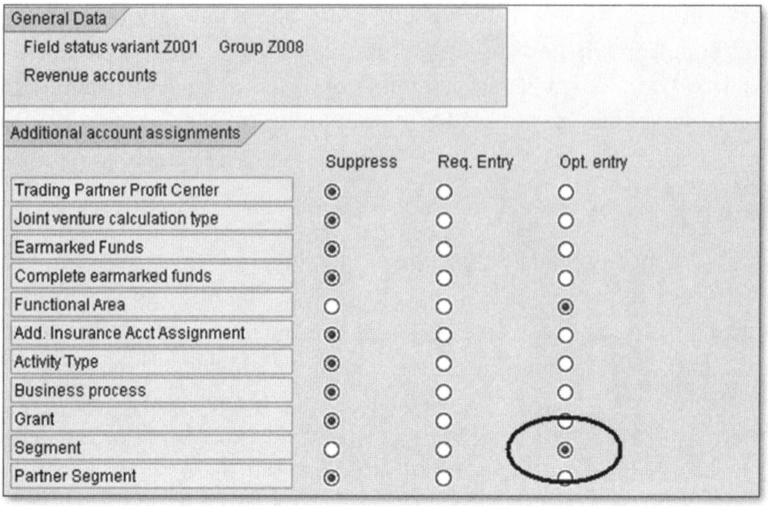

Figure 2.24 Segment Field Added in the Field Status Group

2.3 Summary

In this chapter, we covered the basic configuration of the main enterprise structure elements, which is sometimes referred to as *baseline configuration*. Baseline configuration refers to those configuration items that should not be easily changed once configured because they form the cornerstone of your overall design. Understanding the roles of each of the objects discussed in this chapter will enable you to make good decisions concerning how to use them within your solutions.

Now that you've completed this chapter, you should understand the following:

▶ The role of the components of the enterprise structure in order to decide how to use them.

▶ How to configure the main enterprise structure elements.

▶ The FI and CO master data objects.

In the next chapter, we look at the integration involved in the sales-order-to-cash process.

This chapter runs through the sales-order-to-cash-receipt cycle and explains how each stage integrates with SAP ERP Financials. This is our first look at the Financials-Logistics integration points that are frequently encountered in SAP ERP projects.

3 Integrating the Sales-Order-to-Cash-Receipt Process

In this chapter, we cover the sales-order-to-cash-receipt (S2C) business process and explain the integration points that are relevant for an SAP ERP Financials consultant, including the integration of the process with the Finance component.

> **Note**
>
> We make reference to the Controlling (CO) component but focus mainly on integration with Financial Accounting (FI).

This process begins in Sales and Distribution (SD) and continues through Accounts Receivable (AR); as such, this chapter should be of interest for consultants who want to understand the configuration and design of SD and AR, as well as the integrated business process.

To explain how integration works, we'll look at the design and configuration of the following topics:

- SD organizational elements
- Master data
- Sales orders and billing documents
- Account determination
- AR invoices and payments

The chapter starts by explaining the purpose and configuration of the organizational elements and master data in SD and then looks at how these building blocks fit into the overall process. Because the basis of this book is SAP ERP Financials, it is beyond the scope of this chapter to provide an explanation of *every* SD configuration; however, the chapter covers all of the key configuration activities relevant to the S2C process.

The SD and Materials Management (MM) components overlap a great deal, especially in the area of material master data. This chapter is our first look at Logistics, including MM; when you read Chapter 4, Integrating the Purchase-Order-to-Payment Process, you'll see a detailed review of MM.

3.1 Process Overview

The S2C process is the way in which you manage your relations with your customers, including how customers order goods/services, how you bill them, and how you collect their payments. The process is summarized in Figure 3.1.

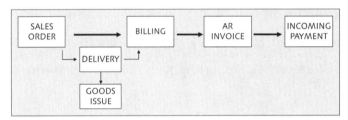

Figure 3.1 S2C Process Flow

In our diagram, the sales order appears to be the start of the S2C process, but in some organizations, the process may begin with a customer inquiry or a customer quotation.

In this section, we provide an overview of the key stages of the S2C process so that you can understand the purpose of each.

3.1.1 Sales Orders

The purpose of the *sales order* is to capture what the customer is ordering; it contains all of the essential sales information, including customer, materials, quantity, prices, delivery dates, and more. This information is used as the basis for the subsequent processes and documents that are needed to complete the entire process.

Sales orders can be created both manually and automatically. Some organizations, for example, manually create sales orders from customer phone calls, or, alternatively, from paper-based customer order forms that originate in the field. Most commonly, though, organizations create sales orders via an interface feed from a non-SAP system, such as a point-of-sales system. Whichever method suits your business best, the sales order is the start of the process for the purposes of our discussions in this chapter.

3.1.2 Delivery Notes

A *delivery note* records the fact that the goods/services in the sales order have been delivered to the customer. In SAP ERP Financials, the system records that the items have been picked, packed, and sent out of the warehouse, thus reducing stock. In some cases, sales orders are split up into many deliveries; in other words, a 1:1 relationship does not have to exist between a sales order and a delivery note. The delivery process is essentially the movement of goods out of the warehouse to the customer; in SAP ERP terms, we call this a *goods issue*. The goods issue transaction generates general ledger postings to record these changes in stock.

3.1.3 Billing Documents

The *billing document* is, as the name suggests, the bill that is issued to the customer. Think of the sales order as an internal document that controls all of the sales processes, and think of the billing document as the external invoice. The two most important functions of the billing document are to generate the physical output, and to be the bridge to pass information from SD to SAP ERP Financials. The details of these two processes are determined based on the rules configured within the automatic account assignment tables, which we discuss later in this chapter.

3.1.4 Accounts Receivable Invoices

Although part of the S2C process, the AR invoice is solely a finance document for debtor management; in other words, it determines when invoices are due for payment. Again, the information here all flows from the original sales order; no information is entered manually. Because SAP ERP is an integrated system, the same document also updates the financial information, that is, SAP General Ledger.

Now that we've presented an overview of the key stages of the S2C process, let's review the configuration of the organizational elements.

3.2 Configuring and Integrating Sales and Distribution Organizational Elements

In this section, we discuss the steps for configuring SD organizational objects and integrating them with SAP ERP Financials.

To begin, let's build on the enterprise structure configuration that we started in Chapter 2, SAP Enterprise Structure, and review the specific areas of SD that need to be configured from an S2C perspective. When we originally configured the enterprise structure for our SAP ERP Financials solution, you may recall seeing folders for SD. After we configure the SD organizational objects (explained in this section), we assign them back to our SAP ERP Financials objects to enable the integration between the systems.

When we decided how to set up the SAP ERP Financials enterprise structure, we had to consider legal entities and statutory requirements. However, this is not the case in the Logistics component; here we are free to define our structure to suit our internal organizational requirements. Although it isn't necessary to have the SAP ERP Financials objects in place before you configure your SD objects, it makes sense to configure the SAP ERP Financials objects before the SD objects. This makes it easier to complete the overall configuration.

The configuration discussed in this section is completed in the area of the IMG shown in Figure 3.2. This figure also shows all of the menu paths for the rest of this section.

3.2.1 Configuring Organizational Objects

Next we discuss the different organizational objects that must be configured in SD.

Sales Area

Sales area is a concept commonly used to describe the organizational relationship of a sales document. It describes the combination of the sales organization, distribution channel, and division for which this transaction is processed; thus, by default, each SD document is specific to a sales area.

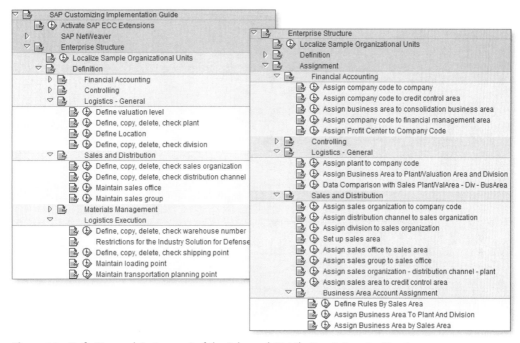

Figure 3.2 Definition and Assignment of the Sales and Distribution Enterprise Structure in the IMG

Sales Organization

The *sales organization* is the highest organizational object in the SD structure and is the level at which you define your rules and controls for the sale and distribution of goods and services in your organization. At this point, you must decide how many sales organizations you need. Companies that want to put in different controls or simply segregate their sales force can set up sales organizations to enable this.

Within a sales organization, you can define controls around processes and master data. For example, you can set up your customer master differently for each sales organization, which may relate to different customer regions; you can also differentiate pricing by sales organization. As such, it should make sense that sales organizations are assigned to company codes. A company code may have many sales organizations assigned to it (e.g., to represent the different sales regions or service areas in that company code), but a sales organization can only be assigned to a single company code. Therefore, you must individually set up master data and controls for individual sales organizations.

Like other main organizational objects, the sales organization configuration screen is a placeholder to which we can assign other objects. The configuration screen shown in Figure 3.3 is accessed via SPRO • ENTERPRISE STRUCTURE • DEFINITION • SALES AND DISTRIBUTION • DEFINE, COPY, DELETE, CHECK SALES ORGANIZATION.

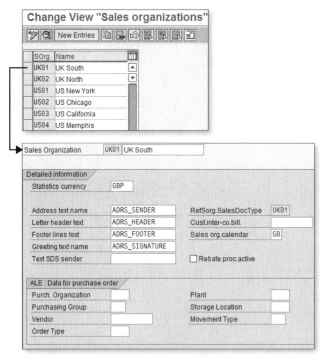

Figure 3.3 Sales Organization Definition

Each sales organization has a sales-specific calendar assigned to it, which enables you to define billing dates specific to that sales organization. If you define calendar monthly billing dates within your sales organization, you cannot also define, say, a 5-4-4 weekly billing convention. For this, you need to set up a separate sales organization with a separate calendar.

At the sales organization level, you also activate customer intercompany billing. This is used when you want to use SD to bill other internal sales organizations as an internal trading solution.

Now that the sales organization is defined, you can assign the sales organization to the company code. As you can see from Figure 3.4, you can assign many sales organizations to the same company code or have a 1:1 assignment. Figure 3.4 is accessed via SPRO • ENTERPRISE STRUCTURE • ASSIGNMENT • SALES AND DISTRIBU-TION • ASSIGN SALES ORGANIZATION TO COMPANY CODE.

SOrg.	Name	CoCd	Company Name	Status
UK01	UK South	UK	SAFA UK	
UK02	UK North	UK	SAFA UK	
US01	US New York	US	SAFA US	
US02	US Chicago	US	SAFA US	
US03	US California	US	SAFA US	
US04	US Memphis	US	SAFA US	

Figure 3.4 Assigning Sales Organizations to Company Codes

As we move through the rest of this chapter, you will see that a number of configuration objects are assigned to the sales organization.

Distribution Channels

You should think of the distribution channel (DC) as being your way of reaching your customers; in other words, it is the route to your market. A DC is a sublevel below the sales organization, and you must set up at least one, even if it's a single default DC for all your transactions. In your organization, you may need different DCs to differentiate between retail sales or Internet sales, for example.

Within the DC, you define and assign a number of parameters, including sales order types, default printers, and DC-specific master data (including customer and material master records). The DC can also be used as a reporting dimension for sales statistics. All elements entered within your sales order have a specific relationship with the DC.

A DC covers the whole process, from the warehouse to the customer. For the DC, you define master data as well as DC-specific conditions and pricing. Table 3.1 shows the four DCs that represent the different routes to market in our example organization.

DC	Description	Purpose
01	Direct Sales	Direct sales to customers
02	Internet Sales	Direct sales to customers
03	Wholesale Sales	Sales to retailers who sell to their customers
04	Clearance Sales	Damaged or faulty goods are sold on to a business partner

Table 3.1 Purpose of Distribution Channels

As we move through the configuration in this chapter, you will better understand how the DC fulfills its purpose. Figure 3.5 shows the configuration of DCs and is accessed via SPRO • ENTERPRISE STRUCTURE • ASSIGNMENT • SALES AND DISTRIBUTION • ASSIGN DISTRIBUTION CHANNEL TO SALES ORGANIZATION.

Change View "Distribution channels"

Distr. Channel	Name
01	Direct Sales
02	Internet Sales
03	Wholesale Sales
04	Clearance Sales

SOrg.	Name	DChl	Name	Status
1000	Germany Frankfurt	16	Factory sales	
1020	Germany Berlin	20	Store chain	
1020	Germany Berlin	22	Industrial customers	
1020	Germany Berlin	24	Pharm. customers	
1030	Germany Berlin	24	Pharm. customers	
2000	UK Heathrow/Hayes	10	Final customer sales	
2000	UK Heathrow/Hayes	12	Sold for resale	
2000	UK Heathrow/Hayes	14	Service	
2000	UK Heathrow/Hayes	30	Internet Sales	
2200	France, Paris	10	Final customer sales	·
2220	France, Paris	10	Final customer sales	
2300	Spain, Barcelona	10	Final customer sales	

Figure 3.5 Configuration and Assignment of Distribution Channels

Our DCs sit below a sales organization, but you can also share a DC across a sales organization. When this occurs, the DCs are called *common* distribution channels. These are defined using Transaction VOR1: SPRO • SALES AND DISTRIBUTION • MASTER DATA • DEFINE COMMON DISTRIBUTION CHANNELS. You can also configure common divisions here, which we discuss next.

Divisions

Whereas the DC helps you reach your customers, the division is specifically concerned with materials and services. You need at least one division in your system to complete the order-to-cash cycle. Divisions tend to represent a range or portfolio for a specific product or service. In SAP ERP, when you make a sale or a purchase, the products have a material master record. The material master record is a very complicated object, and a number of screens (or *views*) represent the different parts of the system. We'll explain the accounting, sales, and purchasing sections when we look at the material master record in Chapter 4. Later in this chapter, we look in some detail at the sales-relevant information contained in material master data.

Divisions are assigned to sales organizations, as shown in Figure 3.6. Their configuration is done within the Logistics-General area of the IMG: SPRO • ENTERPRISE STRUCTURE • DEFINITION • LOGISTICS – GENERAL • DEFINE, COPY, DELETE, CHECK DIVISION.

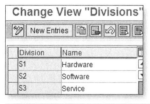

Change View "Divisions"	

Division	Name
S1	Hardware
S2	Software
S3	Service

Assignment Sales Organization - Division			
SOrg.	Name	Dv	Name
UK01	UK South	S1	Hardware
UK01	UK South	S2	Software
UK01	UK South	S3	Service
UK02	UK North	S1	Hardware
UK02	UK North	S2	Software
UK02	UK North	S3	Service
US01	US New York	S1	Hardware
US02	US Chicago	S2	Software
US02	US Chicago	S3	Service
US03	US California	S1	Hardware
US03	US California	S2	Software
US03	US California	S3	Service
US04	US Memphis	S1	Hardware
US04	US Memphis	S2	Software
US04	US Memphis	S3	Service

Figure 3.6 Configuration and Assignment of Divisions

Materials can only be assigned to a single division, which is an assignment made within the material master record (Transaction MM03) on the SALES ORG 1 view (Figure 3.7).

You may wonder: If a material can only be assigned to a single division, does this mean that we need to set up the same material in each division? In fact, you can set up common divisions to be used across sales organizations (Transaction VOR2): SPRO • SALES AND DISTRIBUTION • MASTER DATA • DEFINE DIVISIONS.

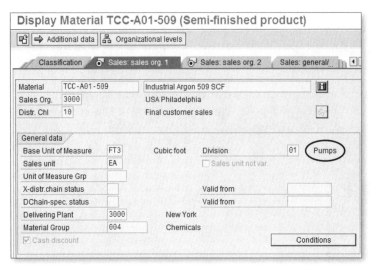

Figure 3.7 Material Assignment to a Division

You can also define conditions and pricing at the division level. Material pricing groups are assigned to materials on the SALES ORG 2 screen; we talk about this in more detail later in this chapter.

Plants

In discussing the distribution of goods from the warehouse, we mentioned that material master records are MM objects. We now look at another MM object, the *plant*, which is a place where materials are stored. A plant can be a warehouse storage facility, or an assembly or manufacturing facility. In SD terms, we are interested solely in the fact that the plant is the location from where we distribute goods, although it could be a location for "nonwarehouse" activities as well.

In MM, plants are used for valuating material. They are assigned to a single company code but can be a distribution or shipping point for any sales organization. This is shown in Figure 3.8, which is where we set up the possible combinations for distribution within our sales organizations: SPRO • ENTERPRISE STRUCTURE • ASSIGNMENT • LOGISTICS – GENERAL • ASSIGN PLANT TO COMPANY CODE.

Change View "Plants": Overview

Plnt	Name 1	Name 2
UK01	UK London	UK London
UK02	UK Birmingham	UK Birmingham
US01	US New York	US New York
US02	US Chicago	US Chicago
US03	US California	US California
US04	US Memphis	US Memphis

Change View "Assignment Plant - Company Code"

Assignment Plant - Company Code

Co	Plnt	Name of Plant	Company Name
UK	UK01	UK London	SAFA UK
UK	UK02	UK Birmingham	SAFA UK
US	US01	US New York	SAFA US
US	US02	US Chicago	SAFA US
US	US03	US California	SAFA US

Figure 3.8 Definition and Assignment of Plants

Plants also need to be assigned to the combination of the sales organization and DC to link them for sending out deliveries (Figure 3.9): SPRO • ENTERPRISE STRUCTURE • ASSIGNMENT • SALES AND DISTRIBUTION • ASSIGN SALES ORGANIZATION - DISTRIBUTION CHANNEL – PLANT.

Change View "Assignment Sales Organization/Distribution Channel - Plan

Assignment Sales Organization/Distribution Channel - Plant

SOrg.	Name	DChCust/Mt	Name	Plnt	Name 1	Status
UK01	UK South	01	Direct Sales	UK02	UK Birmingham	
UK01	UK South	02	Internet Sales	US02	US Chicago	
UK01	UK South	03	Wholesale Sales	UK01	UK London	
UK01	UK South	04	Clearance Sales	UK02	UK Birmingham	
UK02	UK North	01	Direct Sales	UK02	UK Birmingham	
UK02	UK North	02	Internet Sales	US02	US Chicago	
US01	US New York	01	Direct Sales	US01	US New York	
US01	US New York	02	Internet Sales	US02	US Chicago	
US01	US New York	03	Wholesale Sales	US01	US New York	

Figure 3.9 Assignment of Sales Organization and DC to Plant

We briefly mentioned shipping points earlier in this chapter. Although they have nothing to do with SAP ERP Financials integration, you should know that they are positions within the plant from which an outbound delivery is processed. If your organization is using delivery notes or shipping advices, it may issue a document with the details of the shipping point from which your stock is issued.

3.2.2 Linking Organizational Objects

We have now configured all of the main SD objects necessary to complete our sales area configuration. As we said earlier, the sales area is the combination of sales organizations, divisions, and distribution channels specific to your sales order. In this activity, we link the objects together and so define the permissible combinations. Figure 3.10 shows the combinations that have been set up; they represent our permissible sales areas. This screen is accessed via SPRO • ENTERPRISE STRUCTURE • ASSIGNMENT • SALES AND DISTRIBUTION • SET UP SALES AREA.

Change View "Assignment Sales Org. - Distribution Channel - Division":

SOrg.	Name	DChl	Name	Dv	Name	Status
UK02	UK North	03	Wholesale Sales	S1	Hardware	
UK02	UK North	03	Wholesale Sales	S2	Software	
UK02	UK North	04	Clearance Sales	S1	Hardware	
UK02	UK North	04	Clearance Sales	S2	Software	
US01	US New York	01	Direct Sales	S1	Hardware	
US02	US Chicago	02	Internet Sales	S2	Software	
US02	US Chicago	03	Wholesale Sales	S1	Hardware	
US02	US Chicago	03	Wholesale Sales	S2	Software	

Figure 3.10 Defining Permissible Sales Areas

We have now established our internal sales structure, and the way in which we sell and distribute our goods and services to our customers. The last step we need to take is to link these sales areas back to the credit control areas that were set up by the Finance team.

3.2.3 Assigning Sales Areas to Credit Control Areas

When we looked at the configuration of the credit control area (in Chapter 2), we explained that a credit control area is needed to manage credit within an organization. To link the SD and SAP ERP Financials components and check credit between them, we need to ensure that this configuration link is completed. Keep in mind that this configuration provides only a link; the detailed configuration of credit control was covered in Chapter 2. Figure 3.11 shows the configuration entries and

is accessed via SPRO • ENTERPRISE STRUCTURE • ASSIGNMENT • SALES AND DISTRIBU-
TION • ASSIGN SALES AREA TO CREDIT CONTROL AREA.

SOrg.	DChl	Dv	CCAr
UK01	01	S1	1000
UK01	01	S2	1000
UK01	01	S3	1000
UK02	01	S1	1000
UK02	02	S2	1000
UK02	03	S1	1000
UK02	03	S2	1000
UK02	04	S1	1000
UK02	04	S2	1000
US01	01	S1	2000
US02	02	S2	2000
US02	03	S1	2000
US02	03	S2	2000
US02	04	S2	2000
US03	01	S1	2000

Figure 3.11 Assignment of Credit Control Area to Sales Area

Next, we look at business area account determination, which is sometimes required
in a SD design.

3.2.4 Assigning Business Area Accounts

As the use of Profit Center Accounting (PCA) has become more widespread, business areas are less frequently used; however, they are still in use in some places.
As an account assignment object, business areas can be used to provide management analysis about the nature of cost and income in an organization. This area
of configuration can be accessed via the following menu path: SPRO • ENTERPRISE
STRUCTURE • ASSIGNMENT • SALES AND DISTRIBUTION • BUSINESS AREA ACCOUNT
ASSIGNMENT.

The business area can be used as an account assignment object within the FI component, independent of the CO component. It can be determined from the sales
document, based on the organizational object you select. After you have decided
how to assign business areas, define which rule you want to activate. Your options
are shown in Figure 3.12.

This completes our review of the SD organizational objects. In the next section,
we discuss some important master data objects.

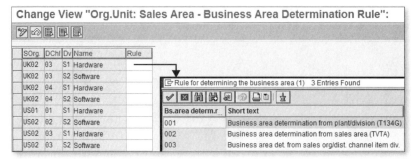

Figure 3.12   Sales Area: Business Area Determination Rule

3.3   Setting Up S2C Master Data: Customer Master Data

The master data needed to support the S2C process is spread between SD, AR, and SAP General Ledger. In this chapter, we specifically look at the customer and material master data, which are central to the entire process. We begin with customer master data.

There are some basic configuration steps that you should be aware of before beginning this section. These steps are covered in detail in our previous book (*SAP ERP Financials: Configuration and Design*); for the purposes of this book, though, we will simply review them quickly.

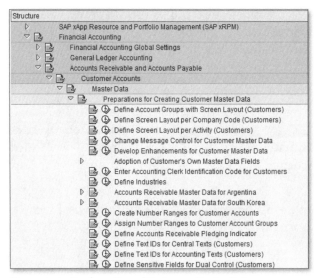

Figure 3.13   Configuration of Customer Master Data

The configuration of customer master data is completed in the IMG as shown in Figure 3.13.

All new customer master records require a number, which can be system-generated or manually entered. The rules concerning customer numbers are governed by the configuration and assignment of number ranges. Figure 3.14 shows the process of creating a new number range.

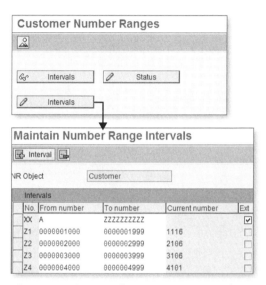

Figure 3.14   Create and Assign Customer Number Ranges

After you configure the number range, the next step is to assign it to a customer account group. To manage customer master records, you set controls in the customer account group. These controls are configured to determine what information needs to be entered when creating a new customer record in the system, and they are set up based on the type of customer record. You do this by completing the field status group configuration in each account group.

From an SAP ERP Financials point of view, the customer master record is shared between SD and AR. As an SAP ERP Financials consultant, you are likely familiar with what needs to be set up from an AR point of view; as such, we will skim through these and spend more time focusing on the SD view of the customer. Looking at Figure 3.15, you can see that the customer master record is split into three groups of data: general data, company code data, and sales data.

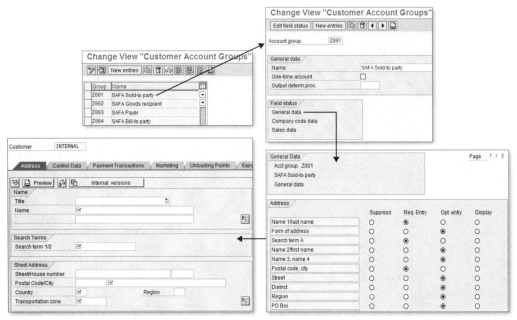

Figure 3.15 Configuration of Customer Account Field Status

You create and manage your customer database via the SAP Easy Access menu: ACCOUNTING • FINANCIAL ACCOUNTING • ACCOUNTS RECEIVABLE • MASTER DATA. From this area, you see that you can use Transaction FD01 to create a customer. This transaction only allows you to manage the general and accounting views of the customer. To fully manage the customer, which you do in an integrated S2C business process, use the transactions in the following area: ACCOUNTING • FINANCIAL ACCOUNTING • ACCOUNTS RECEIVABLE • MASTER DATA • MAINTAIN CENTRALLY.

Next, we review the key fields that appear on the different views of the customer master record. (A more detailed explanation is included in our previous book, *SAP ERP Financials: Configuration and Design.*)

3.3.1 General Data

The general data view holds all of the information related to the general characteristics of the customer, such as name and address. This information is used as a source of information in any customer correspondence. In our example customer (Figure 3.16), we have different locations for different partner functions; this way, the system can identify the different address setups for each partner function.

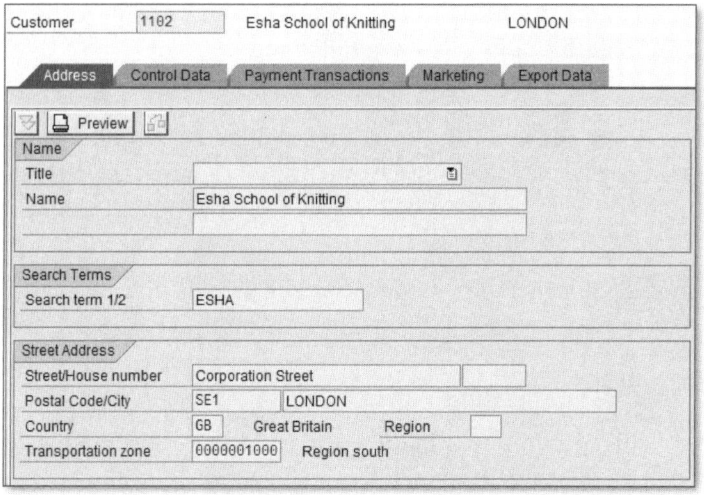

Figure 3.16 Customer Master Record: General Data, Address Tab

In the following lists, we briefly outline the most important fields in the ADDRESS tab and CONTROL DATA tabs, respectively. The ADDRESS tab holds the address information for the customer. This information depends on the partner function that you are creating; for the ship-to, you should enter the warehouse address, and for the bill-to, you should enter the AP department.

The ADDRESS tab includes the following fields:

▶ NAME
This is the main name the customer is known by. Two lines are given here, and you can use both lines.

▶ SEARCH TERM 1/2
Short name that is used to set up a matchcode.

▶ STREET/HOUSE NUMBER
Street address.

▶ POSTAL CODE/CITY
ZIP code and city information.

▶ COUNTRY
Two-digit country identifier.

▶ REGION
Two-letter state abbreviation.

The CONTROL tab contains information about taxes; to fill this out correctly, consult your local tax rules. Fields on this tab include the following:

▶ VENDOR
If this customer is also a vendor, enter the vendor number here. This allows you to match payables and receivables against each other (if you adopt this policy in your company).

▶ VAT REG NO
Specify the customer VAT registration number, which allows you to charge them tax in some countries. You should consult your local tax laws on this matter.

▶ TAX NUMBER 2
The use of this field changes by country; in the United States, it is the employee identification number. In the United Kingdom, it is the national insurance (NI) number. Because it has different uses across Europe, refer to the help file to determine your specific country requirement.

On the PAYMENT TRANSACTION tab, you can enter the customer's bank information (see Figure 3.17). This screen is important if you collect customer payments by direct debit, which is becoming more common for customers who want to make payments over periods of time. Collecting payments electronically from customers is becoming more common in many sectors; nowadays, people frequently pay by direct debit.

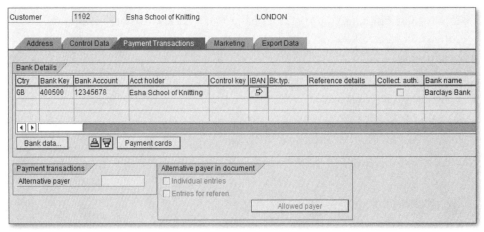

Figure 3.17 Customer Master Record: General Data, Payment Transactions Tab

We briefly address direct debits later in this chapter, at which point, we will return to Figure 3.17.

3.3.2 Company Code Data

The information required in the company code data view is used to complete accounting-based transactions, including AR invoices and incoming payments. These transactions also update the general ledger, so this is where you define the ledger control accounts, or reconciliation accounts. Your organization may have more than one company code; if each is dealing with the same customer, they could have different sets of data on these screens for each company code. This may initially seem confusing, but it may be that you have different terms or general ledger accounts set up for each company code.

The following list explains the most important fields on the ACCOUNT MANAGE-MENT tab, which is shown in Figure 3.18.

▶ RECON. ACCOUNT
This should always be a mandatory field because it controls the posting between the AR subledger and SAP General Ledger. This is explained in some detail later in this chapter.

▶ SORT KEY
When an AR document is created, a value is entered into the assignment field on that document. This field is the default sorting parameter when running a customer line-item report. Whatever you select as the sort key is the value entered into this customer's assignment field.

▶ HEAD OFFICE
The head office functionality is used to group together customers for reporting and analysis. When you have a complex arrangement and want to link up branches with a head office, you can use this field; in this case, postings to the branch are posted to the head office account instead. Note: This functionality is slightly different from partner functions. For example, certain customers use factors to pay their bills on their behalf (this is a debt collection process used by some companies). You can use HEAD OFFICE within AR solely to collect debt from another person. This concept is explained in more detail in Section 3.11.1, Credit Management later in this chapter.

▶ PREV. ACCT. NO.
This can be a useful field to populate when migrating customers from an old system to a new system. It may also be used for customers who have had their account number changed in the SAP ERP system.

▶ CASH MGMT GROUP
If you are using the liquidity analyses reports (available through SAP Cash and Liquidity Management in the SAP FSCM component), this field can be used to control the update of the receivable section of liquidity-forecast reporting.

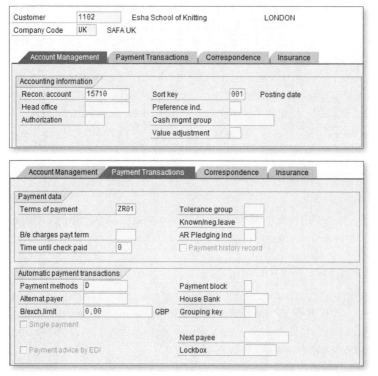

Figure 3.18 Customer Master Record: Company Code Data. Account Management

The following list describes the key fields on the PAYMENT TRANSACTIONS tab, which controls the processing of items within AR only.

▶ TERMS OF PAYMENT
Agreed payment terms with the customer should be used here. This value defaults into each customer invoice you create. It is possible to change the payment terms in the invoice, so you are not restricted to this value.

▶ TOLERANCE GROUP
A tolerance group can be assigned to a customer to control the value of transactions that can be processed, as well as the tolerance within which small differences can be written off. This is explained in more detail later in this chapter.

- ► ALTERNATIVE PAYER

  If you know someone else pays this customer's invoices, you can use this box to link an alternate payer to this record. The alternate payer must be set up in the system as a valid customer record. Because this field is in the area specific to the company code of the customer record, the alternate payer needs to be set up for each company code as necessary.

The following describes the key fields on the CORRESPONDENCE tab, which is used for recording important information in relation to the dunning-related correspondence with the customer. (*Dunning* is a process whereby you monitor outstanding invoices and produce SAP-generated reminder letters to be sent out to the customer; it is explained in detail in Section 3.11.2, Dunning, toward the end of this chapter.)

> **Note**
>
> Although we don't discuss them, there are other fields on this screen that record contact details for correspondence with the customer.

- ► DUNNING AREA

  The dunning area is an assignment made to a rule within the dunning procedure.

- ► DUNNING PROC

  This field is used to assign the dunning procedure relevant to this customer.

- ► DUNNING BLOCK

  If we want to exclude all of this customer's items from the dunning process, we can put a block on the record in this field.

- ► DUNN.RECIPIENT

  If dunning letters for this customer are to be sent elsewhere, an alternative customer master record can be assigned in this field.

We will come back to these fields as we move through the chapter.

3.3.3   Sales Area Data

As you saw in the previous section, the customer can be set up differently for each company code. The same is true for the sales area; that is, the customer can have different settings per sales areas (remember that a sales area is a combination of a sales organization, distribution channel, and division). The key configuration in Figure 3.19 is the pricing configuration, which is essential to control which pricing procedure the system should apply when you create a sales order for the customer. In addition, if you allow this customer additional discounts or other agreements, the relevant price list can be selected here.

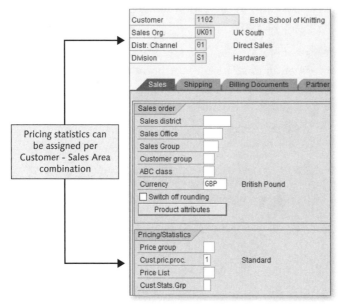

Figure 3.19 Customer Master Record: Sales Tab

Figure 3.20 shows the BILLING DOCUMENTS tab, and the following list describes the most important fields in this tab.

▶ INCOTERMS
Incoterms specify certain internationally recognized procedures that the shipper and the customer must adhere to for the shipping transaction to be recognized as completed successfully. These terms are specific to the location from where the goods are issued (in our example, we use London).

▶ TERMS OF PAYMENT
The payment terms entered here can be different from those entered on the company code screen for this customer that we discussed earlier. The difference is that these are used when creating SD documents (sales orders), whereas the company code terms are relevant only for documents created in FI.

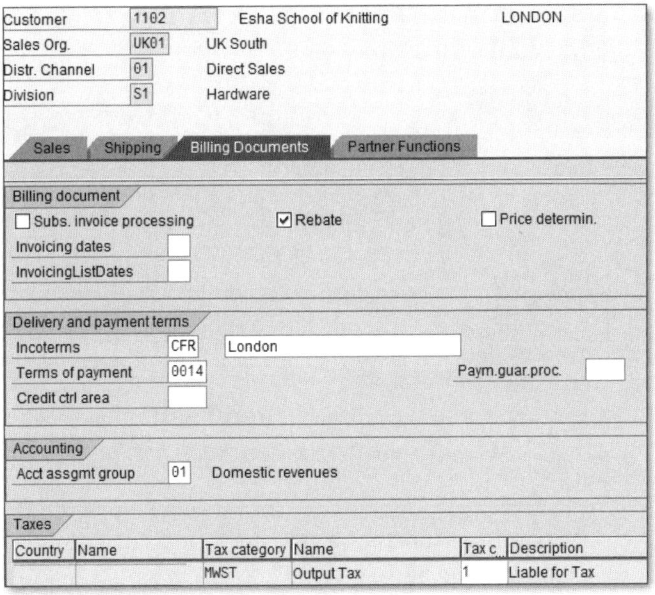

Figure 3.20 Customer Master Record: Billing Documents Tab

▶ CREDIT CTRL AREA
Because more than one credit control area can be assigned to a customer, this field is where you provide the default value for this sales area.

▶ ACCT ASSGMT GROUP
For this sales area, you can define a (customer) account assignment group that is used in the (general ledger) account determination when posting to the ledger. We discuss this in more detail later in the chapter.

▶ TAXES
At the bottom of the screen, you can indicate the customer tax liability. This, combined with the tax classification on the material, determines which tax code appears on the final invoice to this customer.

The last tab is the PARTNER FUNCTIONS tab, which enables you to configure the complicated real-life relationships you may have with your customers. For example, the person placing the sales order may be at a different location than where the goods are delivered, and the accounts department that pays the invoice may be at yet another location. By capturing these addresses, the system can add them to the relevant documentation that is sent out. SAP ERP requires you to set up these partners with their own customer master records in their own right. Table 3.2 explains the common partner functions in this process.

Partner	Function
Sold-to-party	Places the order
Ship-to-party	Receives the goods/services
Bill-to-party	Receives the invoice
Payer	Pays the invoice

Table 3.2 Possible Customer Partner Functions

To establish customer functions, you must set up additional customer master records to represent each partner function in the system and then assign them to the sold-to party.

After you set up and assign the various partners for a customer, you must define a set of rules for determining the appropriate partner function. To do so, use SPRO • SALES AND DISTRIBUTION • BASIC FUNCTIONS • PARTNER DETERMINATION • SETUP PARTNER DETERMINATION.

3.4 Setting Up S2C Master Data: Material Master Data

We mentioned material master data earlier in this chapter and described it as the record for the different products (goods or services) you buy and sell in your organization. The material master data includes all of the information needed to enable the sale and distribution of your product. In this section, we focus on the material master record screens that are required for order-to-cash integration. (A more complete explanation of material master data is given in Chapter 4.)

The transaction codes for material master data are MM01 (create), MM02 (change), and MM03 (display).

3.4.1 Basic Data 1 Tab

The BASIC DATA 1 tab provides the basic information for a material. The main fields are described in the following list:

▶ MATERIAL NUMBER

The master record code. This configuration is discussed in more detail in Chapter 4.

▶ MATERIAL DESCRIPTION

The name of the master record.

▶ UNIT OF MEASURE

The unit in which this material is supplied; examples include "each," "piece," "pack."

▶ DIVISION

Materials are assigned to a single division.

3.4.2 Sales Org 1 Tab

This is the first of the sales-based views, which is shown in Figure 3.21. The following list describes its main fields:

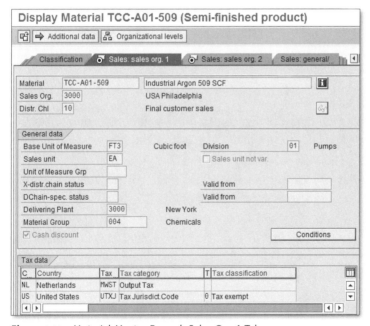

Figure 3.21 Material Master Record: Sales Org 1 Tab

▶ SALES UNIT
This refers to the unit in which the material is sold.

▶ DELIVERING PLANT
This refers to the plant from which this material is distributed or delivered.

▶ DIVISION
All sales materials must be assigned to a single division.

▶ Tax Data
In this section of the screen, you define the settings for tax classification.

For the purposes of sales, you must assign a tax classification to materials. Indicate whether the product is relevant for tax, and, if so, decide the level of tax (full, half, or low). This combines with the tax classification on the customer to determine which tax code appears on the invoice.

3.4.3 Sales Org 2 Tab

This is the second sales-based view, which is shown in Figure 3.22. The following list describes the key fields:

▶ MATERIAL PRICING GRP
The rules for pricing are controlled through condition records. We discuss pricing later in Section 3.5.2.

▶ ACCT ASSIGNMENT GRP
This is where you assign the rules that control the account assignment determination. We discuss this later in the chapter in Section 3.8.

▶ ITEM CATEGORY GROUP
This setting enables the determination of item categories within the sales document.

▶ PRODUCT HIERARCHY
Materials can be grouped together into a hierarchy to reflect product lines. This reporting hierarchy is accessed through the Controlling-Profitability Analysis (CO-PA) component.

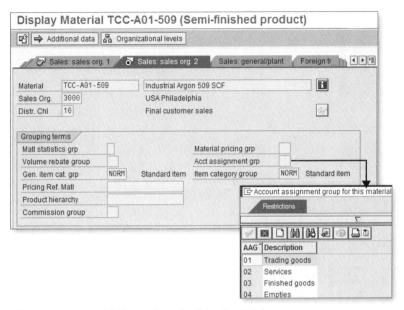

Figure 3.22 Material Master Records: Sales Org 2 Tab

We have now briefly reviewed the importance of the material and customer master records. In the next section, we begin looking at the sales order.

3.5   Sales Order

The first document that we will look at is the sales order, which captures what the customer wants to order and is created after a customer inquiry and quotation. Generally, sales orders are manually created at the point of sale, which may or may not be something that occurs within the SAP ERP system.

Sales orders are created on the application side of the system, as shown in Figure 3.23.

Like most SAP ERP documents, the sales order has header and line item sections, as shown in Figure 3.24. As we look at examples later in this chapter, you will understand what information is contained within each of these sections.

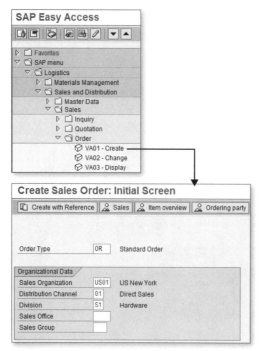

Figure 3.23 Sales Order Management Transactions

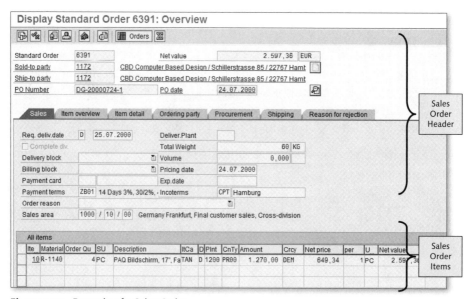

Figure 3.24 Example of a Sales Order

3.5.1 Sales Order Type

The sales order type is the first thing you need to decide when creating your sales order. This important piece of configuration helps you determine a number of important rules about the sales order. We will explain these rules as we move through this chapter, but, in general, we can say that this configuration controls the sales document header information, including the following:

▶ Pricing

▶ Text determination

▶ Item categories

▶ Billing document types

▶ Incompleteness

The configuration rules assigned to the sales document type are essential to the completion of the sales order. You probably recognize the terms we just listed, but we will talk about them briefly later in the chapter.

The configuration of sales order types is completed in the following area of the IMG (Transaction VOV8): SPRO • SALES AND DISTRIBUTION • SALES • SALES DOCUMENTS • SALES DOCUMENT HEADER • DEFINE SALES DOCUMENT TYPES. The configuration screen has a number of configuration items; Figure 3.25 shows the most important ones.

This configuration allows you to view all sales document types, but we are looking specifically at the OR type, which is a standard sales order. Rather than go through each item, the following list highlights the key functionalities that this screen enables:

▶ NO. RANGE
These fields allow you to assign different ranges for internal and external assignments, if required.

▶ ITEM NO. INCREMENT
This field represents the increment between lines in a sales order. In a standard SAP ERP system, the lines in a sales order appear as 10, 20, 30, and so on (i.e., increments of 10).

▶ REFERENCE MANDATORY
Here you can indicate whether it's mandatory to create the sales order with reference to another document. If you make a selection here, you are saying that sales orders can only be created with reference to an inquiry, quotation, or another sales order.

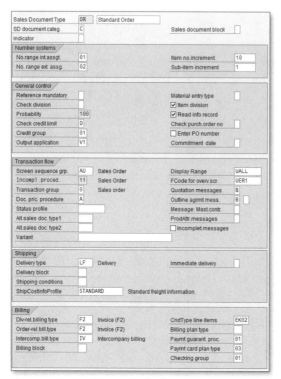

Figure 3.25 Configuration of Sales Document Types

▶ CHECK CREDIT LIMIT
This field controls whether the system does a credit check when creating the sales order. This is dependent on the configuration of automatic credit control.

▶ ENTER PO NUMBER
If you select this option, the system enters the document number in the PO field when saving (if the PO field is blank).

▶ DOC PRIC PROCEDURE
This field controls the pricing procedure for this specific sales document. We explain this configuration later in the chapter.

▶ DELIVERY TYPE
Here you assign the default delivery type that is relevant for this sales order.

▶ BILLING area
In this area, you link the sales order to the billing document. We discuss billing documents later in this section.

▶ In the BILLING BLOCK field, you can assign a default block to a sales order type, which requires a manual release. Some organizations may want to use this for items that require additional levels of control, for example, credit and debit memos.

▶ In the CDNTYPE LINE ITEMS field, you define which condition type is used to determine the results of the sales order pricing activity.

The basic principle you need to understand when configuring sales orders is that the various elements of functionality that we have listed can be assigned to a specific sales order type. As you will see in the sections that follow, the configuration of these functionalities are assigned to the document type.

As a general rule of thumb, organizations tend to adopt the majority of what is in SAP ERP standard order type OR and copy it into their own Z-order type for use. In the Z-order type, they can then make minor adjustments to the various assignments that we have introduced previously and will explore in more detail in the sections that follow.

3.5.2 Pricing

You determine the price a customer pays for goods and services via the pricing procedure, which is determined by the combination of customer and material within a price list. These combinations come together as data within pricing conditions.

We do not discuss pricing configuration in detail here because this topic is beyond the scope of the book. Instead, we focus on the setup of the condition records, which are on the application side of the system.

New conditions can be defined for custom purposes, and are configured in the following area of the IMG (Transaction VOK0): SPRO • SALES AND DISTRIBUTION • BASIC FUNCTIONS • PRICING • PRICING CONTROL • DEFINE CONDITION TYPES • MAINTAIN CONDITION TYPES.

This transaction is used to set up the conditions relevant for a sales order, including the following:

▶ Price

▶ Freight

▶ Tax

▶ Discounts

Having set up the condition types, you can now assign values through the application side of the system by setting up records, as seen in Figure 3.26.

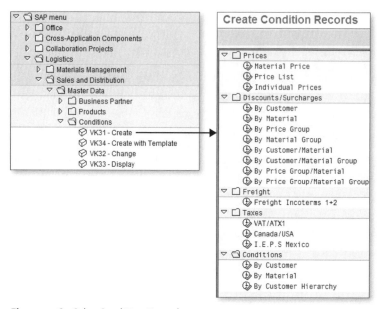

Figure 3.26 Sales Condition Records

If you are changing the price of a material, or amending discounts, tax, or freight information, then these parameters need to be set up as conditions. (The other option is to use manual pricing, in which you have no pricing condition but must type the price directly into the sales order. There is a header condition type, HM00, which allows you to enter the order value manually; alternatively, PN00 allows you to enter the price for each individual item.) You can also set up conditions specific to customers, which allows you to offer different terms to your better customers.

Tax is an important item to discuss in a little more detail here. In the tax configuration settings, you configure the tax codes that are used to calculate tax on customer invoices; this configuration is needed for you to charge the correct amount of tax for the product and customer you are including in your sales order. This information is determined based on two important classifications:

▸ On the SALES ORG 1 tab of the material master record, you define the level of taxation applicable to this material. Most goods and services are subject to full tax; however, you will have instances where you assign other classifications, such as no tax or low tax.

▶ In the BILLING DOCUMENTS tab of the customer master record, you define what level of taxation this customer is subject to.

The actual tax rate is held within condition record MWST, which you must set up accordingly.

The process through which the price for a good or service is determined is known as the *pricing procedure*. When a sales order is created, the system follows the pricing procedure relevant to (1) the document sales area, (2) the customer, and (3) the sales document type that has been selected.

Within the pricing procedure, there are a list of valid condition types — for example, PR00 (material price) and MWST (output tax) — that determine the access sequence. This is nothing more than the order in which the condition tables are read, which determines the price that appears on the sales order. Each condition table holds the combinations of records that are searched to determine price. To define condition tables, use the following menu path: SPRO • SALES AND DISTRIBUTION • BASIC FUNCTIONS • PRICING • PRICING CONTROL • DEFINE CONDITION TABLES (Figure 3.27). (Note: This activity requires a developer key, and should be completed by someone with ABAP knowledge.)

Figure 3.27 Condition Tables

The same fields exist in our example access sequence, but the order defined here is the order in which the system does the price determination, as seen in Figure 3.28.

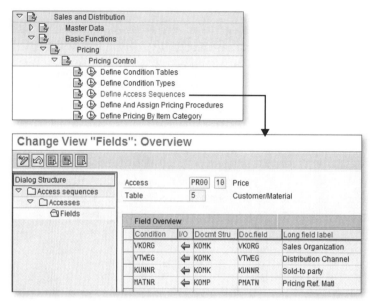

Figure 3.28 Access Sequence PR00

The access sequence and condition tables are brought together in the pricing procedure, as shown in Figure 3.29.

When you create your sales order, in the Pricing screen, the system automatically selects applicable condition types (price, tax, discount, etc.) for your sales order transaction.

For a more detailed discussion of these topics, we recommend consulting a Sales and Distribution book (for example, *Optimizing Sales and Distribution in SAP ERP*, SAP PRESS, 2010).

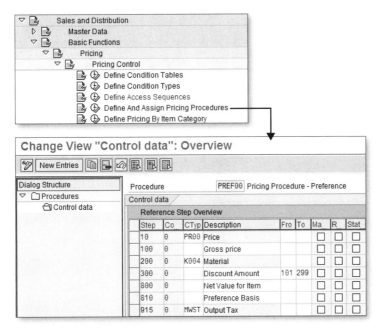

Figure 3.29 Pricing Procedure

3.5.3 Text Determination

Customer correspondence is a key element of the S2C business cycle. Because businesses are constantly communicating with customers, there must be an efficient way to produce correspondence (also known as output), as well as determine what the correct source of information is for the different correspondence you want to produce.

In this section, we look specifically at the text of a sales order and explain how to define header and line item text (both of which affect correspondence output). To get started, use SPRO • SALES AND DISTRIBUTION • BASIC FUNCTIONS • TEXT CONTROL. From this central area, you can configure all text types, the most important of which are listed in Table 3.3.

For sales order header texts, go to the sales document header configuration screen and look specifically at TEXTDETERMPROC (Figure 3.30). This shows you the different texts that are available for you to use. In this same configuration screen, you assign the text procedure to a sales document type, which gives you the flexibility to use the same field for different purposes in different sales document types.

93

S2C Object/Document	Text Type
Customer	Central texts
	Contact person
	Sales and Distribution
Pricing Conditions	Agreements
	Conditions
Sales Document	Header
	Item
Delivery	Header
	Item
Billing Document	Header
	Item

Table 3.3 Common Text Types

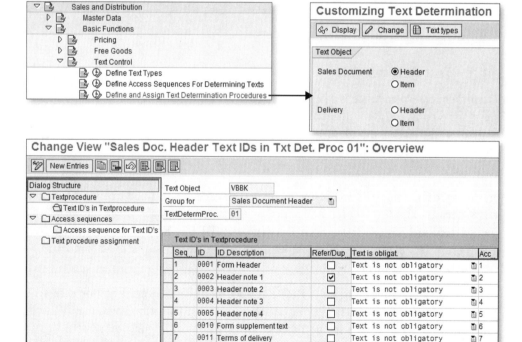

Figure 3.30 Sales Document Header Text Determination

From this same configuration activity, you make available the texts that you want to include in the final customer output. This configuration activity is combined with the copy control functionality to produce texts on the final customer invoice, as explained in the next section.

3.5.4 Sales Document Copy Data

The copy control functionality (SAP refers to this as "copying control" in the IMG) is used to provide the link between different documents. In this specific case, we are looking at copying data from the sales order to the billing document; however, there are a number of copy control functions that you should be aware of, including sales order to sales order, contract to sales order, and delivery to billing (this last one is relevant if you decide to have a delivery-based billing process).

In our S2C business process, we saw that the sales order was converted into a billing document. It's important that this process is automated so that you don't have to manually enter information into the billing document; instead, the information is automatically copied from the source document (the sales order). This is configured in the following area of the IMG: SPRO • SALES AND DISTRIBUTION • BILLING • BILLING DOCUMENT • MAINTAIN COPYING CONTROL FOR BILLING DOCUMENTS.

These relationships are maintained by document types, so you can define different rules based on the different sales order types you've set up in your system. We've already seen the sales document types. Billing documents have their own set of document types, and the first activity in this configuration step is to link the two, as shown in Figure 3.31.

Dialog Structure	Header				
▽ ⛶ Header		Tgt	Billing Type	Source	SalesDocType
⬜ Item		F2	Invoice (F2)	PS2	PS: Billing Request
		F2	Invoice (F2)	OR	Standard Order
		F2	Invoice (F2)	TAV	Standard Order (VMI)
		F2	Invoice (F2)	TSA	Telesales
		F2	Invoice (F2)	SC	Service and Maint.
		F2	Invoice (F2)	YTA	Standard Order BEV
		F2	Invoice (F2)	ZA	Internet order

Figure 3.31 Copying Control for a Standard Order Header to Billing Document

Now that we've established the document type relationship, we next define the rules around the copying of information. These are set separately for header and item information, and you are required to select the copying requirements routine that you want to apply (Figure 3.32).

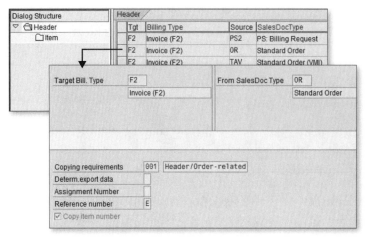

Figure 3.32 Copying Control for a Standard Order Item to Billing Document

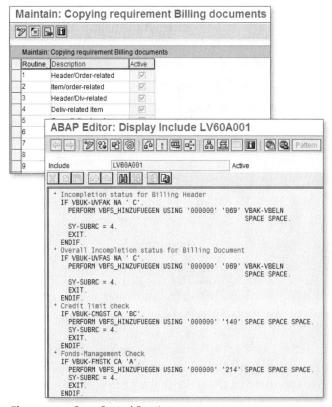

Figure 3.33 Copy Control Routines

In this example, you can see that we have selected SAP standard routine 001. You can also configure your own rules; for example, you may want to copy the information differently by including or excluding other fields. You can also define your own routine; these require ABAP code and are set up via Transaction VOFM.

In Figure 3.33, we show how a standard routine is defined; you can see that a number of mappings or rules are defined within the routine.

Now that you understand how copy control works, you can configure changes to the information flow from the sales order through to the billing document and on to the customer invoice output.

3.5.5 Item Categories

The purpose of an item category is to define the rules to determine how the line item is treated within the sales order. The item category is defined with respect to the sales material, so when it is entered in a sales order, it provides the rules for how the item should be treated. These rules include the following:

- The pricing for the item
- Whether the item is a material or text item
- Which fields are relevant for this item in the incompletion log
- What partner functions are allowed
- Whether the item is relevant for billing

Item categories are determined based on the sales document type and the item category group defined on the material. A more detailed explanation of item categories is outside the scope of this book, so we need not go into any deeper detail here.

3.5.6 Incompletion Procedure

Incompletion procedures are control checks that can be assigned to sales order types to be triggered when the sales order is saved. This check only ensures that there is a value entered in these fields and assumes that other system validations will ensure that the correct information has actually been entered.

For each field, you also define whether incompletion leads to an error or a warning. This configuration is done in the following area of the IMG: SPRO • Sales and Distribution • Basic Functions • Log of Incomplete Items. You can define a separate procedure for the header and the line items, as shown in Figure 3.34.

Table View Edit Goto Selection Utilities(M) System Help
Display View "Groups": Overview
Dialog Structure
Groups
Procedures
Fields
Incompletion groups
Group
Description
A Sales - Header
B Sales - Item
C Sales - Sched. Line
D Partner
F Sales Activity
G Delivery header
H Delivery item

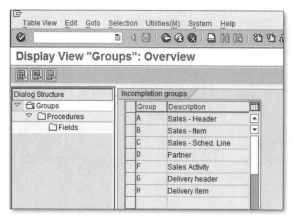

Figure 3.34 Incompletion Groups

Incompletion groups are eligible for all sales documents. In group A, for example, you can select procedures specific to all of the different sales documents available in the SD component. In Figure 3.35, you can see those figures that are included on the sales order header incompletion procedure.

Display View "Fields": Overview
Dialog Structure
Groups
Procedures
Fields
Error proc. 11
Incompletion fields
Table Fld name Description Scr. Status Warning Seq.
VBAK AUDAT Document Date KKAU 01 0
VBAK WAERK Document Currency KBUC 03 0
VBKD INCO1 Incoterms KDE3 04 0
VBKD PRSDT Pricing date KKAU 04 0
VBKD ZTERM Terms of Payment KDE3 03 0

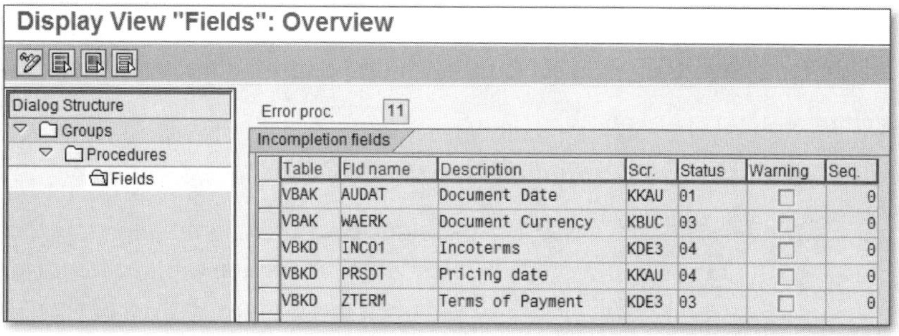

Figure 3.35 Incompletion Fields for Sales Order Header Procedure

Incompletion procedure assignment is made for a variety of different objects, commonly sales document types. The following list of objects can also have an incompletion procedure assigned to them:

- Item categories
- Partner functions
- Sales activities

Incompletion procedures are very useful at ensuring that all necessary information is contained within a sales order. For example, recently we wanted to capture a certain piece of customer information so that it could be issued on an invoice back to that customer. We achieved this by using a field on the sales order, including this field in the incompletion procedure for that sales order type, and also including it in copy control to get it into the billing document. This situation is a perfect example of using different elements of functionality to address a specific business requirement.

3.5.7 Account Assignment Groups

We've already discussed the application of customer and material account assignment groups to master data in Section 3.3, Setting Up S2C Master Data: Customer Master Data (refer to Figures 3.20 and 3.22). These groups are defined in the following area of configuration (Transaction OVK5) (Figure 3.36): SPRO • SALES AND DISTRIBUTION • BASIC FUNCTIONS • ACCOUNT ASSIGNMENT/COSTING • REVENUE ACCOUNT DETERMINATION • CHECK MASTER DATA RELEVANT FOR ACCOUNT ASSIGNMENT.

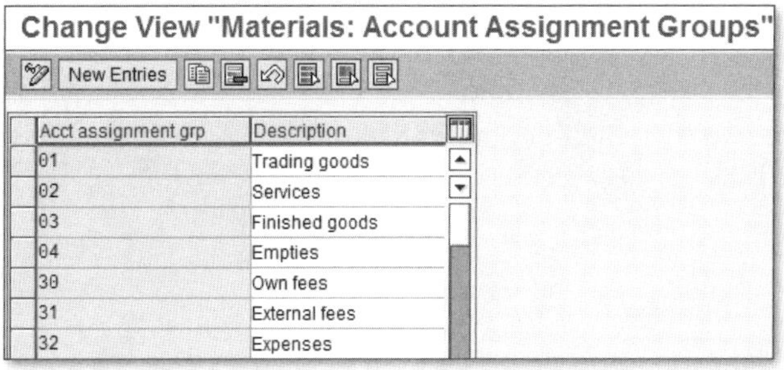

Acct assignment grp	Description
01	Trading goods
02	Services
03	Finished goods
04	Empties
30	Own fees
31	External fees
32	Expenses

Figure 3.36 Material Account Assignment Groups

These categories are used to help you define different rules for the account determination for customers and materials. Later in this chapter, we'll explain how these account assignment groups can be used to determine general ledger account assignment; at this point, though, you just need to know how and where these are set up.

3.6 Delivery

The delivery document serves two main purposes. First, it captures the information necessary to produce a delivery note; second, it updates the stock ledger to indicate that the goods have been issued. However, not every scenario requires a delivery, so some SAP ERP solutions go straight to the accounting document from the billing document.

The delivery document is created based on the information captured in the sales order. The most important information is as follows:

- The material and quantity being shipped
- The ship-to party (who receives the delivery)
- Picking information, that is, the plant and storage location from where to pick the items for this delivery

This information is brought into the delivery document, and, typically, output LD00 (delivery note) is generated.

In addition, the *post goods issue* function updates the ledger to reflect the fact that the materials have gone out of the warehouse. Looking closely at the goods movement information, you can see that movement type 601 is referenced on the line (Figure 3.37). Note that the goods issue creates the general ledger postings in respect to changes in stock, which generates a separate SAP ERP financial document.

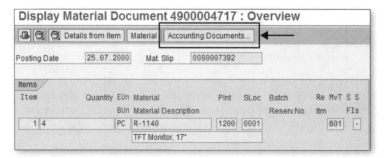

Figure 3.37 Delivery Document

This movement type represents the issue of goods to customers in the form of a delivery. (We explain the purpose of movement types in more detail in Chapter 4, when we look at Materials Management.) The delivery represents an issue out of stock, so we see the following accounting entries:

▶ Debit: costs (or cost of sale)
▶ Credit: inventory

3.7   Billing Documents

Billing is the process by which you invoice the customer for the goods and/or services; it is standard for the customer invoice to be generated from the information in the billing document. In SAP ERP terms, we refer to the billing document as the *invoice* and subsequently create an accounting document (an AR document) that may also be referred to as the customer invoice. Keep this in mind because it may cause confusion between SD and Finance people.

There are different ways of billing. A simple sales order being transferred to a billing document produces a bill based on the dates you specify in the sales order. If you are using a sales contract, you define a billing plan for periodic billing. The billing document also determines the way in which the information is transferred to SAP ERP Financials.

Billing documents have a header and item section, and the information held in each is similar to the header and item of the corresponding sales order. The header section contains the general information for the document, including the following:

▶ Company code
▶ Sales area
▶ Document currency
▶ Pricing procedure
▶ Header conditions
▶ Customer account assignment group
▶ Header text

Figure 3.38 shows an example of a billing document header.

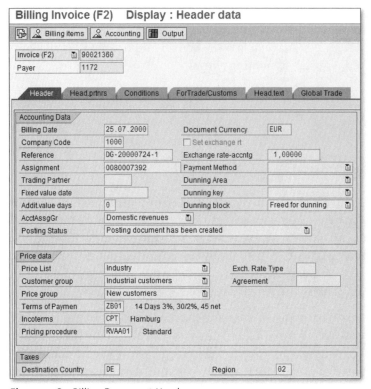

Figure 3.38 Billing Document Header

In Figure 3.39, you can see the different levels of information relating to the billing document line item.

The line item information is specific to each line item on the billing document. Whereas the header holds general information about the overall sale (e.g., customer details), the line item holds specific information, such as the following:

▶ Quantity of material being sold

▶ Pricing condition for this line item and material

▶ Account assignment (profit center, WBS, order, CO-Profitability Analysis segment)

▶ Texts

You can see the link between the billing document data and the AR invoice data in Figure 3.40, and thus get an understanding of how the information transfer works.

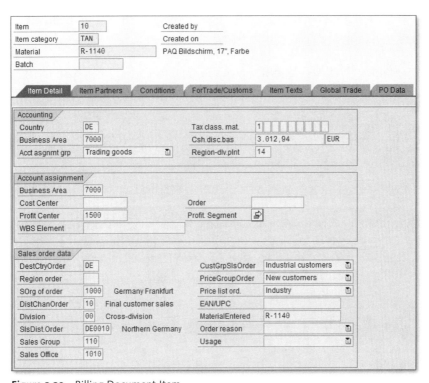

Figure 3.39 Billing Document Item

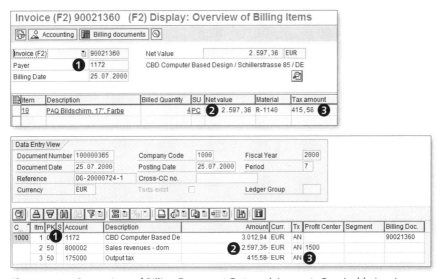

Figure 3.40 Comparison of Billing Document Data and Accounts Receivable Invoice

Table 3.4 explains the linking of the fields on the billing document to the fields on the AR invoice highlighted in Figure 3.40.

❶	The SD payer becomes the *customer* in AR. This is the person from whom you require payment.
❷	The net value in the billing document is posted to the revenue general ledger account to record the sale.
❸	The tax amount in the billing document is posted to the tax general ledger account to record the tax liability.

Table 3.4 Linking Billing Documents to Accounts Receivable Invoices

As you saw when we were looking at sales orders, a billing document is a major sales document type, which means that a lot of the configuration that we looked at previously is also relevant to billing documents. Billing-related configuration is completed in the area of the IMG shown in Figure 3.41.

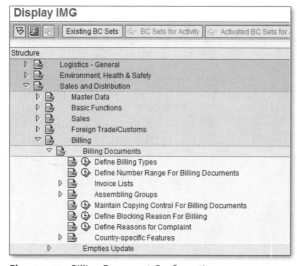

Figure 3.41 Billing Document Configuration

The main (SAP ERP standard) billing document types are as follows:

- F1, F2: Invoice
- G1, G2: Credit Memo
- L1, L2: Debit Memo
- IV: Intercompany billing

When discussing copy control, you saw how information is copied from a sales order into a billing document. As such, no new information is being entered into the system at this point in time. Because no data entry is required, the standard SAP document types are generally sufficient.

Figure 3.42 shows the main configuration items in the billing document configuration screen. The following list highlights the key fields relevant to our discussion.

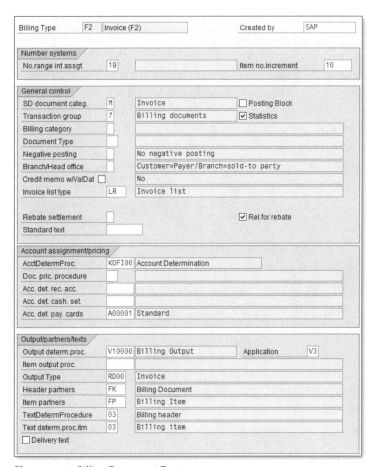

Figure 3.42 Billing Document Type

▶ No. Range Int. Assgt

The billing document number range is always internally assigned because the document is not created manually.

▶ DOCUMENT TYPE

The most important configuration to be aware of in this section is the document type. When this billing document type transfers to SAP ERP Financials, this is the document type that is created. In Figure 3.42, you can see that this field is currently blank. The standard SAP default rule is that if this field is left blank, the system creates an RV document type.

If you wanted to use document types to differentiate between different sources of sales, you would need to use custom sales order types mapped to custom billing document types, and then assign different SAP ERP Financials document types.

▶ BRANCH/HEAD OFFICE

The branch and head office relationship is usually left blank, which means that the payer is updated in SAP ERP Financials. Any relationship on the SAP ERP Financials view of the customer is ignored. There are other options here that you may want to consider, but any settings other than blank should be reviewed when you decide your customer master strategy.

▶ CANCELL. BILLING TYPE

This section is not displayed in Figure 3.42, but it is relevant for the scenario where a customer cancels an order. You can decide the following settings:

▶ Whether a billing document is created when a cancellation is processed (invoice cancellation document)

▶ The copying control rules

▶ The information that is passed to the reference field

▶ The Information that is passed to the assignment field

▶ ACCTDETERMPROC.

In this section, you specify which account determination procedure is referenced when you transfer information from the billing document to SAP ERP Financials. In the example shown, you can see that the assignment is to KOFI, which is the commonly-used procedure.

Although it may seem advisable to assign different procedures here, you'll realize that it's sensible to have a single procedure when we look at the configuration of account determination.

▶ OUTPUT/PARTNERS/TEXTS

The billing document is where you assign the output determination procedure and an output type for each billing document. (This should make sense because you would have different outputs for invoice and credit document types.) At the bottom of this section, you define the text determination procedures, which we talked about earlier (Section 3.5.3).

The last configuration you make here is to the partner determination, which is the rule that determines the bill-to party. We also talked about partner determination earlier (Section 3.3.3, Table 3.2).

3.8   Account Determination

Like all master data information, account assignment information is also passed from the sales order to the billing document. It's important to see this information here because general ledger accounts and profit centers are the basis upon which the SAP ERP Financials postings are determined. In the previous section, you saw how the billing document type is assigned to an account determination procedure, KOFI00.

Account determination is based on the following configurations:

▸ Chart of accounts

▸ Sales organization

▸ Customer account assignment group

▸ Material account assignment group

▸ Account key

This is possibly the most important SAP ERP Financials integration process to understand; unfortunately, it is also one of the most difficult. Next, we explain the process of account determination, including the important integration points. We specifically look at procedure KOFI because this is the most commonly used.

3.8.1   Account Determination Procedure KOFI

Account determination is part of the billing process. At this point, you should make the following double entry posting:

Debit	Customer
Credit	Sales

This seems like a very straightforward posting to make because the customer details are included in the sales order, and the sales general ledger account number can be entered into a table somewhere. However, the topic becomes complicated by the fact that there are different levels of requirements here — some organizations will post all of their income to a single general ledger account and be done with it, others may need a range of general ledger accounts depending on material, and still others may need a range depending on the customer. Some customers might even use a combination of both material and customer to determine a general ledger account.

These rules are defined in logical tables that allow the system to determine the general ledger account based on the information entered into the sales order. SD consultants refer to this as the *access sequence*, or, put simply, the sequence in which the different configuration tables are accessed. In other words, as you perform billing, the system looks through the tables for a valid combination. When it finds the combination, it determines the general ledger account that should be posted for each line of the sales order. This is explained in Figure 3.43, reproduced from SAP Academy material.

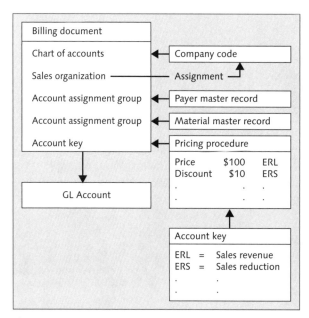

Figure 3.43 Account Determination Procedure

We talked about a number of these configurations already:

▶ Customer account assignment groups were covered in Section 3.3.1, General Data.

► Material account assignment groups were covered in Section 3.3.2, Company Code Data.

Account keys are used as part of pricing, which is beyond the scope of this chapter. Suffice it to say that, as part of pricing, there are various components that make up the sales price of a material; for example, there may be a freight charge or specific discounts. Each of these can be posted to separate general ledger accounts if the entries are maintained in the account determination table. We explain this further in the sections that follow.

Let's now look at how the configuration table is put together. The configuration is completed in the following area of the IMG (Transaction VKOA): SPRO • SALES & DISTRIBUTION • BASIC FUNCTIONS • ACCOUNT ASSIGNMENT/COSTING • REVENUE ACCOUNT DETERMINATION • ASSIGN GL ACCOUNTS.

There are five configuration tables with different combinations of information: Table 1 has the most complex combination, whereas Table 5 (Figure 3.44) has the least complex combination. Decide which of these tables to configure based on how complicated you want to make your account determination procedure. To explain this more thoroughly, let's look at the tables in some detail.

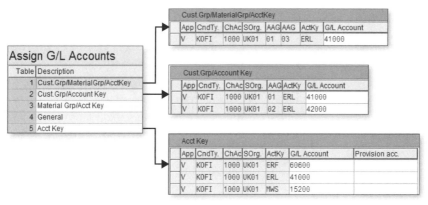

Figure 3.44 Tables in Transaction VKOA

Table 1 has the most complex combinations in that it determines general ledger accounts by the combination of customer and material account group and account key. This means for a combination of a material and customer, we can decide which general ledger accounts are determined for each account key. Figure 3.45 shows how the combinations are linked to other configuration items.

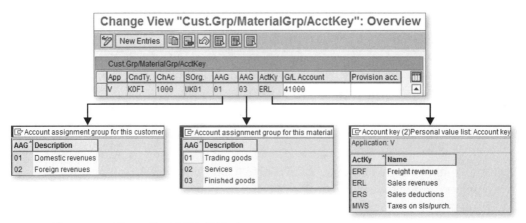

Figure 3.45 Transaction VKOA: Table 1

If you don't want to use this complex scenario, you may want to reduce the number of general ledger accounts you post to, which requires a less complex setup. You can therefore select Table 2 or Table 3, which allows you to define account determination based solely on the customer or the material account assignment group. In this case, you must use either the customer or the material, not both, to determine general ledger accounts. Tables 2 and 3 do not allow both combinations to be used (for this, you would need to use Table 1).

In comparison, Tables 4 and 5 are "catch-all" configurations, meaning that they have the least possible complexity in them. With Table 4, you can only assign a single general ledger account for the sales organization; as a result, this table is a catch-all for postings to the whole process of account determination. Table 5 has a single general ledger account per account key, which means that income is posted to this general ledger irrespective of the customer or material. Making settings in Table 5 means that if the settings in Tables 1, 2, or 3 do not determine a general ledger account, it is determined by the entries in Table 5. You may prefer to put entries in Table 5, rather than Table 4, and treat Table 5 as your catch-all.

Remember, too, that you can use combinations of these tables; for instance, you can enter a value in Table 5 as the default general ledger account for all income postings, and then enter combinations in Tables 1, 2, and 3 with respect to specific general ledger accounts for sales postings.

When looking at your billing document (Transaction VF03), you can see the route that was followed to determine the general ledger accounts. This is demonstrated in Figure 3.46.

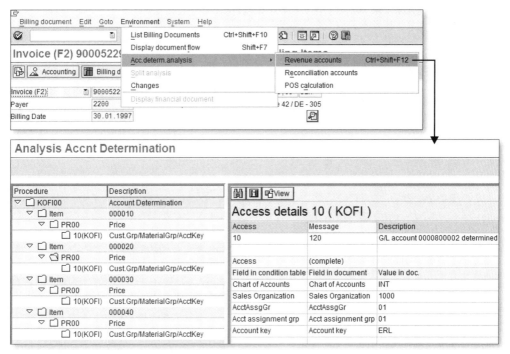

Figure 3.46 Successful Account Determination

Figure 3.46 shows how we are following procedure KOFI00 for this billing document. More specifically, for this line, we've determined general ledger account 800002, based on the combination of the following:

▶ Chart of accounts

▶ Sales organization

▶ Customer account assignment group

▶ Material account assignment group

▶ Account key

You should now understand the SD account determination process. To solidify this knowledge, it's essential that you practice the configuration by entering values into the tables and then running billing. You should then be able to follow through the logic sequence that the system adopts in determining your general ledger account to get a better understanding of the whole process. It is very important that you test this configuration in detail to improve your understanding of this very complicated area.

3.8.2 Errors in Account Determination

As we've said previously, a billing document transfers information into a Financial Accounting document via account determination. If there is an error in the account determination, it doesn't stop the creation of the billing document, but does prevent the creation of the Financial Accounting document. To see any errors, select ACCT. DETERM. ANALYSIS from the billing document header. From within Transaction VF03 (display billing document), you can see where the determination has happened and where it has failed. Figure 3.47 shows how to review the different procedures to locate an account determination failure.

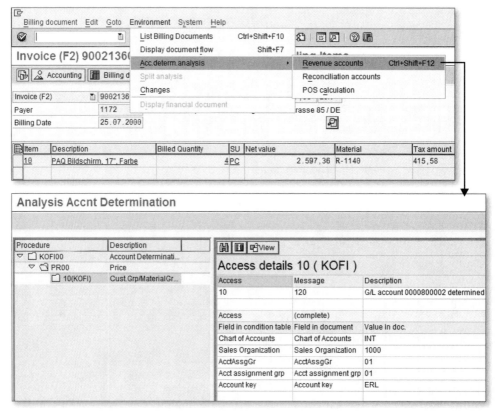

Figure 3.47 Account Determination Failures

This completes our review of the billing document. The next stage in the process is the invoice in the AR component, which is part of SAP ERP Financials.

3.9   Accounts Receivable Invoice

When we talked about the billing document, we mentioned that it is, effectively, a customer invoice. You may wonder, then, what the purpose of the AR invoice is. Very simply, the AR invoice is used for the business processes that occur after the invoice has been generated, including the following:

▶ Ledger postings to the debtors account and the other ledger account

▶ Credit control and debt collection activities

▶ Incoming payment processing

> **Note**
>
> You can find a detailed discussion of this topic in Chapter 6 of our previous book, *SAP ERP Financials: Configuration and Design*.

In this section, we review this area from the order-to-cash point of view, specifically concerning the AR invoice in our Financial Accounting documents. This discussion is applicable to all Financial Accounting documents, including the following:

▶ **DA:** Customer document

▶ **DZ:** Customer payment

▶ **RV:** Billing document transfer

▶ **ZV:** Payment clearing

We start our discussion by looking at the key information that appears on the AR invoice, starting with the header. We then explain document line items and payment terms.

3.9.1   Accounts Receivable Invoice Header

The AR invoice header records control information related to the posting; there is no transactional information in the header. The information in the AR invoice header is strongly driven by the configuration settings made in the billing document type (see Section 3.7, Billing Document). Next, we discuss the most important areas of the invoice header.

Document Type

The most important information is the Financial Accounting document type. If you did not specify the accounting document type when configuring the billing document, the system automatically determines RV as the Financial Accounting document type. The number range is associated with the document type, both of which are configured in the following area of the IMG: SPRO • FINANCIAL ACCOUNTING (NEW) • FINANCIAL ACCOUNTING GLOBAL SETTINGS (NEW) • DOCUMENT.

This folder has three different transactions for editing document types. With SAP General Ledger and the use of the document splitting functionality, you now get two views of the document, the entry view and the general ledger view. The entry view shows the information as you entered it, and the general ledger view is the document after your document splitting rules have been applied.

The third option here is to create a document type in a ledger. If you are operating multiple ledgers, you can set up a document type to be used in a specific ledger only. You can set these up for your additional ledgers only, not your leading ledger.

The configuration of document types requires setting up the simple rules to govern the way in which this document type can be used. We covered this extensively in *SAP ERP Financials: Configuration and Design.*

Figure 3.48 shows the configuration settings for document type RV. Looking closely at the document type RV, you can see that this is assigned to a number range 01, from which the system automatically assigns document numbers (we discuss this next). If you reversed an RV document (e.g., by Transaction FB08), the system posts an AB document. If this field is left blank, the reversal is done by the same document type.

Document Number Ranges

When we made the settings for the billing document type, we assigned a number range, which was selected from the sales document number ranges. For the AR invoice, we can also assign a number range, but this is assigned from the available Financial Accounting number ranges, as shown in Figure 3.49.

Change View "Document Types": Details

🖉 | New Entries | 🗐 🖫 🗠 🖫 🖫 🖫

| Document Type | RV | Billing doc.transfer |

Properties

Number range	01		Number range information
Reverse DocumentType	AB
Authorization Group	

Account types allowed

☑ Assets
☑ Customer
☐ Vendor
☐ Material
☑ G/L account

Special usage

☐ Btch input only

Control data

☐ Net document type
☐ Cust/vend check
☑ Negative Postings Permitted
☐ Inter-company postgs
☐ Enter trading partner

Default values

Ex.rate type for forgn crncy docs [ ]

Required during document entry

☐ Reference number
☐ Document header text

Joint venture

Debit Rec.Indic [ ]
Rec.Ind. Credit [ ]

Figure 3.48   Accounts Receivable Document Type Configuration

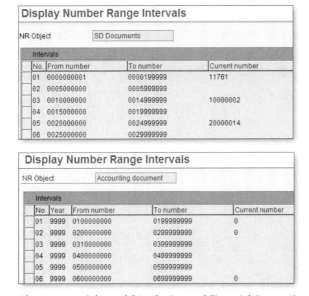

Display Number Range Intervals

| NR Object | SD Documents |

Intervals

No.	From number	To number	Current number
01	0000000001	0000199999	11761
02	0005000000	0005999999	
03	0010000000	0014999999	10000002
04	0015000000	0019999999	
05	0020000000	0024999999	20000014
06	0025000000	0029999999	

Display Number Range Intervals

| NR Object | Accounting document |

Intervals

No	Year	From number	To number	Current number
01	9999	0100000000	0199999999	0
02	9999	0200000000	0299999999	0
03	9999	0310000000	0399999999	
04	9999	0400000000	0499999999	
05	9999	0500000000	0599999999	
06	9999	0600000000	0699999999	0

Figure 3.49   Sales and Distribution and Financial Accounting Number Ranges

The accounting document number range configuration is completed as shown earlier in Figure 3.48, and the SD number range is configured in the following area of the IMG: SPRO • SALES AND DISTRIBUTION • BILLING • BILLING DOCUMENTS • DEFINE NUMBER RANGES FOR BILLING DOCUMENTS.

Because SD documents are separate from Financial Accounting documents, their number ranges may not be configured in the same way. This can be a problem because the customer gets the SD invoice, and the Financial Accounting invoice (the AR document) is used to chase debts. However, you can ensure that the billing document number is the same as the AR invoice number, which resolves the issue because the customer's invoice number will be the same as the number on your billing document in the system. On the Financial Accounting number range side, define the same number range and make it externally defined; this is what enables the Financial Accounting document to take the number range from the billing document.

> **Note**
>
> Remember that the AR invoice document is not to be confused with the billing document. We had a brief look at this as part of Figure 3.40 in Section 3.7, Billing Documents, where we compared the two documents.

Although SAP ERP provides the functionality to set up number ranges for a specific fiscal year and then allows you to reuse them next year, this is not a good auditable practice. In reality, most companies set up a single customer invoice number range (e.g., from 100000000 to 199999999), and this will suffice for the next 10 years. Thus, if you set up number ranges for fiscal year 9999, they become applicable for all years. In addition to number ranges, the AR invoice also contains debtor information.

3.9.2 Document Line Items

Document line items hold transactional information, so ledger postings are seen here. For each AR invoice, you should see at least one customer item and one ledger posting; in addition, there may be tax lines and additional ledger postings, as explained in Table 3.5.

Debit	**Customer:** Total amount the customer owes you.
Credit	**Sales (income):** Total amount posted to the sales (income) general ledger account(s).
Credit	**Tax:** Total tax amount posted to the tax general ledger account.

Table 3.5 Document Line Items

Next we look at each line in turn to fully explain its purpose.

Customer Line

The customer line is a little confusing at first because when you look at the document overview (refer back to Figure 3.40), you can see that the posting is actually made to the customer; whereas when you drill down on the customer line (double-click), you can see that the posting is actually made to the customer reconciliation account that was assigned to this customer (Figure 3.50). As you may recall, reconciliation accounts are balance sheet postings, and the related rules apply in this situation.

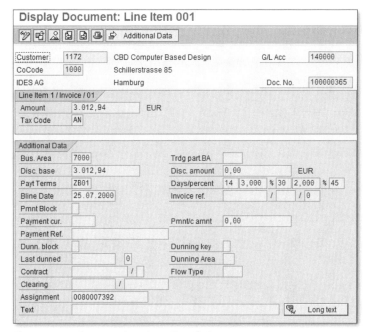

Figure 3.50 Customer Line Item Details Screen

Looking at Figure 3.50, you can see that the gross amount is posted to the customer (including the tax amount). This is because the customer is liable for the full amount of the invoice. The other information on the customer line includes the fields described in the following list.

▶ PAYT TERMS
This field determines when the invoice is due for payment with information drawn from the customer master record.

▶ BLINE DATE
The system captures the baseline date when the AR invoice is created and uses this to determine when the invoice should be paid. Looking at your payment terms, you can define the payment due date based on the baseline date (there is more information about this later in this section).

The system determines the due date for an invoice based on the baseline date and payment terms.

▶ DISC. AMOUNT, DAYS/PERCENT
Based on the payment terms, the invoice may be eligible for a payment discount if the payment is made within the stated periods. This information is displayed within the invoice.

▶ DUNN. BLOCK, LAST DUNNED, DUNNING KEY, DUNNING AREA
This section of the invoice holds information relating to dunning, which will become clearer when we discuss dunning later in this chapter.

The only other information that we have not yet seen in relation to this customer item is the account assignment, which would be a profit center because this posting is a balance sheet item.

Sales (Income) Line

The purpose of the sales line is to record the sales posting to the ledger, which goes to the general ledger account that was determined via account determination. This posting usually goes to the income general ledger account, which should be a P&L account type with a corresponding revenue cost element assigned. The information contained in this line is fairly straightforward, as shown in Figure 3.51.

The line holds the net amount and tax code, and not much else. The sole purpose of this line is for updating the ledger, so the only other information that is missing is the account assignment object.

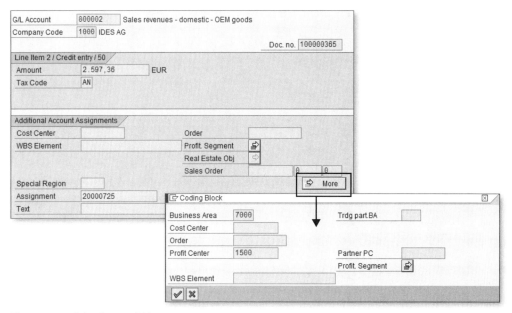

Figure 3.51 Sales (Income) Line

Tax Line

The tax line is created automatically based on the tax codes that have been entered for the customer in the initial line. The main information on this line is the base amount and tax code. The *base amount* is the amount against which the tax is calculated; in the example in Figure 3.52, it is the net amount of the invoice. The amount field represents the actual tax calculated, which is posted to the tax account.

Assignment Field

In some of the figures in this chapter, you may have noticed the use of the ASSIGN-MENT field. When you run a customer line item report, the ASSIGNMENT field is the standard sort criteria for that report. The data in the ASSIGNMENT field is determined when you set up a customer master record. Then, in the COMPANY CODE — ACCOUNT MANAGEMENT screen, populate the SORT KEY field. This is what goes into the ASSIGNMENT field for this customer's transactions. You can configure sort keys in the following area of the IMG: SPRO • ACCOUNTS RECEIVABLE & ACCOUNTS PAY-ABLE • CUSTOMER ACCTS • LINE ITEMS • DISPLAY LINE ITEMS • DETERMINE STANDARD SORTING FOR LINE ITEMS.

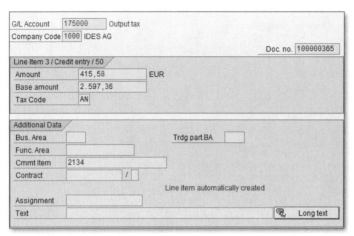

Figure 3.52 Tax Line

While in this screen, you'll see a number of other configuration activities that can help with your line item display for customer items, such as defining sort variants, total's variants, and additional fields for reporting.

3.9.3 Payment Terms

The payment terms you extend to your customers represent your agreement about the time they have to pay their debt. SAP ERP does not differentiate between payment terms for vendors and customers, so both are configured in the same location in the system: SPRO • Financial Accounting (new) • Accounts Receivable and Accounts Payable • Business Transactions • Outgoing Invoices/Credit Memo's • Maintain Terms of Payment (Transaction OBB8).

For each entry, define these key settings:

▶ Sales Text
Enter the short description of the payment term; this can be printed on the invoice sent out to the customer.

▶ Own Explanation
Enter a long description of what the payment term actually is.

▶ Baseline Date Calculation
The baseline date, plus the payment terms, are used to determine the net due date.

Leaving this blank means that the setting you make in the Default for Baseline Date field is applicable.

► DEFAULT FOR BASELINE DATE

The baseline date is based on the selection you make here. In Figure 3.53, we selected POSTING DATE.

► PMNT BLOCK/PMNT METHOD DEFAULT

These options allow you to attach a payment block or a payment method to this payment term. For example, you may want to use this option if you are offering customers better terms in return for a cash payment.

► PAYMENT TERMS

In this part of the configuration screen, enter the specific terms of the agreement. In this example, we are offering a 3% discount for paying within 14 days.

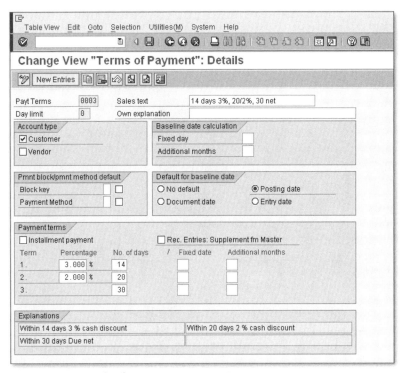

Figure 3.53 Example of a Customer Payment Term

3.10 Incoming Payments

The processing of incoming payments is also referred to as *customer receipting* and is the end of the S2C process. AR has two options for allocating customer payments against invoices: You can manually enter a customer payment in the system, or you can upload a bank statement. Integration has specifically to do with the first of these options, so we focus on that in this section.

To manually enter customer payments, the standard AR system offers Transaction F-28 (or F-26 for its fast entry version). Figure 3.54 shows you the F-28 screen where you enter the necessary data.

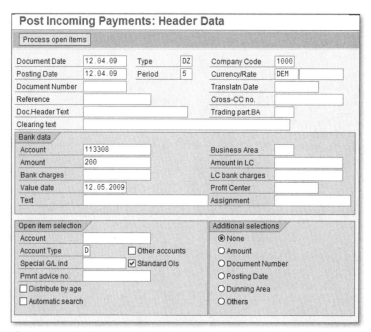

Figure 3.54 Posting Incoming Payments

When you receive a customer payment, enter the information shown in Figure 3.54. In the OPEN ITEM SELECTION area of the screen, enter the customer account number. If you cannot identify the correct customer account, leave the ACCOUNT field blank; when you click PROCESS OPEN ITEMS, the system displays Figure 3.55 and allows you to select from other options.

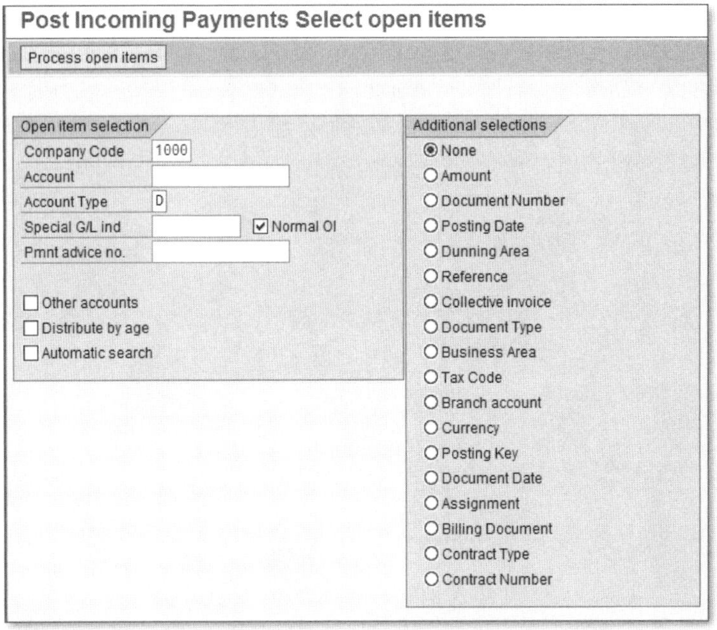

Figure 3.55 Additional Selection Items for Incoming Payments

In the resulting screens, select the invoices against which you want to make the payment, and post the payment. You can also make partial payments to the customer account with a reference to the invoice.

To configure the settings for incoming payments, you use the following area of the IMG: SPRO • FINANCIAL ACCOUNTING (NEW) • ACCOUNTS RECEIVABLE AND ACCOUNTS PAYABLE • BUSINESS TRANSACTIONS • INCOMING PAYMENTS • MANUAL INCOMING PAYMENTS.

Next, we review two additional steps in configuring incoming payments: customer tolerances and automatic clearing.

3.10.1 Configuring Customer Tolerances

Customer tolerances are set up to control the processing of incoming payments, specifically where there are differences between the payment amount and the invoice amount. You may recall that when we configured payment terms, we defined the discounts that may be applied to a customer invoice. At this point, you can also specify what the permitted payment difference is. You can set up a range of tolerances to suit the different scenarios you need and then assign them to directly to customer master records in the PAYMENT TRANSACTION tab of the company code view (see Section 3.3.2, Company Code Data). Define tolerances via SPRO • FINANCIAL ACCOUNTING (NEW) • ACCOUNTS RECEIVABLE AND ACCOUNTS PAYABLE • BUSINESS TRANSACTIONS • INCOMING PAYMENTS • MANUAL INCOMING PAYMENTS • DEFINE TOLERANCES (CUSTOMERS) (TRANSACTION OBA3) (Figure 3.56).

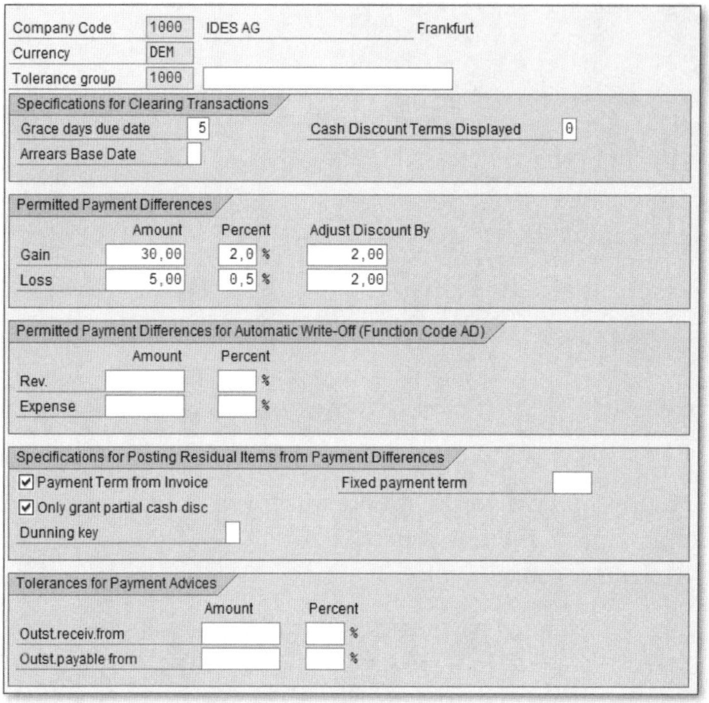

Figure 3.56 Configuring Customer Tolerances

The differences that fall within the defined tolerance limits are automatically posted to clearing accounts, which you define in the following area of the IMG: SPRO • FINANCIAL ACCOUNTING (NEW) • ACCOUNTS RECEIVABLE AND ACCOUNTS PAYABLE • BUSINESS TRANSACTIONS • INCOMING PAYMENTS • MANUAL INCOMING PAYMENTS • CLEARING DIFFERENCES • DEFINE ACCOUNTS FOR CLEARING DIFFERENCES (Transaction ZDI). We will discuss this in more detail as part of Chapter 4.

When processing open items, the system looks at the tolerance settings you configured and determines whether or not items must match exactly. Tolerance settings enable invoices and payment to clear even if there is a difference.

The configuration for processing open items includes line layouts and selection fields that are to be used for processing open items. The configuration settings are accessed via SPRO • FINANCIAL ACCOUNTING (NEW) • ACCOUNTS RECEIVABLE AND ACCOUNTS PAYABLE • BUSINESS TRANSACTIONS • INCOMING PAYMENTS • MANUAL INCOMING PAYMENTS • MAKE SETTINGS FOR PROCESSING OPEN ITEMS.

3.10.2 Automatic Clearing

In the standard AR functionality, SAP ERP offers a way to automatically clear customer receipts against invoices in the system. To take advantage of this, you must define the fields that should be used to match customer receipts to invoices, which is done in the following area of the IMG: SPRO • FINANCIAL ACCOUNTING (NEW) • ACCOUNTS RECEIVABLE AND ACCOUNTS PAYABLE • BUSINESS TRANSACTIONS • OPEN ITEM CLEARING • PREPARE AUTOMATIC CLEARING.

> **Note**
>
> You can also run *only* manual clearing, should your organization prefer that. Even if you do run automatic clearing, though, you usually have to manually clear some items.

In the example shown in Figure 3.57, we identify three criteria out of a possible five:

- **BELNR:** Document number
- **XBLNR:** Reference
- **WRBTR:** Amount

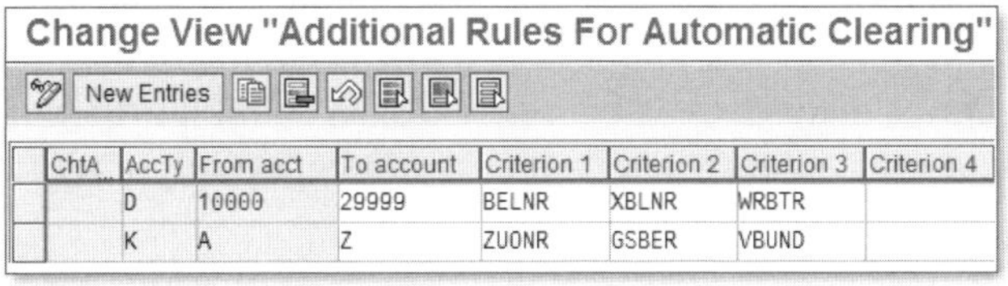

	ChtA	AccTy	From acct	To account	Criterion 1	Criterion 2	Criterion 3	Criterion 4
	D	10000	29999	BELNR	XBLNR	WRBTR	
	K	A	Z	ZUONR	GSBER	VBUND	

Figure 3.57 Define Automatic Clearing Rules

As you can see from Figure 3.57, you can make settings for different account types, not just customers (account type = D). To do the actual clearing, use the standard SAP ERP clearing program (SAPF124) from Transaction F.13, which is shown in Figure 3.58. This is a generic clearing program that is used to clear a variety of account types.

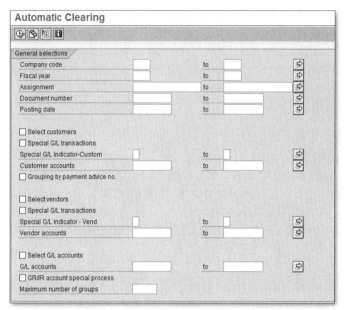

Figure 3.58 Automatic Clearing Program

In the next and last section of the chapter, we look at the debtor management processes. These are technically outside of the order-to-cash process, but it's important to cover the integration of this process as part of this chapter.

3.11 Debtor Management

SAP ERP offers functionality not only to manage customer credit limits but also to actively chase customers who have overdue debts. In this section, we look at two subjects in particular: credit management and dunning. We look at each in turn and discuss the configuration and design as well as the integration across the S2C cycle.

3.11.1 Credit Management

Although SAP ERP offers Financial Supply Chain Management (SAP FSCM) for credit control, this is a fairly new component at the time of this writing. Because most users do not use this functionality, we do not cover it in this book. If you would like to explore it yourself, though, Figure 3.59 shows the menu path for configuring this functionality.

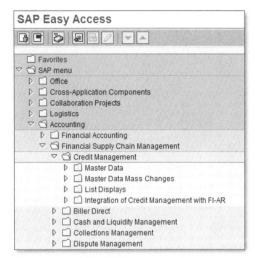

Figure 3.59 SAP FSCM Components

The more commonly used SAP Credit Management offers excellent functionality for creating credit limits and applying credit control procedures. It is part of the AR component (Figure 3.60) and covers a range of functionality that should be more than sufficient for most organizations. The concept here is simple: SAP ERP links the business processes of sales orders and confirming credit exposure. This moves debtor management to the beginning of the process, so you can advise customers of their credit status right when they place an order. This allows you to decide whether or not you want to process the order. As you can see from Figure 3.60, a number of reports are available in the credit management info system to support this process.

Next, we look at the process and options available to you in the design and configuration of this area.

Defining Credit Limits

The credit master record is simply an extension of the customer master record, so when you look at Figure 3.60, you don't see a CREATE option, only CHANGE and DISPLAY options. When you go into Transaction FD32, select an existing customer master record and define the credit limits for this customer; you can define an overall value for this customer, as well as values for specific credit control areas. If you only have one credit control area, you can define values on each screen, as shown in Figure 3.61.

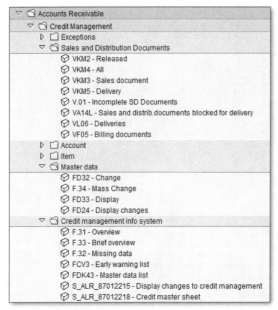

Figure 3.60 Credit Management Transactions in Accounts Receivable

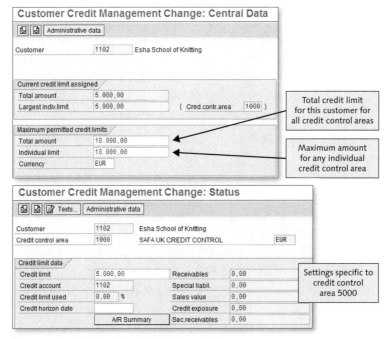

Figure 3.61 Defining Credit Limits for a Customer

Configuring Credit Update Settings

Now that we've set a credit limit for the customer, let's consider the other factors that influence the credit checking procedure. First we revisit the credit control area, which we saw in Chapter 2. As part of the enterprise structure, we configured the credit control area and then assigned it to a company code (SPRO • ENTERPRISE STRUCTURE • DEFINITION • FINANCIAL ACCOUNTING). If you look back at this configuration setting, you can see that we made a decision regarding the UPDATE field, which we revisit in Figure 3.62.

Cred.contr.area	1000	SAFA UK CREDIT CONTROL
Currency	EUR	

Data for updating SD
Update	000012
FY Variant	Z1

Default data for automatically creating new customers
Risk category	
Credit limit	
Rep. group	

Figure 3.62 Credit Control Area Configuration Settings

The update settings are actually the credit update settings. Here you have four options:

▶ **<BLANK>:** No update from SD documents.

▶ **000012:** Open sales order value, delivery document value, and billing document value.

▶ **000015:** Open delivery and billing document value.

▶ **000018:** Open delivery value for sales order and open billing document value.

If you're using SD, which we have been doing in this chapter, 000012 is the correct setting; it ensures that all open sales orders are included in the credit check. In practice, the setting you choose depends on your organization's individual requirements. If you exclude all updates from SD documents (i.e., if you leave the field blank), credit checking is only performed on AR documents.

Configuring the Risk Category Field

One of the most important fields in Figure 3.62 is the RISK CATEGORY field. The values you enter here are the default values that are assigned to each new customer created within this credit control area. Therefore, if you have designed a process where all new customers have a default credit limit of 1000, enter this value here. You can also enter a default value for the risk categories. If necessary, these default values can then be edited in the credit master record, as shown in Figure 3.63.

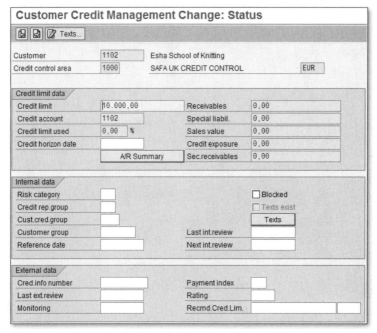

Figure 3.63 Credit Master Record, Internal and External Data

Risk categories are set up in the following area of the IMG: SPRO • Financial Accounting (new) • Accounts Receivable and Accounts Payable • Credit Management • Credit Control Account. The following are some possible risk categories you might consider using in your organization:

▶ High Risk: For customers considered very risky, for example, a new customer, a small company with an unproven record, or a company with a history of making late payments.

▶ Medium Risk: For customers who have some history with the company but still warrant some caution.

▶ Low Risk: For customers who consistently pay on time.

▶ New Customer: For customers who have no history with the company.

Once defined, you then assign categories to credit master records (Figure 3.64), if they have not already been defined by default (which may be the case).

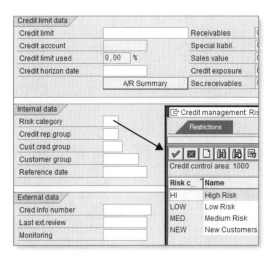

Figure 3.64 Assigning Risk Categories to Credit Master Records

Configuring Automatic Credit Control

You can now set up the rules for automatic credit checking: SPRO • SALES AND DIS-TRIBUTION • BASIC FUNCTIONS • CREDIT MANAGEMENT/RISK MANAGEMENT • CREDIT MANAGEMENT • DEFINE AUTOMATIC CREDIT CONTROL (Transaction OVA8). When you set up a new variant, the screen initially looks like Figure 3.65.

Let's start by looking at the CHECKS section. For each item, we recommend that you read the full help message because we have only summarized the key facts for this discussion. Follow these steps:

1. Decide which type of checks you want to perform. For instance, the dynamic check only concerns open sales order values, whereas the static check looks at the values of open sales, billing, and AR documents. For our scenario, we want to perform a dynamic check.

2. The next thing to decide is the system's reaction if the limit is reached: should it issue a warning message or an error message? Because this variant is being set up for high-risk customers, we make this an error message.

3. For the Status/Block setting, decide whether you want to place an automatic block on the document. If you do, check this indicator.

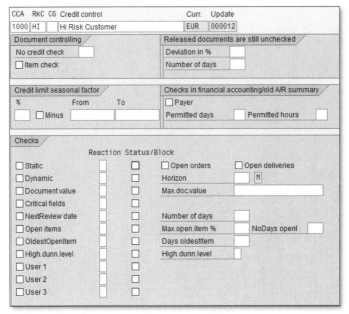

Figure 3.65 Automatic Credit Control Configuration

4. For dynamic checking, you must also configure the Horizon field, which, in this example, is in months. This means that the check is only conducted on those items that are due for delivery within the time horizon defined here.

In Table 3.6, we summarize the settings you need to understand when configuring credit control.

Field	Possible Entries	Effect
REACTION	<BLANK>	No message (no credit check occurs).
	A	Warning.
	B	Error.
	C	Warning + value that is exceeded by.
	D	Error + value that is exceeded by.
STATUS/BLOCK	Checkmark	If you select this option, a block is also applied to sales documents.

Table 3.6 Possible Settings for Automatic Credit Control Configuration

Field	Possible Entries	Effect
STATIC	Checkmark	The system looks at the value of: Open sales orders* + Open delivery docs* + Open billing docs + Open AR items. (*These two values are optional.)
DYNAMIC	Checkmark	This only checks open sales order values.
DOCUMENT VALUE	Checkmark	This option enables a credit check based on a maximum document value.
CRITICAL FIELDS	Checkmark	This setting checks whether critical fields (payment terms, additional value days, fixed value date) have been changed within the sales document.
NUMBER OF DAYS	Checkmark	If a released sales order is subsequently changed, it is rechecked for credit after this number of days (default value = 3 days).

Table 3.6 Possible Settings for Automatic Credit Control Configuration (Cont.)

There are other things that you may want to consider on this screen (e.g., the CREDIT LIMIT SEASONAL FACTOR field allows you to define a period of time when a customer is allowed to exceed its credit limit), but we have focused on those that are applicable to most people.

Now that you've completed these configuration activities, your system can automatically check credit limits when processing transactions.

In the next section, we look at dunning, which is the process we follow for customers who have overdue debts.

3.11.2 Dunning

Dunning is the process by which you chase customers who have overdue debts. This section explains the configuration of the dunning program and reviews the available functionality. Figure 3.66 shows the menu paths relevant to our discussion.

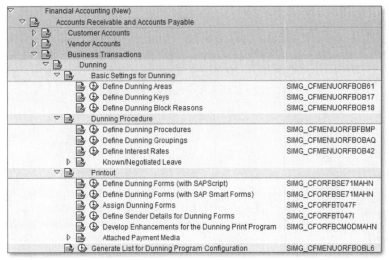

Figure 3.66 Dunning Configuration

Defining Dunning Areas

Dunning areas allow you to apply different rules to different customers; for example, you can separate customers by their AR clerks, so each clerk can run his own dunning routines for his own set of customers.

Defining Dunning Blocks

You may want to exclude specific invoices or customers from dunning runs. These blocks can be assigned to either the customer master record, which applies a blanket block across all items, or to individual invoices.

Note that standard reports can be run for customers or invoices that have dunning blocks, so you can see what items have been excluded. You can also develop workflow routines, so you may want a routine that requests approval for putting on dunning blocks or that sends a workflow message a certain number of days after a dunning block is applied. This could be used to provide a follow-up reminder to the person who applied the block.

Defining Dunning Procedures

Let's now examine the process of defining a dunning procedure, which is the set of rules governing the determination of overdue items. You can set up a number of procedures here and then assign customers to a procedure (Figure 3.67). If no assignment is made, the customer is not selected as part of the dunning run.

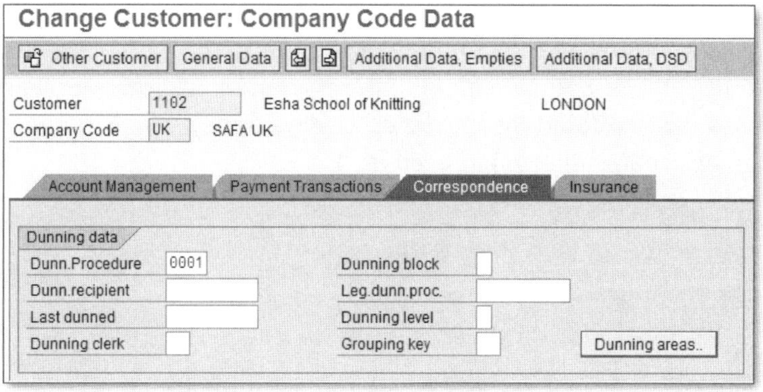

Figure 3.67 Customer Dunning Procedure Assignment

When you configure the dunning procedure, define the following basic parameters (which can also be seen in Figure 3.68):

▶ DUNNING INTERVAL IN DAYS: Defines the frequency between dunning runs.

▶ NO. OF DUNNING LEVELS: Determine the number of levels in the procedure, and then within the procedure, define the details for each level.

▶ INTEREST INDICATOR: Allows you to charge interest on overdue items.

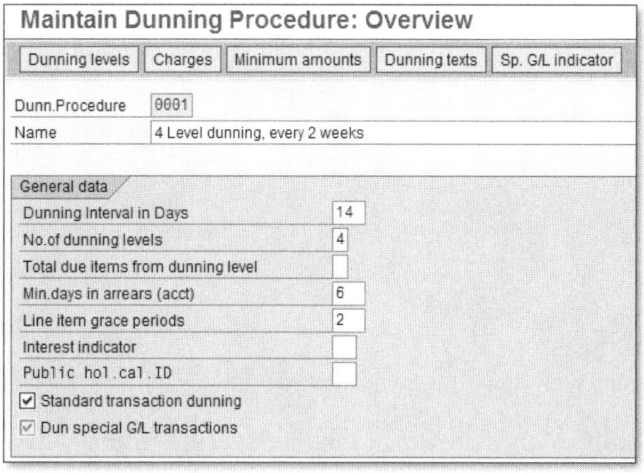

Figure 3.68 Define Dunning Procedure

At the top of the screen, you can see the buttons for configuring elements of the procedure. When you click the DUNNING LEVELS button, the resulting screen (Figure 3.69) allows you to define the days in arrears as the way in which invoices are assigned dunning levels; for example, based on the configuration in Figure 3.69, invoices that are 8 days overdue fall into dunning procedure 1. The days in arrears should be related to the industry you are in and the payment terms you offer. For example, if you have already offered the customer 28 days to pay, it's reasonable to reduce the days in arrears for dunning procedure 1.

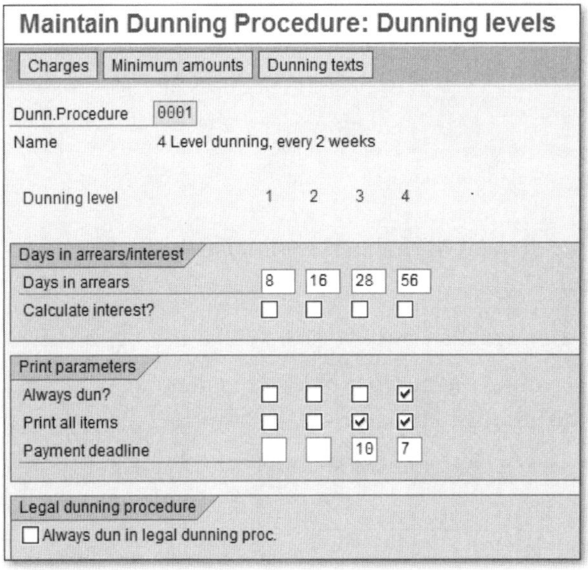

Figure 3.69 Dunning Levels

In our example, we've set up four dunning levels that cause the following actions:

▸ **Level 1:** Telephone call.

▸ **Level 2:** Telephone call.

▸ **Level 3:** Firm reminder letter.

▸ **Level 4:** Final reminder letter.

For each dunning level, you can establish settings that are specific to that level; for example, the CALCULATE INTEREST? option can be activated for individual levels only. You can also run a dunning procedure and have a customer invoice selected in multiple dunning runs. In this situation, the dunning program produces an error that says the invoice has already been selected in the previous dunning run; until that run is processed to completion, it cannot be dunned again.

You can also select the PRINT ALL ITEMS option, which tells the system to print all open items for this account.

If you click the MINIMUM AMOUNTS button, you can specify the minimum amount an invoice needs to be before it reaches a dunning level. This is an important element to define because costs are associated with each dunning level; for example, it costs money to send out reminder letters, so you may not want to do so for a nominal amount of money. If you look at Figure 3.70, you can see how we have configured this option in line with our requirements.

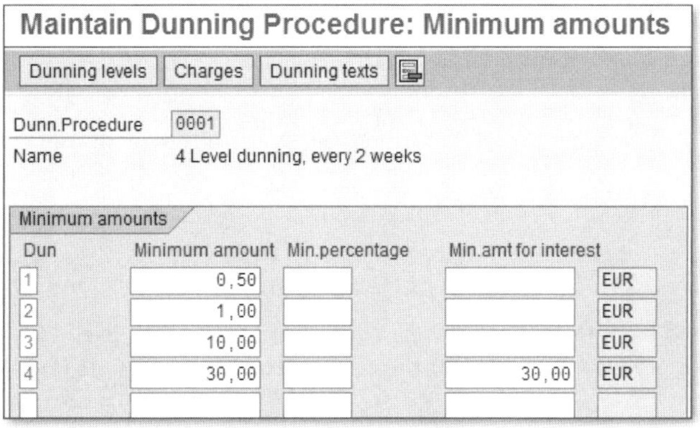

Figure 3.70 Minimum Amounts for Dunning

The final configuration activity is to assign the output, or the dunning text. If we want to generate letters for levels 3 and 4, and we want different letters to go out for each, we need to set up two outputs. These are developed through SAPscript forms, as shown in Figure 3.71.

This now completes our configuration in this area. Dunning procedures are run through Transaction F150, which you can run manually or via batch jobs that run on set days every month.

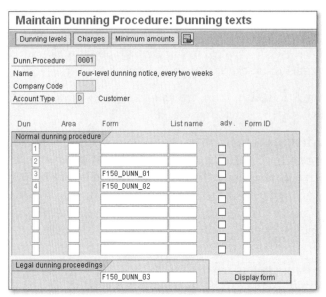

Figure 3.71 Assigning Dunning Texts

3.12 Summary

The objective of this chapter was to cover the configuration and design of the sales-order-to-cash-receipt (S2C) cycle from the point of view of an SAP ERP Financials integration. In the next chapter, we look at the purchase-order-to-payment (P2P) cycle.

This chapter covers the complete integration between SAP ERP Financials and the Materials Management component. The organizational structure, master data, and processes that take place in Financial Accounting and Materials Management integration are discussed in detail, from the creation of the purchase order to payment to the vendor.

4 Integrating the Purchase-Order-to-Payment Process

In this chapter, we cover the purchase-order-to-payment (P2P) business process and explain the integration points that are relevant for an SAP ERP Financials consultant, including the integration of this process with the Financial Accounting (FI) components (SAP General Ledger and Controlling). The P2P cycle begins in Materials Management (MM) when the purchase order is created, and it moves to Accounts Payable (AP), where the invoices are raised and payments made to the vendors for the purchases.

During these process steps, we highlight the key integration points and explain how to configure them in the system. The majority of the P2P configuration in MM is explained, including the following areas:

- MM organizational elements
- Master data
- Purchase orders
- MM account determination
- Goods receipts
- Invoice verifications
- Outgoing payments

The chapter starts with a brief overview of the P2P process. We then explain the MM organizational elements, highlight the importance of the relevant master data, and then delve into each of the P2P process steps. Note that a lot of overlap occurs between the Sales and Distribution and MM components, especially in the area of material master data. As a result, some of the concepts you saw in Chapter 3, Integrating the Sales-Order-to-Cash-Receipt Process, will also be discussed in this chapter.

4.1 Process Overview

In a P2P cycle, you capture the business processes between your organization and your vendors. This cycle covers all of the business processes that occur, starting from the point that the purchase order is created, to the end where payments are made to the vendor. Figure 4.1 provides a high-level view of the five key stages within this cycle. In this section, we explain the process behind each stage:

► Purchase order

► Goods receipt

► Invoice Verification

► AP invoice

► Outgoing payment

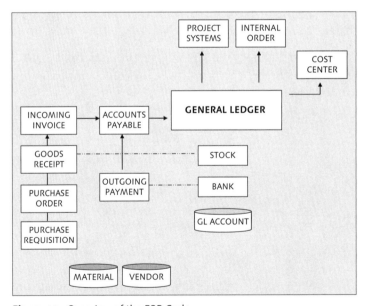

Figure 4.1 Overview of the P2P Cycle

4.1.1 Purchase Order

A purchase order (PO) is the process by which you purchase goods from a supplier (a *vendor*). It forms a legal contract between the buyer (within your organization) and the vendor, who agrees to supply the goods you need, and contains a list of the items you are buying (materials), as well as quantities, prices, and delivery information.

A PO may be created based on a purchase requisition or a previous PO, which is used in some business processes. Information is pulled from info records that contain purchasing-related information for the vendor-material combination.

The PO details the materials that you are procuring. A material is assigned an account assignment object, such as a profit center, which ensures that it is properly represented in reports. For example, one common business requirement is that a company must be able to split out inventory (stock) valuation by profit center; as such, many organizations design their solutions to get this figure.

4.1.2 Goods Receipt

A goods receipt is posted in the system when materials are received into inventory (stock). The main purpose of this process is to ensure that the items you have received match the information that was originally part of the PO. For example, you may have created a PO for 50 items at $5 each, for a total of $250. When you receive the items in more than one delivery, the goods receipt is used to monitor the receipt of goods into inventory.

At the time the invoice is received, you can see whether it covers all 50 items, or whether it is a partial invoice for the items that have actually been received. In SAP ERP, this is known as *three-way matching*, which refers to the fact that you are matching the original PO with the goods receipt and the vendor invoice. This process of three-way matching is completed at the point of Invoice Verification, which is explained next.

4.1.3 Invoice Verification

In invoice verification, you validate your vendor invoices before any payments are made to them. This is a key business process for many organizations because it enables them to make payments for valid invoices only when the goods (or services) have been received. Many organizations choose to activate invoice verification based on goods receipt and follow a three-way matching policy (among the invoice, the goods receipt, and the PO).

If you have activated invoice verification based on goods receipt, the system checks that the invoice you are entering corresponds to the goods that have been received. The system not only validates the quantity but also checks the value of the invoices; if there are any variances, the system creates variance postings. The accounts department carefully monitors these variances to keep strong control over their buyers and procurement officers. Variance postings to the general ledger are controlled by the settings made within the MM automatic account determination tables, which we discuss later in this chapter.

4.1.4 Accounts Payable Invoice

The invoice verification process takes place within MM, but this generates an AP invoice within the AP subcomponent. When paying an invoice, the payment program determines the payment information by looking at the payment method, bank details, vendor address, and so on from the vendor master record (covered later in this chapter).

Your company may decide to use POs for all inventory-related purchases and create an AP invoice for non-inventory-related purchases, which would mean that there won't be any PO or goods receipts process for these sorts of items in the SAP ERP system.

4.1.5 Outgoing Payments

Outgoing payments can be made manually or by using the automatic payment program. We discuss both of these processes later in the chapter. The key concept in automatic payment is that it combines the selection criteria provided with the vendor master records and open items to generate payments and then clears the open items at the same time.

Now that we've briefly covered the key stages in the P2P cycle, let's expand our discussion of the key stages to explain the FI and MM integration in greater detail, as part of a process rather than an isolated concept. We begin with the main MM organizational elements, which are covered in the next section.

4.2 Configuring and Integrating Materials Management Organizational Elements

We introduced the concept of organizational elements, or building blocks, in Chapter 2, SAP Enterprise Structure. Recall that the main organizational elements from an integration point of view are as follows:

- Purchasing organizations
- Purchasing groups
- Plant
- Storage locations

Next, we discuss each of these elements.

4.2.1 Purchasing Organizations

A purchasing organization is an important element in the procurement process and is comprised of a collection of purchasing activities that relate to all or part of an organization. Depending on the requirements of your company, you can configure a very simple or an extremely structured purchasing function; complex purchasing functions are often required when large amounts of money are spent on purchasing different types of material each year. These purchases can relate to many companies within an organization (centralized purchasing), or just one company (decentralized purchasing). Decentralized purchasing is most suited for companies that have a presence in many countries around the world.

The main configuration activities related to purchasing organizations are as follows:

- Creating purchasing organizations
- Assigning purchasing organizations to one company code or multiple company codes
- Assigning purchasing organizations to plants

We discuss these three main activities next.

Creating Purchasing Organizations

The menu path for creating a purchasing organization is: SPRO • ENTERPRISE STRUCTURE • DEFINITION • MATERIAL MANAGEMENT • MAINTAIN PURCHASING ORGANIZATION (Figure 4.2).

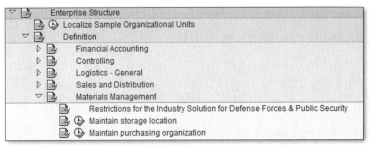

Figure 4.2 Maintain Purchasing Organization

Figure 4.3 shows the main screen for creating a purchasing organization in SAP ERP. Click the NEW ENTRIES button, and enter the four-character purchasing organization number, together with the long description for the purchasing organization in the NEW ENTRIES screen.

Figure 4.3 Creating a Purchasing Organization

Depending on your company's requirements, you can have different types of purchasing organizations set up in the SAP ERP system. These types determine the next step in setting up purchasing organizations, which is to assign your newly created purchasing organization to one company code, multiple company codes, or a plant. Next, we discuss the process of assigning purchasing organizations to a company code or codes.

Assigning Purchasing Organizations to Single or Multiple Company Codes

If your company has a central purchasing department that is responsible for all companies within your organization, you can create one purchasing organization and assign all your company codes to that one purchasing organization. If your company does not have a centralized purchasing function, and each company within your organization is responsible for its own purchases, you can make a one-to-one assignment of purchasing organization to company code. This is completed using the menu path shown in Figure 4.4: SPRO • ENTERPRISE STRUCTURE • ASSIGNMENT • MATERIAL MANAGEMENT • ASSIGN PURCHASING ORGANIZATION TO COMPANY CODE.

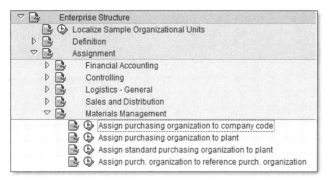

Figure 4.4 Menu Path for Assigning Purchasing Organizations to Company Codes

In the screen shown in Figure 4.5, enter the purchasing organization ID. In the company code (CO) column, enter the company code to which this purchasing organization should be assigned. This same screen is used for single and multiple company code assignments.

Change View "Assign Purchasing Organization -> Company Code"

Assign Purchasing Organization -> Company Code

POrg	Description	Co	Company Name	Status	
0006	IDES USA	0006	IDES US INC New GL		
0007	IDES Deutschland	0007	IDES AG NEW GL 7		
0008	SAFA UK	UK	SAFA UK		

Figure 4.5 Assigning Purchasing Organizations to Company Codes

Assigning Purchasing Organizations to Plants

If large plants within your organization make purchasing decisions locally , assigning purchasing organizations to company codes might not be appropriate. In this scenario, the company should link the purchasing organization at the plant level. This also means the company code is then determined indirectly by the assignment of the plant to the company code.

Note

We explain the concept of a plant later in this section; for now, let's just focus on how to assign a purchasing organization to a plant.

Purchasing organizations can be assigned to a plant using the following menu path: SPRO • ENTERPRISE STRUCTURE • ASSIGNMENT • MATERIAL MANAGEMENT • ASSIGN PURCHASING ORGANIZATION TO PLANT.

In the screen shown in Figure 4.6, enter the plant ID details in the purchasing organization row, and click SAVE.

Change View "Assign Purchasing Organization to Plant": Overview

New Entries

Assign Purchasing Organization to Plant

POrg	Description	Plnt	Name 1	Status	
0006	IDES USA	0006	New York		
0007	IDES Deutschland	0007	Werk Hamburg		
0008	SAFA UK	UK01	UK London		
0008	SAFA UK	UK02	UK Birmingham		

Figure 4.6 Assigning Purchasing Organizations to Plants

4.2.2 Purchasing Groups

A purchasing group can refer to a person or a group of people who are dealing with a specific material or group of materials purchased through the purchasing organization; purchasing groups are used to reflect the structure of your purchasing department below the level of the purchasing organization. They are configured via SPRO • MATERIALS MANAGEMENT • PURCHASING • CREATE PURCHASING GROUPS and defined by a three-character alphanumeric value that is entered with a description and telephone numbers (Figure 4.7).

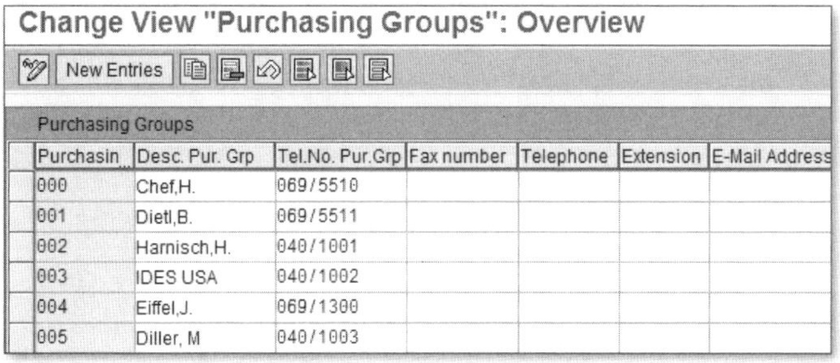

Figure 4.7 Creating Purchasing Groups

After creating and assigning purchasing organizations and creating purchasing groups, you can move to the next important MM organizational element: the plant.

4.2.3 Plants

From an SAP ERP point of view, the definition of a plant varies depending on your organization's requirements. The simplest definition of a plant is a place where you hold valuated inventory, although it does not need to be a manufacturing, storage, or shipping facility for storing materials. (Recall that we also encountered plants during our discussion of Sales and Distribution organizational elements in Chapter 3.)

> **Note**
>
> Before you create a plant in the system, a few prerequisites need to be defined, including a factory calendar, country keys, and region keys. After you've defined these prerequisites, you are ready to create a plant.

Next, we discuss the two main configuration activities involving plants:

▶ Creating plants

▶ Assigning plants to company codes

Creating Plants

A plant is defined by a four-character ID. The menu path for creating a plant is SPRO • ENTERPRISE STRUCTURE • DEFINITION • LOGISTICS – GENERAL • DEFINE, COPY, DELETE, CHECK PLANT (Transaction OX10). In the main screen, click the NEW ENTRIES button; the screen shown in Figure 4.8 appears.

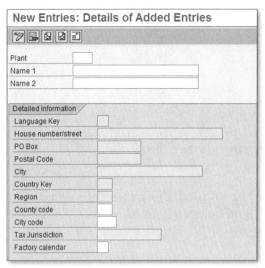

Figure 4.8 Defining a Plant

Enter the information provided in the following list:

▶ PLANT
Enter the four-character plant ID.

▶ NAME1/NAME2
Enter the name(s) of the plant. Use the NAME 1 field as a primary field; if the name is long, you can also use the NAME 2 field.

▶ COUNTY CODE
Enter the county code.

▶ CITY CODE
Enter the city code.

▶ REGION
Enter the region.

▶ FACTORY CALENDAR
Enter the factory calendar ID. (SAP ERP has predelivered calendars that identify workdays, public holidays, and company holidays. If these do not meet your requirements, you can create your own calendars.)

Click SAVE, and the plant is created. In the next step, you assign the plant to a company code.

Assigning Plants to Company Codes

Before you assign the plant to a company code, you must first define a valuation level, which specifies the level at which the materials are valuated for the client. The menu path for this is SPRO • ENTERPRISE STRUCTURE • DEFINITION • LOGISTICS – GENERAL • DEFINE VALUATION LEVEL (Transaction OX14).

You can specify the valuation level at the company code level or plant level, but the plant level is much more common. Be aware that it takes a lot of time and effort to change the level at which the valuation of materials is carried out.

After the valuation level has been completed, you can assign the plant to a company code. This step is important because it establishes a link between the entries for a plant and the FI legal entity (i.e., the company code). The menu path for assigning a plant to a company code is SPRO • ENTERPRISE STRUCTURE • ASSIGNMENT • LOGISTICS – GENERAL • ASSIGN PLANT TO COMPANY CODE (Transaction OX18).

In the main screen, click the NEW ENTRIES button. In the resulting screen, enter the company code and plant in their respective columns, and click SAVE. The assignment is saved, as shown in Figure 4.9.

Change View "Assignment Plant - Company Code"

New Entries

Assignment Plant - Company Code

Co	Plnt	Name of Plant	Company Name
UK	UK01	UK London	SAFA UK
UK	UK02	UK Birmingham	SAFA UK
US	US01	US New York	SAFA US
US	US02	US Chicago	SAFA US
US	US03	US California	SAFA US
US	US04	US Memphis	SAFA US

Figure 4.9 Assigning a Plant to a Company Code

Another important MM organizational element is found within plants: the *storage location*. We talk about storage locations next.

4.2.4 Storage Locations

A storage location is a place where inventory is kept within a plant. This is the lowest level of location within the MM component, and there is always at least one storage location defined for a plant. You can define storage locations via SPRO • ENTERPRISE STRUCTURE • DEFINITION • MATERIALS MANAGEMENT • MAINTAIN STORAGE LOCATION (Transaction OX09).

1. Define your storage location with a four-character ID. In the initial screen, shown in Figure 4.10, enter the plant number.

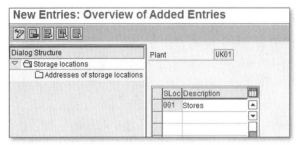

Figure 4.10 Defining a Storage Location

2. Click the New Entries button, and add the storage location number and description.

3. Highlight your newly created storage location, and click the addresses of storage locations in the dialog structure.

4. As shown in Figure 4.11, click the New Entries field to enter up to a three-character number of the storage location address.

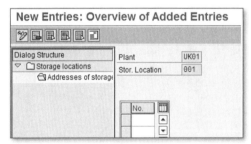

Figure 4.11 Address of a Storage Location

5. After entering this, you are asked to enter the secondary information about the location, such as its complete address and telephone number. Save your entries.

We have now completed the definition, creation, and assignment of purchasing organizations, purchasing groups, plants, and storage locations. In the next section, we explain the importance of master data from an integration point of view.

4.3 Setting Up P2P Master Data: Material Master Data

You'll recall that we first discussed material master data in Chapter 3. From a MM perspective, we are concerned with capturing information such as the material description, base unit of measure, standard price, material group, product hierarchy, and so on. All this information is extremely important and plays an important role in the successful completion of processes (such as P2P, S2C, etc.). In this section, we discuss the process of configuring material master data for the P2P process, as well as the important fields involved in the integration of FI and MM.

4.3.1 Configuring Material Master Data

Several configuration activities must be completed before a material master record can be maintained in an SAP ERP system:

▶ Defining material number formats

▶ Defining material number ranges

▶ Defining material types

Defining Material Number Formats

In SAP ERP, you have two options for maintaining material numbers in the system. The first is to manually enter them, which allows you to keep numbering conventions from your legacy system. The second is to let SAP ERP automatically assign them. If you use this second option, SAP ERP automatically assigns a material number whenever a new material is created; this assignment is based on certain settings in the configuration. Maintain the material number field via SPRO • LOGISTICS – GENERAL • MATERIAL MASTER • BASIC SETTINGS • DEFINE OUTPUT FORMAT OF MATERIAL NUMBERS (Transaction OMSL).

Figure 4.12 shows the configuration screen for defining the output format for material numbers. The most important field here is the MATERIAL NO. LENGTH field, which determines the maximum length a material number can have when it is created in the SAP ERP system. If you've decided to let SAP ERP assign the material numbers, you can enter the required format in the MATERIAL NUMBER TEMPLATE field.

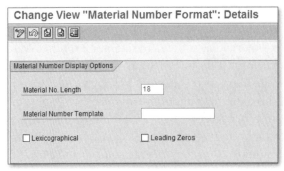

Figure 4.12 Define Output Format of Material Numbers

Defining Material Number Ranges

Material number ranges in SAP ERP can be configured via SPRO • LOGISTICS – GENERAL • MATERIAL MASTER • BASIC SETTINGS • MATERIAL TYPES • DEFINE NUMBER RANGES FOR EACH MATERIAL TYPES (Transaction MMNR).

Figure 4.13 shows how you can enter number ranges for material numbers in the system, and also select the option to make that range either externally or internally assigned. Number ranges are assigned to material types (discussed in the next section), and numbering for new materials are assigned based on these number ranges.

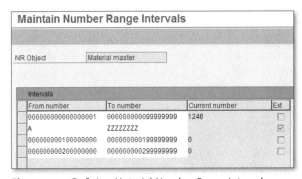

Figure 4.13 Defining Material Number Range Intervals

> **Note**
>
> When all number ranges are entered in the system, we usually do not recommend transporting the number range tables because the transport carries the current number value used up to this point. This often leads to a clash between the sender and target systems. This will also result in issues in the target system, where you'll get error messages when creating documents.

Defining Material Types

A *material type* is a logical grouping of materials that are similar in characteristics. Any material master record created in SAP ERP must be assigned to a material type. The menu path for this is SPRO • LOGISTICS – GENERAL • MATERIAL MASTER • BASIC SETTINGS • MATERIAL TYPES • DEFINE ATTRIBUTES OF MATERIAL TYPES (Transaction OMS2).

One of the important functions of defining material types is that it predefines certain fields in the material master record for any material created under a specific material type, for example, the price control setting, as shown in Figure 4.14.

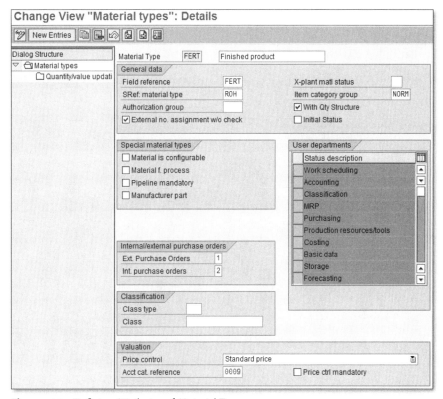

Figure 4.14 Defining Attributes of Material Types

Figures 4.15 and Figure 4.16 show a few examples of material types and their attributes, respectively.

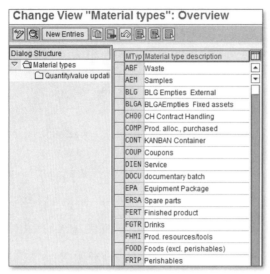

Figure 4.15 Material Types

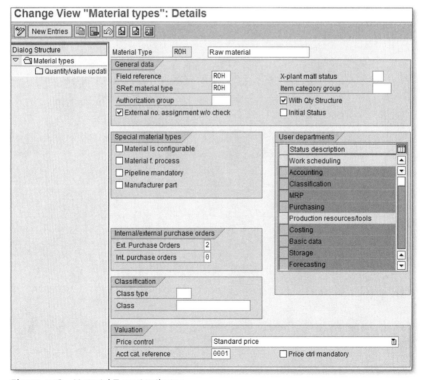

Figure 4.16 Material Type Attributes

After performing the main configuration activities for material master data, you must maintain some fields specific to FI, as discussed next.

4.3.2 Maintaining Financial Accounting Fields in Material Master Records

The data stored in material master records ensures that the system has enough information to enable the successful completion of processes involving a specific material. This information is saved in what we call *views,* for example, BASIC DATA, PURCHASING, FOREIGN TRADE, MRP, WORK SCHEDULING, GENERAL PLANT DATA, ACCOUNTING, COSTING, and so on. For integration, we focus our attention on only the fields within those views that have relevance from a FI point of view: the ACCOUNTING and COSTING views.

Accounting 1 View

The important fields in the ACCOUNTING 1 view, as shown in Figure 4.17, are discussed in the following list.

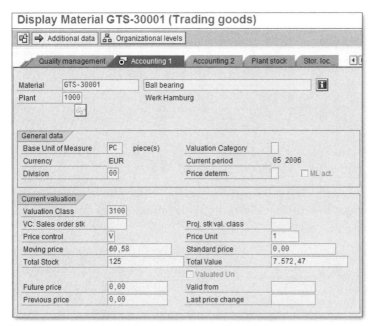

Figure 4.17 Material Master Record: Accounting 1 Tab

▶ VALUATION CLASS

The VALUATION CLASS field is used to link a material to the general ledger accounts. When there is material movement, the linked general ledger accounts are updated because of this setting. You can create a valuation class using the following path: SPRO • MATERIAL MANAGEMENT • VALUATION AND ACCOUNT ASSIGNMENT • ACCOUNT DETERMINATION • ACCOUNT DETERMINATION WITHOUT WIZARD • DEFINE VALUATION CLASSES (Transaction OMSK).

Figure 4.18 shows the configuration screen for creating a new valuation class in the system.

Change View "Valuation Classes": Overview

ValCl	ARef	Description	Description
0710	0001	Equipment 1	Reference for raw materials
1011	0001		Reference for raw materials
3000	0001	Raw materials 1	Reference for raw materials
3001	0001	Raw materials 2	Reference for raw materials
3200	0006	Services	Reference for trading goods
7900	0008	Semifinished products	Ref. for semifinished products
7910	0008	Semi finished - Purchased	Ref. for semifinished products
7920	0009	Finished products	Ref. for finished products
7921	0009	Finished products - extrn	Ref. for finished products
7930	0009	Finished products - purch	Ref. for finished products
9001	0009	Sales Aids & Literature	Ref. for finished products

Figure 4.18 Defining Valuation Classes

▶ PRICE CONTROL

This field is used in the valuation of materials in the system. The two options available are moving price (V) and standard price (S):

▶ MOVING PRICE: The moving price is calculated in the system by dividing the total material value by the total inventory. This price changes with all valuation-relevant movements.

▶ STANDARD PRICE: The standard price represents the price for a material that remains constant; it is not affected by any changes in prices or movements of the materials. You can enter the standard price in this field after you select S for the PRICE CONTROL indicator.

▶ PRICE UNIT

The PRICE UNIT field is used to represent the number of units to which the moving price or standard price relates. This field has more significance for materials with very small prices because it prevents any rounding errors. For example, if there is a material with a standard price of USD $5.58, and the price per unit is 1000, the actual cost per unit is $0.00558.

▶ FUTURE PRICE and VALID FROM

The FUTURE PRICE field is used when a change is required to the standard price of a material. The future price entered takes effect from the date specified in the VALID FROM field.

Costing 1 View

The costing department uses costing views in the material master record to enter information relevant to their work. Figure 4.19 shows the COSTING 1 screen. From a FI point of view, the most important field in this screen is the PROFIT CENTER field, which is where you enter the profit center to which this material relates.

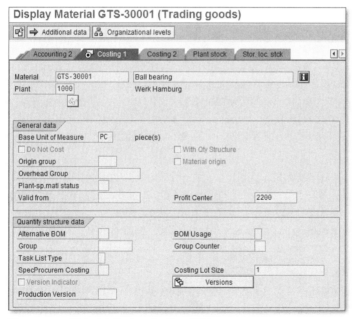

Figure 4.19 Material Master: Costing 1 Tab

4.4 Setting up P2P Master Data: Vendor Master Data

Vendor master data contains all of the necessary information about the suppliers of a company from which materials or services are purchased. SAP ERP has designed a single place for storing all of the important information related to suppliers, thus ensuring that all of the departments are accessing the most updated and correct information about the suppliers.

Vendor master records are divided into three sections:

- **General data**
  This section contains information about the vendor that remains the same for any company dealing with that vendor in the SAP ERP system. The general data entered in this section can include name, search term, address, telephone, fax, email, and so on. Use Transaction XK01 or FK01 to enter this information.

- **Company code data**
  This section contains information about the vendor that is entered at the company code level; it is specific for that company code only. The information entered here can include reconciliation accounts, payment terms, payment methods, dunning information, correspondence info, and so on. Use Transaction FK01 to enter this information in the system.

- **Purchasing organization data**
  This section contains information about the vendor that is entered at the purchasing organizational level. Just as accounting data is specific to a company code and can differ from one company to another, purchasing data is relevant for one purchasing organization and can be different between purchasing organizations. The data entered here includes partner functions, purchasing default

fields, invoice verification indicators, and so on. Use Transaction MK01 or XK01 to enter this data in the system.

Next, we divide our discussion of vendor master data into two parts: the configuration of vendor master records, and the vendor master record fields that are important to FI.

4.4.1 Configuring Vendor Master Data

There are two major configuration activities for vendor master data: defining vendor account groups, and defining vendor number ranges. We discuss both of these activities next.

Defining Vendor Account Groups

Vendor account groups are used to logically group vendors of similar types; for example, foreign, trade, nontrade, and so on. The vendor account group controls the number range assignments for the vendors, the field status of the account fields (which controls the screen layout), and one-time vendors. When creating a vendor master record, you are required to enter the vendor account group for that vendor, so you must define vendor account group configuration before you can create a vendor master record. Account groups can be created via SPRO • FINANCIAL ACCOUNTING (NEW) • ACCOUNT RECEIVABLE & ACCOUNT PAYABLE • VENDOR ACCOUNTS • MASTER DATA • PREPARATIONS FOR CREATING VENDOR MASTER DATA • DEFINE ACCOUNT GROUPS WITH SCREEN LAYOUT (VENDORS).

Figure 4.20 shows the custom vendor account groups in the system, as an example. You can define your own vendor account groups by clicking the NEW ENTRIES button. The screen shown in Figure 4.21 appears.

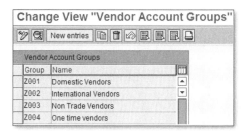

Figure 4.20 Defining Vendor Account Groups

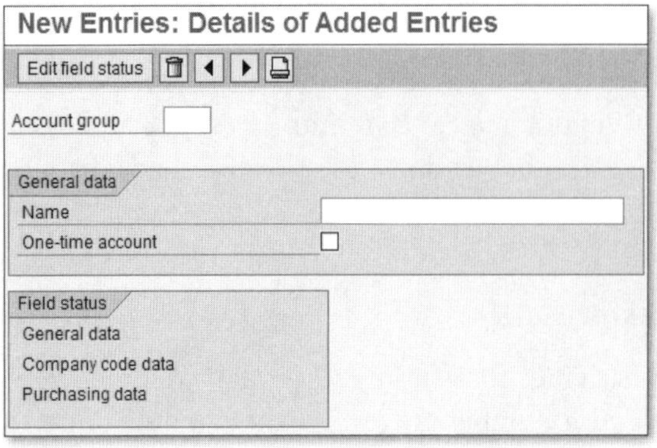

New Entries: Details of Added Entries

Edit field status

Account group

General data
Name
One-time account ☐

Field status
General data
Company code data
Purchasing data

Figure 4.21 New Vendor Account Group Definition

On this screen, you can center the account group key and its description in the ACCOUNT GROUP and NAME fields, respectively. If this is a one-time vendor account group, select the ONE-TIME ACCOUNT flag. After entering this basic information, move on to the FIELD STATUS area, which is where you decide whether the fields are available for entry, just display, required, or completely suppressed. You have the option to change the field status for general data, company code data, and/or purchasing data by highlighting the relevant field status option and then selecting the EDIT FIELD STATUS button.

Figure 4.22 shows the GENERAL DATA screen, which lists specific field status groups available for configuration.

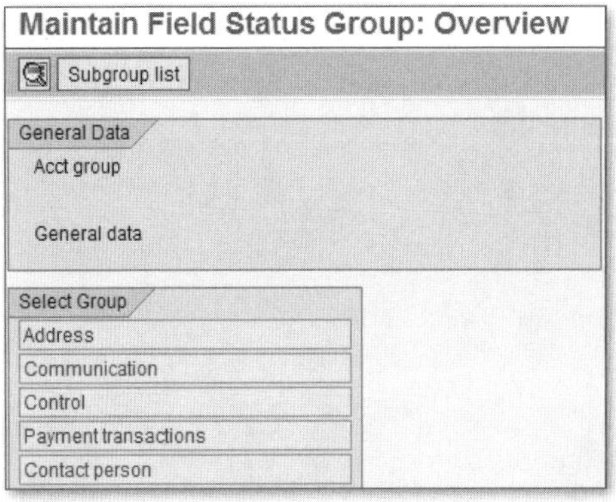

Maintain Field Status Group: Overview

Subgroup list

General Data
Acct group

General data

Select Group
Address
Communication
Control
Payment transactions
Contact person

Figure 4.22 Vendor Account Group: Field Status Group Settings

Double-click the group you want to configure, and, in the next screen (Figure 4.23), indicate whether certain fields should be suppressed (SUPPRESS), required

(Req. Entry), optional (Opt. Entry), or display only (Display). After this configuration, the fields in vendor master records in this account group will appear exactly as you indicated here.

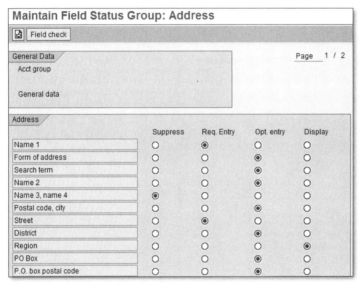

Figure 4.23 Maintain Field Status Group

The layouts of screens can also be configured from a company code point of view by using the following menu path: SPRO • Financial Accounting (New) • Account Receivable & Account Payable • Vendor Accounts • Master Data • Preparations for Creating Vendor Master Data • Define Screen Layout per Company Code (Vendors).

Defining Vendor Number Ranges

In SAP ERP, you have two options for assigning numbers to a newly created vendor in the system. You can either assign them manually (external number assignment), or you can let SAP ERP assign them automatically (internal number assignment). You can create different number ranges for each type of vendor account group, but this decision should be based on careful consideration. The menu path for creating number ranges is SPRO • Financial Accounting (New) • Account Receivable & Account Payable • Vendor Accounts • Master Data • Preparations for Creating Vendor Master Data • Create Number Ranges for Vendor Accounts (Transaction XKN1).

Figure 4.24 shows the configuration screen for creating vendor number ranges. Enter the two-character ID for the number range, together with its lower and upper limit. If you want to manually assign the number for the vendor, set the Ext flag; do not select this flag if you want the system to automatically assign the new number.

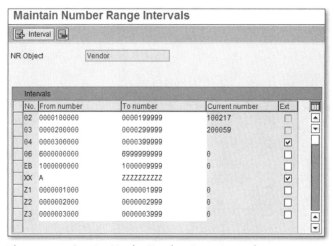

Figure 4.24 Creating Vendor Number Range Intervals

After the number ranges have been created, the next step is to assign them to vendor account groups. This activity can be completed via SPRO • Financial Accounting (New) • Account Receivable & Account Payable • Vendor Accounts • Master Data • Preparations for Creating Vendor Master Data • Assign Number Ranges to Vendor Account Groups.

Figure 4.25 shows the configuration screen for this activity, where you can assign one range to more than one vendor account group, or assign a different number range for each account group.

Now that we've explained some of the basic requirements for creating vendor master records, let's explore some of the vendor master record fields that are important for integration with FI.

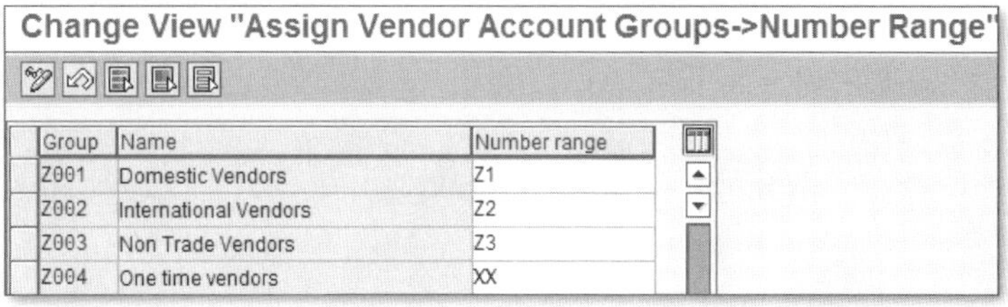

Figure 4.25 Assigning Vendor Account Groups to Number Ranges

4.4.2   Maintaining Financial Accounting Fields in Vendor Master Records

As we mentioned previously, vendor master records have three distinct sections (general data, company code data, and purchasing organization data). From an integration point of view, though, the most relevant sections of the vendor master record are the accounting info and payment transactions in the company code data, and the purchasing data and partner functions in the purchasing organization data. Next we explore some of the important fields in these two sections.

Company Code Data Fields

The company code data section allows the accounting department to enter all accounting-relevant information in the vendor master record, for example, reconciliation accounts, payment methods, and so on. You can use the menu path SAP MENU • ACCOUNTING • FINANCIAL ACCOUNTING • ACCOUNTS PAYABLE • MASTER RECORDS • DISPLAY (Transaction Code FK03) to display the vendor master record. After entering the vendor number and your company code, you should set the ACCOUNTING INFO and PAYMENT TRANSACTIONS flag under the company code data to see their details. In the following list, we briefly explain the most important fields in the ACCOUNTING INFORMATION screen (shown in Figure 4.26):

▶ RECON. ACCOUNT
   Reconciliation accounts connect subledger accounts (such as customers, vendors, and assets) with SAP General Ledger in real time. Essentially, reconciliation accounts are general ledger accounts entered in the business partner master data to record all transactions in the subledger. This way, all postings to the subledger accounts are automatically posted to the linked reconciliation accounts, and the general ledger is always up to date. You can create one reconciliation account to represent all different vendors, or you can create different reconciliation accounts to represent different types of vendors or vendor

163

groups, such as reconciliation accounts on the basis of domestic or foreign trade, group or non-group, and so on.

▶ SORT KEY
This defines the value that fills in the assignment field in your transactions. Normally key 003 is selected for entry in this field.

▶ INTEREST INDIC.
Select an interest calculation indicator in this field if the account is suitable for automatic interest calculation. The menu path to configure interest calculation is SPRO • FINANCIAL ACCOUNTING (NEW) • ACCOUNTS RECEIVABLES AND ACCOUNTS PAYABLE • BUSINESS TRANSACTIONS • INTEREST CALCULATION • INTEREST CALCULATION GLOBAL SETTING • DEFINE INTEREST CALCULATION TYPE.

▶ INTEREST FREQ.
In this field, as shown in Figure 4.26, enter the period for which the interest calculation should run for this vendor. The period can be monthly, quarterly, or yearly, depending on your requirements.

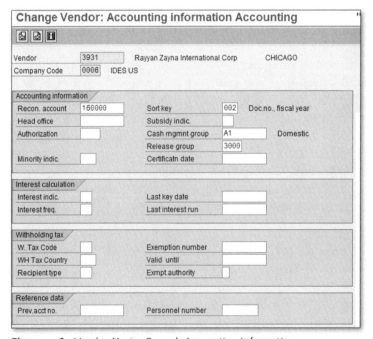

Figure 4.26 Vendor Master Record: Accounting Information

▶ Prev. Acct. No.

Use this to search for a vendor account. It can be used as part of the data conversion, so the legacy system account number can be entered here.

The important fields in the Payment Transactions screen are explained in the following list and shown in Figure 4.27:

▶ Payt Terms

Payment terms represent the amount of time your company has to pay a vendor, for example, 30 days from the date of the invoice, 60 days from the date of the invoice, and so on. You can also use payment term settings to take advantage of the cash discounts offered by vendors for early payments. These settings can be configured in the system when you define payment terms using this menu path SPRO • Financial Accounting (New) • Accounts Receivables and Accounts Payable • Business Transactions • Incoming Invoices/Credit Memos • Maintain Terms of Payment.

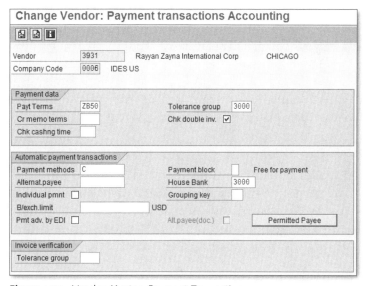

Figure 4.27 Vendor Master: Payment Transactions

▶ Chk Double Inv

The purpose of this indicator is for the system to check for double or duplicate invoices at the time of invoice entry. If this indicator is selected, the system checks whether invoices have already been entered by using certain preset criteria, such as posting date, reference field, and amount.

▶ Payment Methods

In this field, enter the payment method that you will use to pay the vendor invoices, for example, checks, wire transfers, BACS, and so on. When you're performing the automatic payment run, the system uses this field to identify vendors with a specific payment method entered as a parameter in the automatic payment run. We discuss payment method settings in more detail later in this chapter.

▶ Payment Block

If you want to stop payment for a vendor, enter the reason for the payment block in this field; the vendor open items will then not be available for selection in automatic payment runs or during manual payments, unless an authorized accounting clerk can unblock the vendor for payment. The payment block reasons can be configured using this menu path SPRO • Financial Accounting (New) • Accounts Receivables and Accounts Payable • Business Transactions • Outgoing Payments • Outgoing Payments Global Settings • Payment Block Reasons • Define Payment Block Reasons (Transaction OB27).

▶ House Bank

Banks that are used by your company are created as house banks in SAP ERP. You can create one or more house banks, depending on the complexity of your banking arrangements. If the same house bank is used for paying a specific vendor, then that house bank can be entered in this field. Configuration of house banks is covered in more detail later in this chapter.

Purchasing Organization Data Fields

In this section of the vendor master record, the purchasing department maintains purchasing-related information about the vendor, such as the order currency, terms of payment, and so on. You can use the menu path SAP Menu • Logistics • Materials Management • Purchasing • Master Data • Vendor • Central • Display (Transaction XK03) to display the vendor master record. After entering the vendor number and your company code, set the flag for the Purchasing Data and Partner Functions to see the fields we explain next.

The important purchasing data fields are explained in the following list and shown in Figure 4.28.

▶ Order Currency

In this field, you can enter the currency to be used on a PO for a vendor. In most cases, it is the currency of the vendor's country.

Create Vendor: Purchasing data

Alternative data Sub-ranges

| Vendor | 3931 | Rayyan Zayna International Corp | CHICAGO |
| Purchasing Org. | 0008 | SAFA UK | |

Conditions

Order currency	USD	American Dollar
Terms of paymnt	0002	
Incoterms	EXW	
Minimum order value		
Schema Group, Vendor		Standard procedure vendor
Pricing Date Control		No Control
Order optim.rest.		

Sales data

Salesperson	
Telephone	
Acc. with vendor	

Control data

☑ GR-Based Inv. Verif.	ABC indicator	
☐ AutoEvalGRSetmt Del.	ModeOfTrnsprt-Border	
☐ AutoEvalGRSetmt Ret	Office of entry	
☐ Acknowledgment Reqd	Sort criterion	By VSR sequence number
☐ Automatic purchase order	PROACT control prof.	
☐ Subsequent settlement	☐ Revaluation allowed	
☐ Subseq. sett. index	☐ Grant discount in kind	
☐ B.vol.comp./ag.nec.	☐ Relevant for price determ. (del.hierarchy)	
☐ Doc. index active	☐ Relevant for agency business	
☐ Srv.-Based Inv. Ver.	Shipping Conditions	

Figure 4.28 Vendor Master: Purchasing Data

- TERMS OF PAYMNT

  Payment terms represent the amount of time your company has to pay a vendor, for example, 30 days from the date of the invoice, 60 days from the date
  of the invoice, and so on. You can also use payment term settings to take advantage of the cash discounts offered by vendors for early payments. If a specific
  vendor is used for both trade and nontrade purchases, you can enter different
  payment terms in the accounting and purchasing data fields, making it possible
  to have different payment requirements for the same vendor. In this case, however, documents created through the P2P process take the payment terms from
  this view.

- GR-BASED INV. VERIF.

  If you set this indicator, the system performs invoice verification based on the
  goods receipts amounts. As we mentioned earlier, this concept is known as

a three-way match, whereby the PO, goods receipt, and invoice are matched to ensure that the totals are correct and that the invoice should be paid to the vendor.

The PARTNER FUNCTIONS screen shown in Figure 4.29 allows the purchasing user to define the various relationships between the vendor and your company. A vendor can be small in size, such as a sole proprietor, or a large multinational company, and the business partner functionality is used to define the vendor's various operations. This functionality can be defined for both customers (as discussed in Chapter 3) and vendors. The various available vendor partner codes are shown in Table 4.1.

Partner Code	Description
AZ	Alternative Payment Recipient
CA	Contact Address
CP	Contact Person
ER	Employee Responsible
GS	Goods Supplier
OA	Ordering Address
PI	Invoice Presented By
VN	Vendor

Table 4.1 Vendor Master: Partner Functions Information

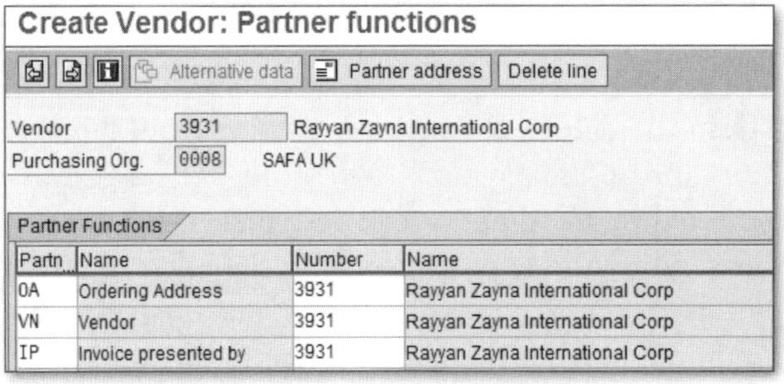

Figure 4.29 Vendor Master: Partner Functions Information

You should now have a basic understanding of the configuration and important fields in both material and vendor master records. In the next section, we begin by looking at the transaction documents that are created as a part of the P2P process.

We begin with the PO because it is a common starting point in the P2P process for almost every solution implemented in companies worldwide.

4.5 Purchase Orders

Purchase orders are created to request specific products from vendors. They are considered to be legal and binding documents, and they contain information about the product, its quantity and price, as well as the PO number, delivery address, payment terms, and currency of the PO.

You can create a PO with or without a purchase requisition, depending on your business requirements. A purchase requisition is basically an internal document created to give notification to the purchasing department of material requirements; it contains information about the quantity of the material, among other things. In this section, we explore the process of creating a PO *without* a purchase requisition because this is more relevant to the integration process.

> **Note**
>
> When you create a PO, no accounting document is created in the system.

We use the option of creating a PO with a known vendor number, using the vendor information explained in the previous sections. To create a PO when you know the vendor number, use Transaction ME21N or the following menu path: SAP MENU • LOGISTICS • MATERIALS MANAGEMENT • PURCHASING • PURCHASE ORDER • CREATE • VENDOR KNOWN. The EnjoySAP transaction is divided in two sections, as shown in Figure 4.30: the header information and line item details. Both these sections can be minimized and expanded as required.

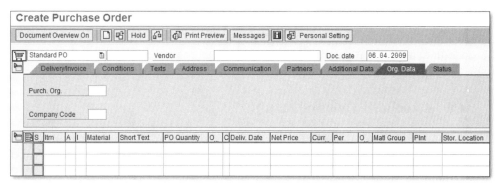

Figure 4.30 Create Purchase Order with Vendor Known

In the main screen, select the PO type, which, in our case, is the standard PO type (NB). Use the following list to enter the other relevant information in the PO:

- ▶ VENDOR
  Enter the number of the vendor receiving this PO.

- ▶ PURCHASING ORG.
  Enter the purchasing organization number in this field.

- ▶ PURCH. GROUP
  Enter the purchase group number in this field.

- ▶ COMPANY CODE
  Enter the company code in this field.

- ▶ MATERIAL
  Enter the material number in this field.

- ▶ PO QUANTITY
  Enter the quantity of the material you need to purchase.

- ▶ DELIV. DATE
  Enter the delivery date for the material.

- ▶ NET PRICE
  Enter the per unit price for the material.

- ▶ PLNT
  Enter the plant ID in this field.

After entering this information, save the PO in the system, and a PO number is generated. The PO should then be sent to the vendor via whatever method was agreed upon between the vendor and your company (e.g., EDI, fax, email, etc.).

Now that the PO is created, the next stage in the process is the goods receipt. However, before that, we need to consider several integration steps because goods receipts and invoice entries both result in FI postings. In the next section, we look at a key configuration that enables the transformation of MM documents into FI documents: account determination.

4.6 Account Determination

To properly understand this configuration area, you should have a holistic appreciation of the various elements involved. We divided this section into various steps that are important to properly understand the concept of integration. These steps build on the discussions earlier in this chapter; bringing this all together will give you a complete understanding of this complex topic.

We need to consider these important steps:

- Defining valuation classes
- Defining account groupings for movement types
- Defining transaction keys
- Defining account determination

We discuss each of these steps next.

4.6.1 Defining Valuation Classes

In SAP ERP, individual materials are grouped in *valuation classes* for the purposes of valuation; similar materials are posted to the same general ledger accounts so that their valuation is appropriately represented in the inventory account. If you look at the material master record shown earlier (refer Figure 4.17), you can see this assignment; this is how you specify which general ledger stock account is posted to when a transaction for this material is processed. The menu path for defining valuation classes is SPRO • MATERIAL MANAGEMENT • VALUATION AND ACCOUNT ASSIGNMENT • ACCOUNT DETERMINATION • ACCOUNT DETERMINATION WITHOUT WIZARD • DEFINE VALUATION CLASSES (Transaction OMSK).

From the screen shown in Figure 4.31, you can see three options that need to be configured. We consider each in turn.

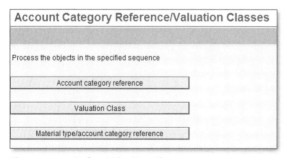

Figure 4.31 Define Valuation Classes

Account Category Reference

An account category reference is a way to group together valuation classes used by the system to determine whether the valuation class entered in the material master record is allowed for maintaining accounting data. Figure 4.32 shows the different types of account category references available in the system. To create your own account category reference, click the NEW ENTRIES button.

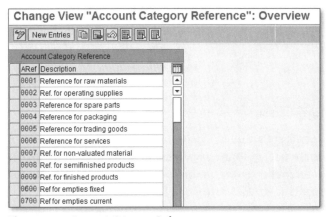

Figure 4.32 Account Category References

In the resulting screen (Figure 4.33), enter the account category reference ID in the AREF column, and enter a brief description in the DESCRIPTION column.

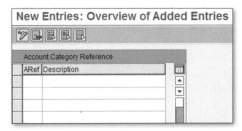

Figure 4.33 Creating an Account Category Reference

Valuation Class

As explained previously in this chapter, the VALUATION CLASS field links groups of materials to a specific general ledger account. You can also say that a valuation class is a group of materials with the same general ledger account determination settings. When there is material movement, the linked general ledger accounts are updated according to this setting.

Figure 4.34 shows the configuration screen for the definition of valuation classes. A valuation class is created with reference to an account category reference, as shown in Figure 4.34.

Change View "Valuation Classes": Overview

ValCl	ARef	Description	Description
1210	0002	Low-value assets RU	Ref. for operating supplies
3000	0001	Raw materials 1	Reference for raw materials
3001	0001	Raw materials 2	Reference for raw materials
3002	0001	Raw materials 3	Reference for raw materials
3003	0001	Raw materials 4	Reference for raw materials
3030	0002	Operating supplies	Ref. for operating supplies
3040	0003	Spare parts	Reference for spare parts
3050	0004	(Returnable) packaging	Reference for packaging
3100	0005	Trading goods	Reference for trading goods

Figure 4.34 Defining Valuation Classes

Material Type/Account Category Reference

As already defined in this chapter, a material type is a logical grouping of materials that have similar characteristics. Similarly, an account category reference is a grouping of valuation classes; essentially, account category references act as a link between material types and valuation classes. Figure 4.35 shows the configuration screen for creating that link.

Change View "Account Category Reference/Material Type": Overview

Account Category Reference/Material Type

MTyp	Material type descr.	ARef	Description
CONT	KANBAN Container	0001	Reference for raw materials
COUP	Coupons	0005	Reference for trading goods
DIEN	Service	0006	Reference for services
DOCU	documentary batch	0008	Ref. for semifinished products
EPA	Equipment Package	0004	Reference for packaging
ERSA	Spare parts	0003	Reference for spare parts
FERT	Finished product	0009	Ref. for finished products
FGTR	Drinks	0005	Reference for trading goods
FHMI	Prod. resources/tools	0008	Ref. for semifinished products
FOOD	Foods (excl. perishables)	0005	Reference for trading goods
FRIP	Perishables	0005	Reference for trading goods
HALB	Semi-finished product	0008	Ref. for semifinished products
HAWA	Trading goods	0005	Reference for trading goods

Figure 4.35 Account Category Reference/Material Type

You've now established the link among account category references, valuation classes, and movement types.

4.6.2   Defining Account Groupings for Movement Types

Movement types in MM are used to differentiate between various business reasons for the movement of goods. Each movement type is configured to reflect the different transaction that is processed and may have a related function such as updating the quantity fields, updating the inventory and consumption accounts, selecting fields used for entering documents, and printing goods receipt/issue slips. More importantly, though, movement types update the inventory account and trigger transactions that result in postings to general ledger accounts. (Movement types are not directly linked to general ledger accounts, but their attributes — such as account grouping — determine what general ledger accounts are posted to for a specific movement of materials.)

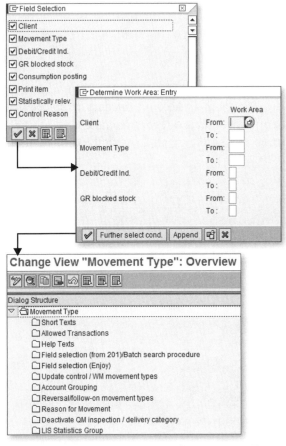

Figure 4.36 Account Groupings Within Movement Types

You can create your own movement types if necessary, but SAP ERP provides many standard options that can be used. The complete configuration of movement types involves many steps, but we restrict this discussion to the account grouping within the movement types, as shown in Figure 4.36 and Figure 4.37. The menu path for configuring account groups is SPRO • MATERIALS MANAGEMENT • INVENTORY MANAGEMENT AND PHYSICAL INVENTORY • MOVEMENT TYPES • COPY, CHANGE MOVEMENT TYPES (TRANSACTION OMJJ).

As you can see in Figure 4.37, the system uses the key entered here to find the account for transactions/events with active account groupings in the table of account keys. In the system, the account grouping has been defined for the following transactions/events:

▶ GBB (offsetting entry for inventory posting)

▶ PRD (price differences)

▶ KON (consignment liabilities)

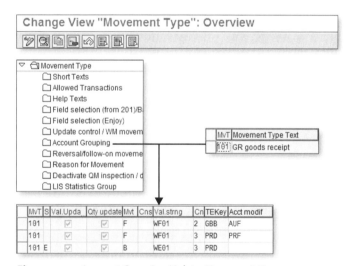

Figure 4.37 Account Grouping Link to Movement Types

Transaction keys in MM automatically determine the general ledger accounts together with the valuation class and posting keys. The transaction keys also reflect specific transactions that occur as part of the P2P process. These are standard system-driven processes; for example, everyone uses inventory posting, although different organizations may use different terms for it. Figures 4.38 and 4.39 show different transaction keys available in SAP ERP.

You can't create new transaction keys in the system. Multiple movement types are grouped into transaction keys that can be used to provide similar general ledger account determination for the same sort of movement types. All transaction keys share the same transaction group (RMK).

Maintain FI Configuration: Automatic Posting - Procedures

Group   RMK   Materials Management postings (MM)

Procedures

Description	Transaction	Account determ.
Rev.from agency bus.	AG1	☑
Sales fr.agency bus.	AG2	☑
Exp.from agency bus.	AG3	☑
Expense/revenue from consign.mat.consum.	AKO	☑
Expense/revenue from stock transfer	AUM	☑
Subsequent settlement of provisions	B01	☑
Subsequent settlement of revenues	B02	☑
Provision differences	B03	☑
Inventory posting	BSD	☑
Change in stock account	BSV	☑
Inventory posting	BSX	☑
Revaluation of other consumables	COC	☑
Delkredere	DEL	☑
Materials management small differences	DIF	☑
Purchase account	EIN	☑
Purchase offsetting account	EKG	☑
Freight clearing	FR1	☑
Freight provisions	FR2	☑
Customs clearing	FR3	☑
Customs provisions	FR4	☑
Purchasing freight account	FRE	☑
External activity	FRL	☑
Incidental costs of external activities	FRN	☑
Offsetting entry for inventory posting	GBB	☑
Account-assigned purchase order	KBS	☐

Figure 4.38 Transaction Keys Under Group RMK (Part I)

Maintain FI Configuration: Automatic Posting - Procedures

Group   RMK   Materials Management postings (MM)

Procedures

Description	Transaction	Account determ.
Price diff. offset. entry (cost object)	KTR	☑
Accruals and defer.acct(material ledger)	LKW	☑
Prepayment	PPX	☑
Price Differences from W/Off WIP	PRA	☑
Differences (AVR Price)	PRC	☑
Cost (price) differences	PRD	☑
Price Differences (Mat. Ledger, AVR)	PRG	☑
Price differences (cost object hierarc.)	PRK	☑
Price Diff. from WIP Written Off (Mat.)	PRM	☑
Product cost collector price differences	PRP	☑
Prod.cost coll.price diff. offsett.entry	PRQ	☑
Material ledger fr.low.levels price dif.	PRV	☑
Cost (price) differences (mater.ledger)	PRY	☑
Expense/revenue from revaluation	RAP	☑
Inv.reductions from log.inv.verification	RKA	☑
Neutral provisions	RUE	☑
Brazilian taxes for transfer posting	TX0	☑
Gain/loss from revaluation	UMB	☑
Gain/loss from revaluation	UMD	☑
Unplanned delivery costs	UPF	☑
Input tax	VST	☑
WGB < missing >	WGB	☑
Goods issue inflation revaluation	WGI	☑
Goods receipt inflation revaluation	WGR	☑
WIP from Price Differences (Int. Acty)	WPA	☑
WIP from Price Differences (Material)	WPM	☑
GR/IR clearing account	WRX	☑

Figure 4.39   Transaction Keys Under Group RMK (Part II)

In Figure 4.40, you can see the link among the concepts of movement type, transaction keys, and account modifier. An account modifier is basically a key that allows you to subdivide the main transaction key for detailed account determination. This means that when a specific movement type is used, the transaction key, together with the account modifier, is used to determine the general ledger account for postings.

At this point, we can now assign general ledger accounts so that when inventory-related transactions take place, the correct general ledger accounts are automatically determined.

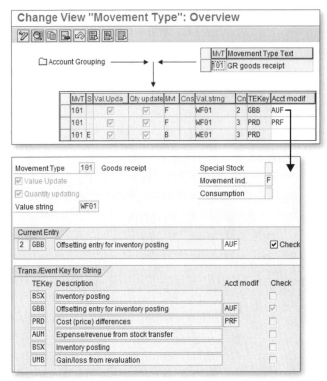

Figure 4.40 Movement Type Link to Transaction Key and Account Modifier

4.6.3 Defining Account Determination

You can configure the inventory-related account determination by following this menu path: SPRO • FINANCIAL ACCOUNTING (NEW) • GENERAL LEDGER (NEW) • PERI-ODIC PROCESSING • INTEGRATION • MATERIALS MANAGEMENT • DEFINE ACCOUNTS FOR MATERIALS MANAGEMENT. Click ACCOUNT ASSIGNMENT, and the screen shown in Figure 4.41 appears. You can also use Transaction OBYC to access this screen directly.

For the keys shown in Figure 4.41, you can configure them in three ways:

▶ POSTING KEY
This lets you define the financial posting keys that are triggered by the keys shown in Figure 4.41.

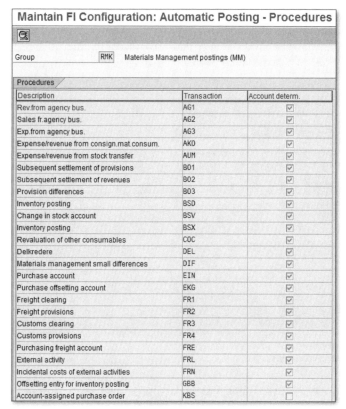

Figure 4.41 Maintain Automatic Account Determination

▶ RULES

This option lets you select the relevant rules for this key. For example, for BSX, you can select both the valuation modifier and valuation class, which allows you to enter the general ledger account for this combination. For some other keys, such as GBB, you can also select the general modifier to be added to this combination, depending on your requirements.

▶ ACCOUNTS

This lets you assign the actual general ledger accounts based on the combination specified within the rules.

You can configure a procedure by double-clicking it, as shown in Figure 4.42. We show just one example key here: BSX.

Note

The use of each key in combination with these rules depends on your business requirements and overall project design across the P2P cycle.

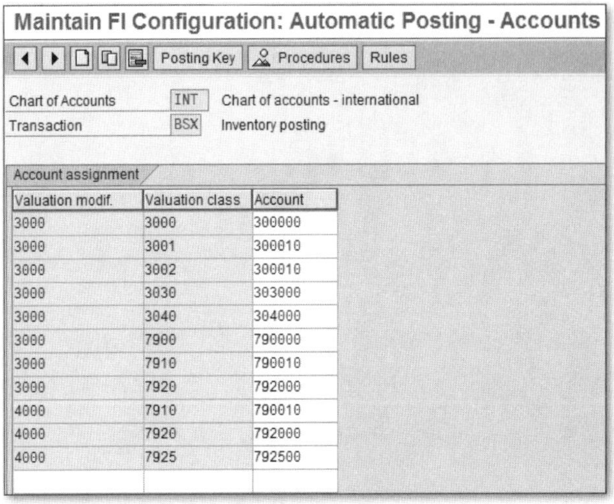

Maintain FI Configuration: Automatic Posting - Accounts

◄ ► ☐ ☐ ☐ Posting Key | ⚬ Procedures | Rules

| Chart of Accounts | INT | Chart of accounts - international |
| Transaction | BSX | Inventory posting |

Account assignment

Valuation modif.	Valuation class	Account
3000	3000	300000
3000	3001	300010
3000	3002	300010
3000	3030	303000
3000	3040	304000
3000	7900	790000
3000	7910	790010
3000	7920	792000
4000	7910	790010
4000	7920	792000
4000	7925	792500

Figure 4.42 BSX Transaction Key Settings

Click the RULES button, and select the rules that you want to activate, as shown in Figure 4.43. By selecting the valuation class as a rule, you can assign different general ledger accounts for each valuation class. As explained previously, these valuation classes are then entered in the material master record and serve the function of controlling the automatic account determination.

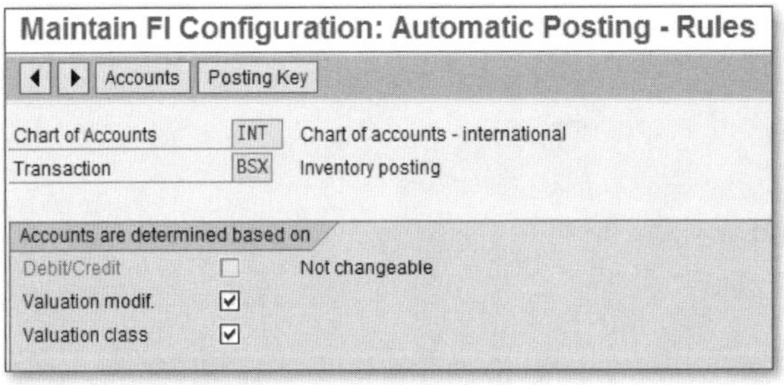

Maintain FI Configuration: Automatic Posting - Rules

◄ ► Accounts | Posting Key

| Chart of Accounts | INT | Chart of accounts - international |
| Transaction | BSX | Inventory posting |

Accounts are determined based on

Debit/Credit	☐	Not changeable
Valuation modif.	☑	
Valuation class	☑	

Figure 4.43 Configuration Settings for BSX Transaction Key: Rules

Next, we look at some of the most important transaction keys (refer Figures 4.38 and 4.39). We discuss them in alphabetical order.

AKO: Expense/Revenue from Consignment Material Consumption

AKO is used when the consignment material is withdrawn. The SAP ERP system uses the price maintained in the purchasing info record, but if the consignment inventory is valuated at a standard price, it might result in a price difference.

AUM: Expense/Revenue from Inventory Transfer

AUM is used when an inventory transfer occurs between materials or plants that have different prices. If the receiving material is priced as standard, the difference in price results in a price difference posting. If the material is valuated at a moving average price, the price difference is posted to inventory accounts (provided that the inventory is still in stock).

BSX: Inventory Postings

BSX is used to link general ledger accounts (balance sheet accounts) that represent the monetary value of inventory owned by your company. An increase/decrease in material inventory due to goods receipt/issue is reflected by a debit/credit posting to these balance sheet accounts. You can choose to use separate general ledger accounts for different types of materials by making the corresponding setting in this key.

BO1, BO2, and BO3: Vendor Rebate Provisions and Settlements

You use BO1, BO2, and BO3 when you have arrangements with your vendors for high-volume purchases. These agreements mean that if the business with the vendor reaches a certain agreed-upon volume, these rebates are not adjusted against the invoice but instead are settled. If the rebate arrangement pricing condition is marked as relevant in the PO calculation schema, you can post a provision for the accrued income. The system uses B01 to post the provision amount to the general ledger accounts assigned to it. If there are any differences in the provision calculations, these differences are posted using BO3. Finally, when the settlement is carried out, you use BO2 to post the values to the revenue accounts.

DIF: Materials Management Small Differences

Use DIF to determine general ledger accounts in which to write off any small differences between the debit and credit balances at the time of invoice postings (as long as the differences are within the tolerance limits defined for this purpose).

FR1 and FR3: Freight Clearing and Customs Clearing

FR1 and FR3 are used to assign accounts that act as clearing accounts for planned delivery costs. These clearing accounts post credit entries for corresponding freight and customs costs at the time of goods receipts. When an invoice is received, these same accounts are debited with clearing entries.

FR2 and FR4: Freight Provision and Custom Provision

FR2 and FR4 are used to link accounts that are posted with provisions for planned delivery costs at the time the PO is created; this enables better liquidity management and planning. In pricing, a condition type is set as provision-relevant; these accounts are used for posting provisional entries for this purpose.

GBB: Offsetting Entry for Inventory Posting

GBB is used to determine the offset account for inventory postings for valuated inventory. There are numerous subkeys within the GBB area that you may choose to use, as shown in Figure 4.44. Table 4.2 provides a comprehensive list of subkeys and their purposes. You should enter the general ledger accounts you want to post to if the relevant key is triggered. We recommend that you leave untouched those you don't want to use.

Maintain FI Configuration: Automatic Posting - Accounts

◀ ▶ ☐ ☐ ☐ | Posting Key | ☒ Procedures | Rules

| Chart of Accounts | INT | Chart of accounts - international |
| Transaction | GBB | Offsetting entry for inventory posting |

Account assignment

Valuation	General m	Valuation cl	Debit	Credit
0001	VAY	7900	894025	894025
0001	VAY	7910	894025	894025
0001	VAY	7920	893015	893015
0001	VAY	7925	893015	893015
0001	VBO	3000	400020	400020
0001	VBO	3001	400020	400020
0001	VBO	3030	400020	400020
0001	VBO	3040	400020	400020
0001	VBO	3050	400020	400020
0001	VBO	3100	400020	400020
0001	VBO	7900	893020	893020
0001	VBO	7920	893020	893020
0001	VBR		400000	400000
0001	VBR	1210	400000	400000
0001	VBR	3000	400000	400000
0001	VBR	3001	400010	400010

Figure 4.44 GBB Transaction Key

The rules for all of these subkeys are defined under the superior key, in that you can segregate the postings rules by the following:

- Debit and credit
- General modifier (subkey; e.g., AUA)
- Valuation modifier
- Valuation class (configurable for materials)

Subkey	Description
AUA	For order settlement.
AUF	For goods receipts for orders (without account assignment), and for order settlement if AUA is not maintained.
AUI	Subsequent adjustment of actual price from cost center directly to material (with account assignment).
BSA	For initial upload of materials to the SAP ERP system.
DST	For physical inventory adjustments that may occur on a periodic or ad hoc basis.
INV	For assigning the general ledger account relevant for posting any gains or losses due to inventory differences.
VAX	For goods issues for sales orders without an account assignment object. This posting must go to a balance sheet code only.
VAY	For goods issues for sales orders with an account assignment object. This posting must go to a balance sheet code only.
VBR	For internal goods issues for internal consumption. This key confirms the account to which your material is being consumed.
VKA	For sales order account assignment in a make-to-order scenario (e.g., an individual PO).
VKP	For project account assignment (e.g., an individual PO).
VNG	For defining the general ledger account that is posted to for any scrapping or destruction write off of inventory.
ZOB	For goods receipts without POs (movement type 501).
ZOF	For goods receipts without production orders (movement types 521 and 531).

Table 4.2 Inventory Offsetting, Transaction GBB Subkeys

PRA, PRF, and PRD: Price Variance Accounts

PRA, PRF, and PRD are used for posting price variances in the procurement process. When using standard prices, there can be many reasons for price variances; for example, there could be a price variance at the time of goods receipt because the PO price was different from the standard price, or at the time of invoice receipt because the invoice price is different from the PO price or standard price. The situation is different for materials that are valuated at a moving average price because large quantities need to be there in inventory to absorb these variances; otherwise, there would be price variance entries posted to the accounts defined for these keys. The keys and account groupings discussed in the following sections are used to assign the general ledger accounts for the following types of movements/postings:

- **Blank:** Goods receipts and invoice receipts against POs.
- **PRF:** Goods receipts against production orders and production order settlements.
- **PRA:** Goods issues and other movements.
- **PRU:** Transfer postings.
- **PRD:** Offsetting entry for inventory postings.

PRK and KTR: Price Differences and Price Differences Offsetting Entry

PRK is used to assign general ledger accounts in which you can settle the costs related to product costings from the highest node of the cost object hierarchy. KTR is used to post the offsetting entry to the settlement performed with PRK. The need for these keys arise in product costing when the cost is collected on objects that cannot be directly assigned to individual cost collectors. In the cost object hierarchy, you can either settle the costs directly from the top node or distribute them to the lower nodes in that hierarchy.

KDM: Materials Management Exchange Rate Difference

Exchange rate differences arise when items are procured in a foreign currency. At the time of the goods receipt, for example, the material price is compared with the corresponding price in an invoice, or the PO price and any variance due to the exchange rate is posted to the general ledger accounts assigned to KDM.

KDR: Materials Management Exchange Rate Rounding Differences

KDR is used to post any rounding differences due to exchange rate conversion and calculation to the general ledger accounts assigned to this key.

KON: Consignment Payables

Consignment transactions involve a vendor providing and storing goods on your location, for which you take ownership but are required to pay only when the items are consumed. Use KON to assign accounts that act as a clearing account between withdrawal from consignment inventory and the settlement of the consignment inventory through an invoice. These accounts act in a similar way to the goods receipt/invoice receipt account explained in the upcoming section titled WRX: Goods Receipt/Invoice Receipt Clearing Account.

RKA: Invoice Reduction from LIV

If you are consistently receiving unacceptably overpriced invoices from a vendor, you can use RKA to assign accounts that will be posted to automatically adjust the payable amount with the appropriate value. These values will then eventually be used to post credit memos to settle the account.

RUE: Neutral Provision

Use RUE to assign accounts that are used for posting any additional types of delivery costs, other than freight and customs, on a PO for which the FR1 and FR3 keys are used.

UMB: Gain/Loss from Revaluation

Use UMB to post any gain or loss arising out of a revaluation of documents posted in previous periods due to changes made to the standard price or moving average price of the material.

UPF: Unplanned Delivery Costs

Use UPF to assign an account to post any unplanned delivery costs at the time of purchasing.

VST: Purchase Input Tax

Use VST to enter accounts that are used to post input tax from purchasing transactions. Usually this tax is included on the invoice received from the vendor. The general modifier used in this key refers to the tax code that enables postings to different general ledger accounts for different purchasing tax codes.

WGI and WGR: Goods Issue/Receipt Inflation Revaluation

In countries with high inflation, you can use WGI and WGR to revaluate inventory using the market price or inflation index maintained in the system. WGI is used for revaluation at the time of goods issue by comparing the price in the goods issue with the newly calculated price and posting any difference to the general ledger accounts assigned to this key. WGR is used for revaluation on the receiving plant by calculating the difference in price and posting inventory adjustments to the general ledger accounts assigned to this key.

WRX: Goods Receipt/Invoice Receipt Clearing Account

WRX is used to define accounts that act as clearing accounts between the goods receipts and invoice receipts in a standard P2P cycle. As you will see when we discuss the posting of goods receipts in the next section, the system credits this account while an offsetting debit entry is posted to the inventory accounts determined by the BSX key. At the time of the invoice receipt from the vendor, this clearing account is debited, and an offsetting credit entry is posted to the vendor Accounts Payable account. At any given time, this account then provides an analysis on goods that have been received but not yet invoiced, as well as goods invoiced but not yet received. At month-end, you can use this information to post accrual entries accordingly.

This concludes Section 4.6, which was quite heavy in terms of configuration concepts. You are now in a position to post goods receipts and invoice receipts, as you will see in the next sections. Based on your knowledge from this section, you should be able to see the links among movement types, valuation classes, and general ledger accounts.

4.7   Good Receipts

The goods receipt process is used to receive materials in the system that relate to a specific PO from an external vendor or as a result of in-house production. This process eventually results in postings to the inventory accounts that were assigned in the previous section and appear in the financial statements of your company. In this section, we discuss the process and the effects of posting a goods receipt against a PO.

4.7.1 Posting Goods Receipts

To post a good receipt, follow these steps:

1. Using Transaction MIGO, enter the goods receipt in the system. (You can use this same transaction code even if you don't know the PO number.)

2. Access the transaction via SAP MENU • LOGISTICS • MATERIALS MANAGEMENT • INVENTORY MANAGEMENT • GOODS RECEIPT • FOR PURCHASE ORDER • PO NUMBER KNOWN.

3. In the resulting screen (Figure 4.45), enter the PO number in the field next to Purchase Order. The information from the PO itself appears in the screen; check the information and make changes if required.

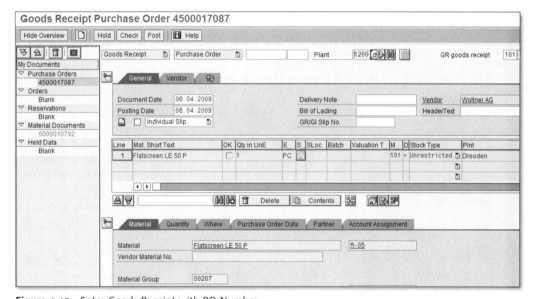

Figure 4.45 Enter Goods Receipt with PO Number

4. If you haven't received all items on the PO, make changes in the Qty in UnE field, providing the actual quantity received for a specific material.

5. After making the required changes in this screen, flag the item OK field, and then save your entry (Figure 4.46). The system posts a few documents and carries out certain actions, which we discuss next.

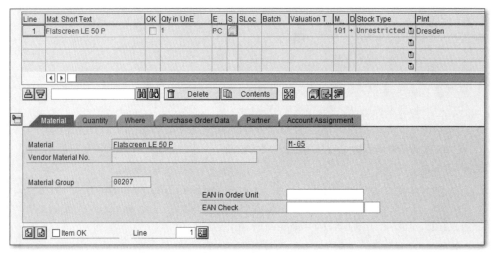

Figure 4.46 Enter Goods Receipt with PO Number

4.7.2 Effects of Posting Goods Receipts

As a result of goods receipt posting, the system carries out the following activities.

Material Document Posting

The system posts a material document as part of the goods receipt step to show the material movement taking place at that time. You can view the material document using Transaction MB03.

Accounting Document Posting

The accounting document is posted at the same time as the material document. It captures the financial aspect of the material movements at the time of material receipt. You can display the accounting document through the material document using Transaction MB03.

Goods Receipt Note Printing

At this stage, you can print a goods receipt note, which can be used by the warehouse to assist them in storing the material in the right location. There are three printed versions within SAP ERP: WE01, WE02, and WE03. You can make modifications to these notes to meet the requirements of your own company.

Changes in Inventory

The goods receipt also results in changes in inventory levels; that is, at the time of goods receipt, the inventory level increases. (Conversely, when goods are returned, the inventory level decreases.)

4.8   Invoice Verification

The invoice verification process in a business can often represent a large volume of transactions. Luckily, the configuration behind this process is consistent with the general SAP ERP Financials configuration. Invoice verification allows you to record the liability for the goods purchased from the vendor and reflect these financial entries in your accounts.

To begin, you must enter the invoice in the system using Transaction MIRO. You can also access this transaction via: SAP MENU • LOGISTICS • MATERIALS MANAGEMENT • LOGISTIC INVOICE VERIFICATION • DOCUMENT ENTRY • ENTER INVOICE. On the screen shown in Figure 4.47, enter the information shown in the following list.

- ▶ INVOICE DATE
  Enter the invoice date in this field.

- ▶ REFERENCE
  Enter any useful information in the reference field. Note that you can set this field to be mandatory; for example, you could force users to enter the vendor invoice number here.

- ▶ POSTING DATE
  Enter the posting date in this field. This is the date that determines the posting period in which the postings will be made to the respective general ledger accounts.

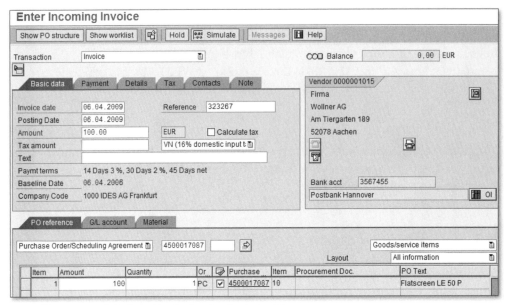

Figure 4.47 Entering a Vendor Invoice Against a PO

► AMOUNT
Enter the total invoice amount in this field.

► TAX AMOUNT
Enter the amount of tax on the invoice in this field. Also, you can select the tax code applicable for this invoice from the dropdown options, and let the system calculate the tax by setting the flag on the CALCULATE TAX option. The system posts to the relevant tax general ledger account based on the settings done using the following menu path: SPRO • FINANCIAL ACCOUNTING (NEW) • FINANCIAL ACCOUNTING BASIC SETTINGS (NEW) • TAX ON SALES/PURCHASES • CALCULATION • DEFINE TAX CODES FOR SALES AND PURCHASES (Transaction FTXP).

► TEXT
You can use this field as a freely definable field for any useful information.

► PURCHASE ORDER/SCHEDULING AGREEMENT
Enter the PO number, and press Enter. The system brings all relevant information from the PO onto this screen.

Select the line items for which you received the invoice, and press $\boxed{\text{Enter}}$. The invoice should match for the value as well as the amount, and the signal light should be green. Click the SAVE icon, and the system generates the invoice number.

Figure 4.48 shows the relationship of the different information that we've maintained throughout this chapter and how it is used during the invoice verification process.

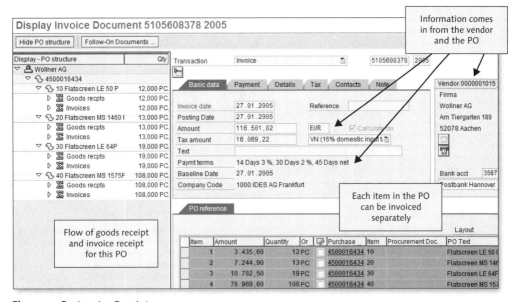

Figure 4.48 Invoice Receipt

Non-PO Invoices

This section explained how to deal with a PO-based invoice, but some organizations use a non-PO invoice process — meaning they enter invoices into the system without a PO. This may happen, for example, with an annual invoice from an accountancy firm whose services you employed.

In such circumstances, an Accounts Payable (only) invoice is entered straight into the system via Transaction FB60. This is very similar to posting a journal transaction in the SAP ERP system; the only difference is that you are entering a vendor item.

You are now ready to pay the invoice. We cover the configuration for making outgoing payments in the next section.

4.9 Outgoing Payments

Outgoing payments can be made either as a manual outgoing payment — for example, when you have to write checks by hand or make cash payments — or by processing an automatic payment run. An automatic payment run is when, based on certain criteria, the system identifies open items and pays them all at once.

In this section, we look at the process of configuring manual and automatic payments, starting with related configurations. What we don't cover in this section is the configuration of core FI settings (document types, number ranges, and so on); for more information about these settings, consult our previous book: *SAP ERP Financials: Configuration and Design*.

In this section, we explain the key configuration steps for outgoing payments and also look at the process of making outgoing payments using both the manual as well as automatic run options. First we explain the concept of vendor tolerances.

4.9.1 Defining Vendor Tolerances

In this step, you define the tolerances for dealing with differences in payments made to vendors that occur during payment settlements. You can define vendor tolerances as a combination of currency amounts and percentages, depending on your requirements.

This is configured in the following area of the IMG: SPRO • FINANCIAL ACCOUNTING (NEW) • ACCOUNTS RECEIVABLE AND ACCOUNTS PAYABLE • BUSINESS TRANSACTIONS • OUTGOING PAYMENTS • MANUAL OUTGOING PAYMENTS • DEFINE TOLERANCES (VENDORS).

In Figure 4.49, you can see that the TOLERANCE GROUP field is left blank and is not given any unique ID. This field is where you assign different values to different user IDs; if you do not assign these IDs, the system assumes that all users are assigned to the generic tolerance group — the blank entry in the table.

The settings specified in this screen also affect the creation of residual items (relevant for manual payments). In Figure 4.49, we've specified that any residual item created should take its payment terms from the original invoice.

Looking at the actual value defined on this screen, the permitted tolerance is very small. If you set larger tolerances in your system, you can make use of reason codes (discussed next).

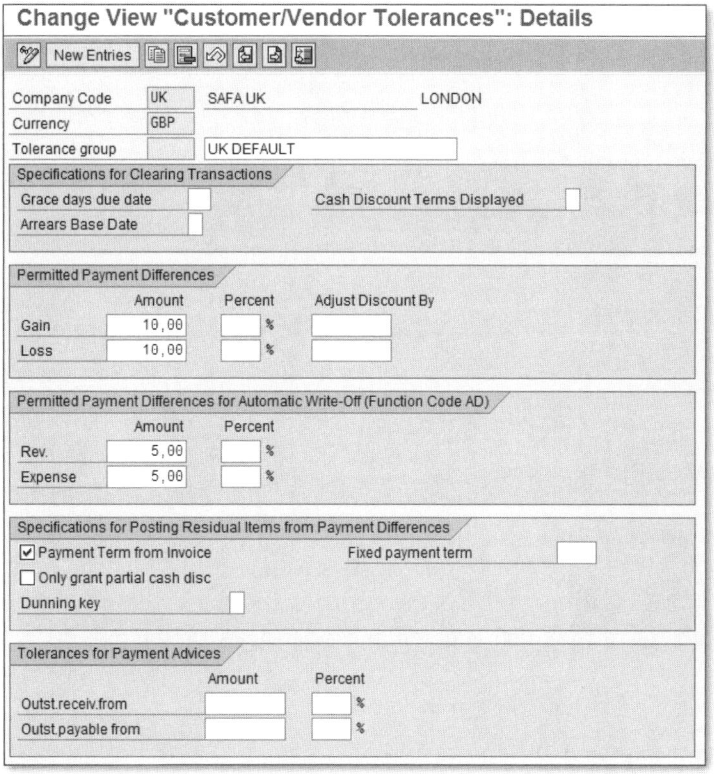

Figure 4.49 Defining the Vendor Tolerance Group

4.9.2 Automatic Posting of Payment Differences

You have two options for posting payment differences. The first is to post all differences to a single general ledger account, and the second is to classify the differences and then use this classification (i.e., reason codes) to determine to which account the payment differences are posted.

Next, we discuss the settings possible in this area of configuration.

Defining Reason Codes

Reason codes are created in the system to explain the reason for a payment difference on an invoice, as shown in Figure 4.50. If you want to regularly use reason codes, you should set large tolerances that enable bigger differences to be posted to the system. Reason codes (relevant for manual postings) are created in the following area of the IMG: SPRO • FINANCIAL ACCOUNTING (NEW) • ACCOUNTS RECEIV-

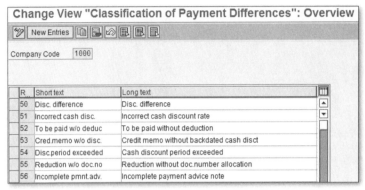

Figure 4.50 Payment Difference Reason Codes

In the next step, you assign general ledger accounts for these reason codes, which automatically control to which general ledger accounts these amounts are posted.

Defining Accounts for Payment Differences

As explained earlier, if you have chosen not to use reason codes for payment differences, you only need to make a single entry here; all your payment differences, both gains and losses, are then posted to this one single general ledger account. To define accounts, follow this menu path: FINANCIAL ACCOUNTING (NEW) • ACCOUNTS RECEIVABLE AND ACCOUNTS PAYABLE • BUSINESS TRANSACTIONS • OUTGOING PAYMENTS • MANUAL OUTGOING PAYMENTS • OVERPAYMENT / UNDERPAYMENT • DEFINE ACCOUNTS FOR PAYMENT DIFFERENCES (MANUAL OUTGOING PAYMENTS).

In Figure 4.51, as you can see, we have taken two reason codes as an example and linked them to an account. You do have the option to define the first line, without the reason code, as a default setting. This is the minimum setting you make if you choose not to use many reason codes. The other lines are indicative of the way in which you assign a specific reason code to an account.

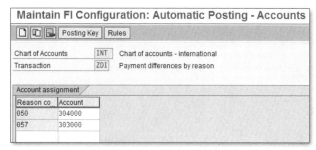

Figure 4.51 Assign General Ledger Accounts to Payment Difference Reason Codes

As shown in Figure 4.51, the second line has a reason code specified, which means that where this reason code is used, the difference is posted to this specific general ledger account.

4.9.3 Defining Payment Block Reasons

Payment block reasons, as shown in Figure 4.52, are defined in the system to ensure that invoices that should not be paid are not paid, for example, during automatic payment runs. This process can be done automatically or manually. Payment block reasons are configured in the following area of the IMG: SPRO • Financial Accounting (New) • Accounts Receivable and Accounts Payable • Business Transactions • Outgoing Payments • Outgoing payments Global Settings • Payment Block Reasons • Define Payment Block Reasons.

You can define a new blocking reason if required, but we recommend that you avoid doing so unnecessarily.

Change View "Payment Block Reasons": Overview

New Entries

Block ind.	Description	Change in pmnt prop.	Manual payments block	Not changeable
	Free for payment	☑	☐	☐
*	Skip account	☐	☐	☐
A	Blocked for payment	☑	☑	☐
B	Blocked for payment	☑	☐	☐
N	IP postprocessing	☐	☐	☐
P	Payment request	☐	☑	☑
R	Invoice verification	☑	☐	☐
V	Payment clearing	☐	☑	☐

Figure 4.52 Create Payment Block Reasons

You can also specify a payment block as a default for a specific payment term, as shown in Figure 4.53.

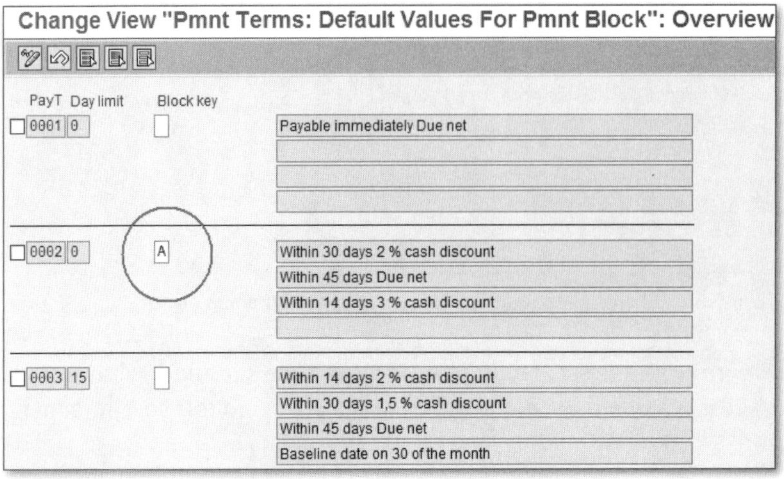

Figure 4.53 Assign a Default Block for a Specific Payment Term

You can configure this setting in the following area of the IMG: FINANCIAL ACCOUNT-ING (NEW) • ACCOUNTS RECEIVABLE AND ACCOUNTS PAYABLE • BUSINESS TRANSACTIONS • OUTGOING PAYMENTS • OUTGOING PAYMENTS GLOBAL SETTINGS • PAYMENT BLOCK REASONS • DEFINE DEFAULT VALUES FOR PAYMENT BLOCK.

We have now completed the basic configuration settings required for both manual and automatic payments. The configuration steps specific to automatic payment runs are covered later in this chapter. Next, let's look at how to process a manual payment in the system.

4.9.4 Processing a Manual (Outgoing) Payment

Manual outgoing payment methods are used when you have to write a check, pay cash out of the petty cash box, or make urgent payments. Manual payments can be processed from Transaction F-53, as shown in Figure 4.54.

In this screen, enter the information provided in the following list:

▸ DOCUMENT DATE and POSTING DATE
Enter the document date (payment date) and the posting date (date of ledger entry).

▸ ACCOUNT (in BANK DATA section)
Enter the bank (general ledger) account from which you are making the payment.

Post Outgoing Payments: Header Data

Process open items

Document Date	☑		Type	KZ	Company Code	1000
Posting Date	06.04.2009		Period	4	Currency/Rate	EUR
Document Number					Translatn Date	
Reference					Cross-CC no.	
Doc.Header Text					Trading part.BA	
Clearing text						

Bank data

Account	☑		Business Area	
Amount			Amount in LC	
Bank charges			LC bank charges	
Value date	06.04.2009		Profit Center	
Text			Assignment	

Open item selection			Additional selections	
Account			⦿ None	
Account Type	K	☐ Other accounts	○ Amount	
Special G/L ind		☑ Standard OIs	○ Document Number	
Pmnt advice no.			○ Posting Date	
☐ Distribute by age			○ Dunning Area	
☐ Automatic search			○ Others	

Figure 4.54 Processing a Manual Outgoing Payment

▶ AMOUNT
Enter the payment amount, based on the currency you have selected.

▶ ACCOUNT (in OPEN ITEM SELECTION section)
Enter the vendor account against which you want to make the payment. The system asks you to select open items from this account.

▶ ACCOUNT TYPE
Enter account type K for vendors. You can select the type of account you are paying from the dropdown list. If you select D (customers), the system allows you to make a payment to a customer (e.g., if you want to send a refund to a customer).

▶ ADDITIONAL SELECTIONS
It is possible to select your open items (invoices for payment) based on other criteria. If the account has a number of open items, you can select additional parameters from the additional selections.

After you enter the header information in the preceding list, you can select open items (unpaid invoices) for which you want to make a payment, as shown in Figure 4.55.

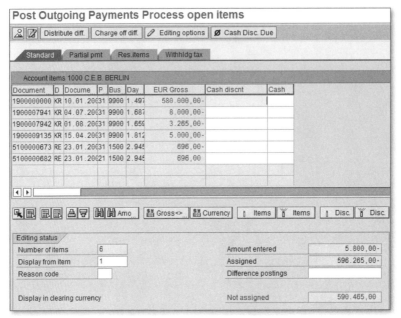

Figure 4.55 Post Outgoing Payments: Process Open Items

After selecting the open items, you can see that the AMOUNT ENTERED field and the ASSIGNED field match, which means that the document is ready to be posted. Click SAVE, and the system generates a payment document and clears the open items from the vendor account.

So far we've explained the background configuration and the process for manual payments. Next, we look into the specific configuration of the automatic payment program.

4.9.5 Configuring the Automatic Payment Program

The automatic payment program is an essential part of every Accounts Payable implementation. The configuration steps are completed using the following menu path: SPRO • FINANCIAL ACCOUNTING (NEW) • ACCOUNTS RECEIVABLE AND ACCOUNTS PAYABLE • BUSINESS TRANSACTIONS • OUTGOING PAYMENTS • AUTOMATIC OUTGOING PAYMENTS • PAYMENT METHOD/BANK SELECTION FOR PAYMENT PROGRAM. You can also use Transaction FBZP, where you will see all of the relevant steps for setting up the automatic payment program.

The configuration of the automatic payment program is divided into the six steps we discuss next.

Step 1: Setting Up All Company Codes for Payment Transactions

You can reach the screen for setting up all company codes for payment transactions using the following menu path: SPRO • FINANCIAL ACCOUNTING (NEW) • ACCOUNTS RECEIVABLE AND ACCOUNTS PAYABLE • BUSINESS TRANSACTIONS • OUTGOING PAYMENTS • AUTOMATIC OUTGOING PAYMENTS • PAYMENT METHOD/BANK SELECTION FOR PAYMENT PROGRAM • SET UP ALL COMPANY CODES FOR PAYMENT TRANSACTIONS, as shown in Figure 4.56. At your system design phase, you need to review whether payments are being made out of a single company code or from many company codes. The first two nodes of this area are required to enable the required company codes for making payments. For each company code, you need to define who the sending company code is (i.e., the company code with the vendor invoices that need to be paid), as well as the paying company code (i.e., the company code that has the bank account from which the payment is going to be made).

Figure 4.56 Setting Up All Company Codes for Payment Transactions

The setting in this screen makes it possible to pay vendor invoices for another company code. Note that you will only be able to make payments for another company code if you have configured the intercompany clearing accounts in IMG using the following menu path: SPRO • FINANCIAL ACCOUNTING (NEW) • GENERAL LEDGER ACCOUNTING (NEW) • BUSINESS TRANSACTIONS • PREPARE CROSS-COMPANY CODE TRANSACTIONS.

Step 2: Setting Up All Paying Company Codes for Payment Transactions

In this step, you set up the paying company codes for payment transactions. We need to make these settings for those company codes that we defined as paying company codes in the previous step.

You can reach the screen for setting up all paying company codes for payment transactions using the following menu path: SPRO • FINANCIAL ACCOUNTING (NEW) • ACCOUNTS RECEIVABLE AND ACCOUNTS PAYABLE • BUSINESS TRANSACTIONS • OUTGOING PAYMENTS • AUTOMATIC OUTGOING PAYMENTS • PAYMENT METHOD/BANK SELECTION FOR PAYMENT PROGRAM • SET UP PAYING COMPANY CODES FOR PAYMENT TRANSACTIONS (Figure 4.57).

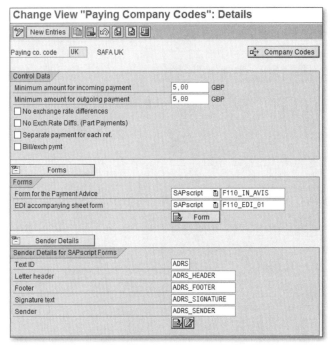

Figure 4.57 Setting Up All Paying Company Codes for Payment Transactions

This configuration step simply allows this company code to be used in the automatic payment program. You must specify the following:

► Minimum amounts for a payment (incoming and outgoing)

► The forms to be used for the remittance advice

► The sender details (which link SAP ERP fields)

The programmer uses this information to create the remittance advice you send out to the vendor.

Step 3: Setting Up Payment Methods per Country for Payment Transactions

In this step, you define which payment methods will be used in each country. This setting allows you to define certain specific methods that are applicable for a given country. All of the company codes assigned to a given country will be able to use one or more of the payment methods defined here. You can reach the screen for setting up payment methods at the country level using the following menu path: SPRO • FINANCIAL ACCOUNTING (NEW) • ACCOUNTS RECEIVABLE AND ACCOUNTS PAYABLE • BUSINESS TRANSACTIONS • OUTGOING PAYMENTS • AUTOMATIC OUTGOING PAYMENTS • PAYMENT METHOD/BANK SELECTION FOR PAYMENT PROGRAM • SET UP PAYMENT METHOD PER COUNTRY FOR PAYMENT TRANSACTIONS.

In the following examples, we look at two payment methods: checks (Figure 4.58) and bank transfers (Figure 4.59), defined at the country level GB (Great Britain) and US (United States), respectively.

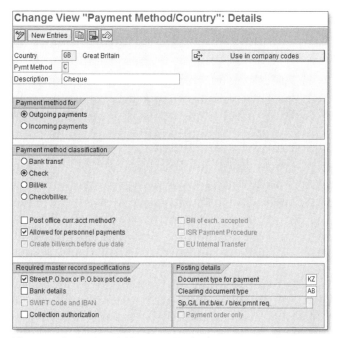

Figure 4.58 Setting Up Payment Methods per Country for Payment Transactions

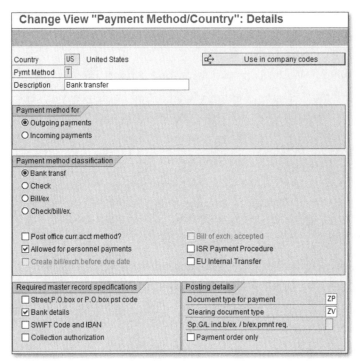

Figure 4.59 Setting Up Payment Methods per Country for Payment Transactions

When you compare the two payment methods, you can see that it is possible to specify different rules for each payment method. We highlight some important points for you here.

▸ Payment methods are classified as being for outgoing or incoming payments. Because we are covering the P2P process in our examples, we are just looking at outgoing payments.

▸ You are required to specify a master record, for example, a street address in the vendor master record. The system uses this as a control to validate that the necessary information exists in the master record. For checks, as you can see in Figure 4.58, you need to have the address information where the check should be sent. For a bank transfer, you need the bank information, as shown in Figure 4.59.

▸ The standard document types for Accounts Payable are ZP (payments) and ZV (clearing documents). If necessary for better analysis, you can set up additional document types and assign them to different payment methods.

- The classic payment medium programs used in SAP ERP for the United States include the following:

    - **RFFOUS_T:** Bank transfers and bank direct debits.

    - **RFFOUS_C:** Check (with check management).

Step 4: Setting Up Payment Methods per Company Code for Payment Transactions

In this step, you define a payment method for a company code for payment transactions. You can reach the screen for setting up payment methods per company code using the following menu path: SPRO • FINANCIAL ACCOUNTING (NEW) • ACCOUNTS RECEIVABLE AND ACCOUNTS PAYABLE • BUSINESS TRANSACTIONS • OUTGOING PAYMENTS • AUTOMATIC OUTGOING PAYMENTS • PAYMENT METHOD/BANK SELECTION FOR PAYMENT PROGRAM • SET UP PAYMENT METHOD PER COMPANY CODE FOR PAYMENT TRANSACTIONS (Figure 4.60).

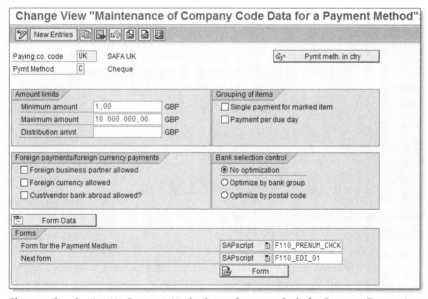

Figure 4.60   Setting Up Payment Methods per Company Code for Payment Transactions

The following list explains the most important fields in the company code settings:

▶ SAPSCRIPT
The most important setting you will make is the definition of the form that is relevant to this payment method. The form is developed using SAPscript, and it determines the payment advice (or remittance advice) that is sent along with the payment.

▶ MINIMUM AMOUNT and MAXIMUM AMOUNT
You can set limits on the minimum amount and maximum amount that can be paid by this payment method.

▶ SINGLE PAYMENT FOR MARKED ITEM
If you want to create an individual payment for each line item in your payment run, select this option.

▶ PAYMENT PER DUE DAY
This field makes the system group together items by payment date. Thus, it groups together items that fall on the same due date and combines their payment.

▶ FOREIGN CURRENCY ALLOWED
This indicator allows you to pay invoices that are in a currency other than your company code currency.

▶ CUST/VENDOR BANK ABROAD ALLOWED?
This setting needs to be activated if you will use this payment method to make payments to the banks located in other countries.

Step 5: Setting Up Bank Determination for Payment Transactions

In this step, we look at the configuration for setting up the ranking order for house banks and house bank accounts. You can reach the screen for setting up bank determination by using the following menu path: SPRO • FINANCIAL ACCOUNTING (NEW) • ACCOUNTS RECEIVABLE AND ACCOUNTS PAYABLE • BUSINESS TRANSACTIONS • OUTGOING PAYMENTS • AUTOMATIC OUTGOING PAYMENTS • PAYMENT METHOD/BANK SELECTION FOR PAYMENT PROGRAM • SET UP BANK DETERMINATION FOR PAYMENT TRANSACTIONS.

In organizations that have a single house bank configuration setup, this is fairly straightforward; for each paying company code, you need to configure the following settings:

- RANKING ORDER

  If you have more than one house bank per payment method, you define the priority in which the system makes payments, as shown in Figure 4.61.

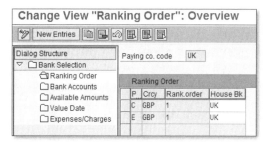

Figure 4.61 Settings for Bank Ranking Order

- BANK ACCOUNTS

  List the available bank accounts for each house bank as well as their assigned bank subaccount (general ledger account) (Figure 4.62).

Figure 4.62 Bank Accounts Available

- AVAILABLE AMOUNTS

  Define the maximum amount you want to be able to pay out of this bank account. The DAYS UNTIL VALUE DATE field is nullified if you enter 999 in it. Companies tend to set very large amounts here because there is no system logic that checks the payment amount going out of a specific bank against this available amount.

- VALUE DATE

  This should be the average amount of time it takes for a payment to be processed. This is useful in treasury and cash management.

- EXPENSES/CHARGES

  Here you configure charges that are to be made as part of the payment. This is used in Spanish bills of exchange scenarios.

Step 6: Defining House Banks

In this step, you define the settings for the house bank to be used for automatic payment runs in your company code. House banks are created in the system to represent the bank accounts that are used to make automatic payments. (A house bank is configured in the system, whereas normal banks are created as master data.) You can define the house bank by using the following menu path: SPRO • FINANCIAL ACCOUNTING (NEW) • BANK ACCOUNTING • BANK ACCOUNTS • DEFINE HOUSE BANKS (Transaction FI12).

In the screen shown in Figure 4.63, enter the HOUSE BANK ID, BANK COUNTRY, BANK KEY (a key under which you store the bank data for a specific country in SAP ERP), and ADDRESS.

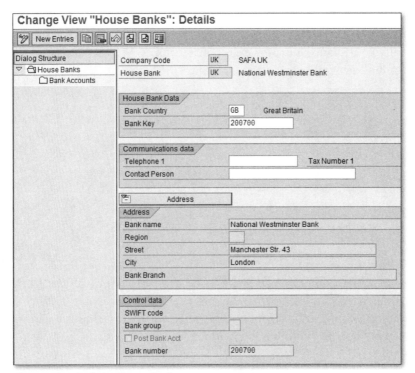

Figure 4.63 Defining House Banks

After the house bank is defined, enter the bank accounts within the house bank that should be linked to the general ledger account in the system. Figure 4.64

shows the screens where you define the bank accounts and the link to the general ledger accounts.

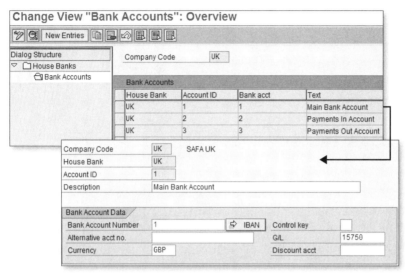

Figure 4.64 Defining House Banks: Bank Accounts

After completing the configuration for the automatic payment program, you are ready to post automatic payments.

4.9.6 Running the Automatic Payment Program

You can access all of the transactions related to the payment program using the menu path shown in Figure 4.65. Run the automatic payment program using Transaction F110.

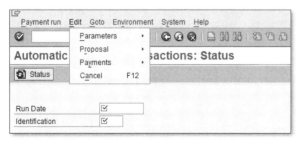

Figure 4.65 Transaction F110: Automatic Payment Run Menu Bar

On the AUTOMATIC PAYMENT TRANSACTIONS: STATUS screen, enter the RUN DATE as the current day's date. In the IDENTIFICATION field, enter a unique ID for this payment run, for example, SMT1. Click the PARAMETER tab, and the screen shown in Figure 4.66 appears. Supply the information described next.

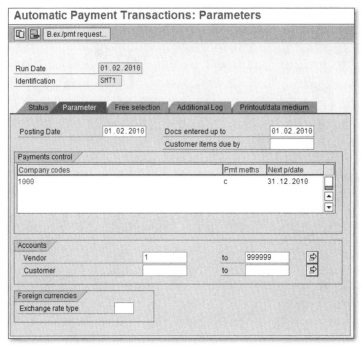

Figure 4.66 Automatic Payment Program: Entering Parameters

Select the PARAMETER tab, and fill the POSTING DATE and DOCS ENTERED UP TO fields. Entry in the DOCS ENTERED UP TO fields filter the open items based on the entry date, not the posting date. Under the PAYMENTS CONTROL section, enter the sending company codes for which you want to run the payment program, as well as the relevant payment methods. In the NEXT P/DATE field, enter the date for the next payment run date; the system uses these entries to identify which items are selected for payment during this run by excluding items with a net due date after the date specified here. Under the ACCOUNTS section, enter the vendor accounts to be selected for this payment run.

Now click the ADDITIONAL LOG tab, and select the flags shown in Figure 4.67.

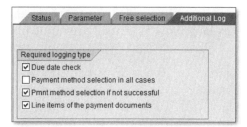

Figure 4.67 Automatic Payment Program: Entering Additional Log Info

After entering this information, click SAVE. Click the STATUS tab, and new icons appear on the screen. These indicate that the program is now ready to be run. Click the PROPOSAL icon shown in Figure 4.68.

Figure 4.68 Automatic Payment Program: Proposal

After the proposal runs, you can review it, and you have the option to edit it by clicking the EDIT PROPOSAL button, as shown in Figure 4.69. If there are any issues with certain selected open items, such as blocked invoices or missing vendor addresses, the system includes them in the exception list, and those items are not available for payment until the issues are resolved. If you are happy with the results, click the PMNT RUN icon, and the system will process the payments by clearing the vendor open items and crediting the bank clearing accounts.

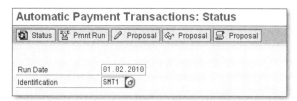

Figure 4.69 Automatic Payment Program: Edit/Display Proposal

When creating your proposal and final payment list, you may want to see a report to analyze the items in the proposal. When you create the proposal, instead of simply selecting the DISPLAY PROPOSAL button, as shown in Figure 4.69, follow the menu path EDIT • PROPOSAL • PROPOSAL LIST. This calls report RFZALI20, which displays the proposal in a way that can be printed or sent electronically for approval.

4.10 Summary

This chapter covered the configuration and design of the purchase-order-to-payment (P2P) cycle for integrating FI and MM. The chapter was not intended to explain every element of MM configuration, but just enough so that you can sufficiently understand the P2P cycle as well as core elements of MM. In the next chapter, we look at the integration of FI with elements of the SAP ERP Human Capital Management component (SAP ERP HCM).

This chapter explains the integration of SAP ERP Human Capital Management and SAP ERP Financials, focusing on two specific areas: Organizational Management and Payroll.

5 Integrating SAP ERP HCM with SAP ERP Financials

This chapter looks at the integration of SAP ERP Human Capital Management (SAP ERP HCM) and SAP ERP Financials. SAP ERP HCM replaces the SAP Human Resources component, which has been significantly expanded and now covers a number of areas.

In this chapter, we focus on the integration-related configuration and design of two SAP ERP HCM topics that have a significant amount of integration with SAP ERP Financials: Organizational Management (OM) and Payroll.

In Section 5.1, Process Overview, we offer an overview of the business processes involved in both topics. We start looking at OM in Section 5.2, where we focus on the building blocks of SAP ERP HCM, which you need to understand to follow the subject of Section 5.3. In Section 5.3, Employee Master Record, we focus on the key screens and fields on the employee master record that are relevant for payroll integration, and so complete our review of OM. Finally, we conclude the chapter with a discussion of the configuration and design of Payroll, as well as the all-important review of the posting of payroll to SAP ERP Financials, and the related integration points.

> **Note**
>
> The employee master record is a key part of integration so we have given it a separate section in this chapter to allow you to focus on all of the complexities that surround it.

Country-Specific Settings

The tricky thing about SAP ERP HCM is that the information sources governing the processes are the employment laws of the country in which you operate. For this reason, after you implement SAP ERP HCM, you must also implement the country-specific settings provided by SAP ERP. To keep on top of changes in statutory rules or regulations, you must keep your records up to date and ensure that you regularly download updates from SAP ERP.

As a result of the country-specific settings of SAP ERP HCM, you will notice that the IMG has country-specific menu paths. In the examples in this chapter, we look at settings for the United States and Great Britain; however, you should consult your own country-specific IMG location to see your own country-specific settings.

5.1 Process Overview

Although many people mistakenly assume that the payroll process is the only area that SAP ERP Human Capital Management covers, the component is actually quite extensive. A comprehensive review (which is out of the scope of this book) would include the following:

- Employee administration
- Recruitment
- Personnel development
- Time management
- Benefits administration
- Talent management

In this section, we provide a process overview of the subjects that are most relevant to integration with SAP ERP Financials: OM and the payroll process. For each, we summarize the process, explain the key steps or objects, and discuss the points of integration.

5.1.1 Organizational Management

Put simply, Organizational Management allows you to draw up your company's organizational structure, that is, charts that show who works where and who reports to whom. If you think of this structure as a tree, each point in the tree represents a position and job role in the company. Using these charts, you can see in which department employees are located, which in turn should correlate to the cost center and hierarchy structure for your organization.

The complexity of these organizational charts varies from company to company. Of course, if you wanted to put a structure together for a company with 1000 employees, it would be a lot simpler than a multinational company operating in different sectors and different countries. However, regardless of its complexity, you can use the information contained in an organizational chart to drive and control a number of processes, such as approval of expenses or performance management.

There are many ways of managing an organizational chart, and SAP ERP is partnered with a number of products that facilitate this process. For the purposes of this chapter, however, we are concerned only with the standard delivered SAP ERP tools. Using these tools, you can define *nodes*, or positions, that represent a certain job in the organization. The system comes preloaded with more than 30 standard objects, but you can also create custom objects as necessary. Following are the main objects with which you should familiarize yourself:

▶ **Organizational unit**
Every company is split into departments that OM represents using *organizational units*. This structure should reflect the way your company is set up, so it's not something that is fixed or defined.

▶ **Position**
Within the organizational structure, *positions* exist to define where people actually sit within the organization: what they do, and whom they report to. This is usually fairly straightforward, in that one person occupies one position within an organization; however, it is possible to set up job sharing, whereby people work in several different positions, each for a certain percentage of their time. Positions can be assigned a specific cost center or can inherit one from a higher position; this defines where costs for this position are posted. A specific position's costs may also need to be distributed to different account assignment objects.

▶ **Job**
A *job* in OM is a simple concept that defines the set of responsibilities belonging to a specific position. For example, the position of AP clerk has a set of

specific responsibilities, which means that, if you have five AP clerks, they should usually be doing the same job.

▶ **Work center**

A *work center* is a location where work is actually done, such as a workstation where a graphic designer is using his PC, a workshop, or a section within a workshop. This information is useful for shift planning, among other things.

▶ **Cost center**

If you are familiar with SAP ERP Financials, you already know that cost centers are the main cost assignment object. Because employees usually incur costs, cost centers are the most common account assignment object to assign these costs to. The most frequent expense is the cost of paying an employee, but there are other costs, such as expenses and/or training, that need to be posted to an account assignment object. You can use other account assignment objects as well, for example, work breakdown structures (WBS) and internal orders (both of these concepts are discussed in more detail in Chapter 6, Integrating Asset Accounting, Investment Management, and Project Systems). In addition, when running balance sheet postings, you usually post to profit centers (as you will recall from Chapter 2, SAP Enterprise Structure).

Before we look at a specific organizational structure, let's consider some basic properties of such structures:

▶ Every person in the structure must have a chief, someone who is responsible for the people below him.

▶ Every position must have a person assigned to it.

▶ Reporting moves upward, so approvals for a certain position go the person above that position.

Figure 5.1 shows an organizational structure with units, positions, and — most importantly — people assigned.

As you can see, each object is assigned a unique eight-digit code, which is the way SAP ERP internally indexes and stores this information.

The organizational structure is used to determine a person's manager. This is important for both SAP ERP HCM and Financials purposes because managers are required to approve costs incurred by their staff.

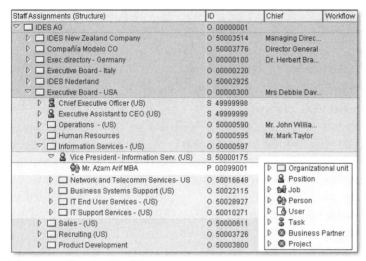

Figure 5.1 Organizational Structure

5.1.2 Payroll

Payroll remains the highest profile area of SAP ERP HCM and is important in understanding Financials and SAP ERP HCM integration. The process starts in SAP ERP HCM, when employees exist and their salary and deductions are calculated. After calculating the overall payroll, we then determine the correct general ledger accounts and account assignment objects before creating the financial postings.

The payroll process involves the following key concepts:

▶ **Payroll Engine**
The *Payroll Engine* is the name given to the program that calculates and posts payroll results. It takes into consideration a number of different things, including the following:

  ▸ A country's statutory requirements

  ▸ An employee's basic pay

  ▸ Time and attendance information

As previously mentioned, SAP ERP provides country-specific templates that can calculate rules for you. These rules are stored within the payroll schema, and, if needed, can be enhanced to include an organization's specific requirements.

▶ **Payroll area**

Payroll areas allow you to control the way in which you pay people. Many organizations have employees that are paid for different time periods (e.g., weekly or monthly). With Payroll, you can pay different payroll areas over different payroll periods. All employees are assigned to a single payroll area.

▶ **Retroactive (retrospective) changes**

You can process retroactive payments in SAP ERP HCM because sometimes corrections to employee data are not known or processed until after payment is made. Thus, if an employee is entitled to back pay, this can be automatically calculated based on the change in circumstances. The HR changes are time specific and date specific, so when you next run payroll, the system calculates the changes and makes the adjustment in the next available period.

Note that changes in configuration do not trigger retroactive changes; only changes to master data trigger these changes. If you need to make a retroactive calculation, you must force the posting through or wait until the next payroll run.

Now that we've explained the key concepts in the payroll process, let's look at its three separate stages: the prerequisite stage, the payroll run, and the closing stage (also known as the *exit payroll* activity).

Prerequisite Stage

The system configuration for Payroll is based around the settings you make for the payroll area and the associated payroll calendar, which dictates the paydays. The process runs across the entire period, starting with the completion of the old payroll posting run. The payroll administrators then move on to the input phase, where they perform the administrative task of making changes to existing payroll records. This action is time-sensitive, meaning that they must start the payroll process at a specified day in the period to meet the time scales for the actual payment run.

All of this information tends to be contained within or linked to the payroll control record, which we discuss in more detail in the configuration part of the chapter (see Section 5.2.4, Payroll Control Record).

Payroll Run

After you start the payroll cycle, the system locks all payroll data and records while it runs a payroll proposal, just as it would run an F110 (automatic outgoing payments) proposal. This is called the *payroll simulation* run. You can run this several times to review the output and then make corrections to data that appears incorrect. Again, the only constraint is the payroll time table, which dictates when you need to run the real payroll posting run.

The Payroll Driver is the program that calculates your pay and references a collection of sources, including the rules defined within your payroll organizational structure, the payroll schema, the data captured on your employee master record, and any time recoding information that may be relevant to your final pay.

The actual calculation of the amount paid is based on what each employee is entitled to be paid, less any deductions they are due to make. Each element of pay is known as a *wage type*; there are wage types for all sorts of things, including basic pay, deductions, and bonuses.

Exit Payroll

When the processing is complete, you must physically exit Payroll, which releases the control record and indicates that payroll administrators can start working on the next payroll period. This ensures that at any given point in time, the payroll is running on a fixed data set. If this were not the case, it would be possible for the actual payroll to differ from the figures in the payroll simulation. Even worse, the system could allow you to run a simulation successfully but then produce an error when you tried to complete the real payroll run.

The completion of the entire payroll process is the posting of a file (or files depending on the size of your payroll) to the ledger. We discuss this in more detail later (see Section 5.4.7, Full Payroll Posting to Finance).

5.2 Configuration and Design of SAP ERP HCM Building Blocks

This section looks at the configuration and design of the core objects that are needed as the basis for this chapter; these objects are the building blocks needed to execute the processes we cover.

> **Note**
>
> In this section, we only cover the building blocks that support our understanding of OM and Payroll.

In this section, we discuss the following objects:

- Personnel area
- Payroll area
- Control record
- Period/date modifier
- Payroll calendar

> **Note**
>
> Remember, as we mentioned earlier, these configuration settings are country specific.

In SAP ERP HCM, these key organizational objects are collectively referred to as the *personnel structure* of a company.

5.2.1 Personnel Area and Subareas

From an SAP ERP Financials perspective, we are used to seeing the company code represent legal entities in line with statutory law. In addition to statutory laws, organizations also need to comply with HR laws, that is, the rules governing the way in which you employ and pay people. The personnel area is the highest object on the HR side, and we should use this to represent our HR rules and regulations. The personnel area is a placeholder against which you can assign the various rules and configuration objects, but you can also run reports against personnel areas. During configuration, personnel areas are assigned to company codes, as you can see in Figure 5.2.

Many types of laws affect HR rules, including the following:

- Tax law
- Benefits law
- Contributions law
- Recruitment law
- Civil law

Whenever there is a situation where there could be a difference in these laws, you may find separate personnel areas being set up.

Within the personnel area, there are other ways of segregating employees; the personnel *subarea* can be used to group together different types of employees. For example, you may have subareas for different parts of the country, or you may choose to set up subareas for salaried versus hourly staff.

Figure 5.2 shows where the configuration of the HR ENTERPRISE STRUCTURE is found within the IMG.

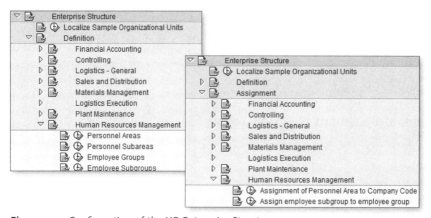

Figure 5.2 Configuration of the HR Enterprise Structure

Personnel areas are set up in the following area of the IMG: SPRO • ENTERPRISE STRUCTURE • DEFINITION • HUMAN RESOURCES MANAGEMENT.

In Figure 5.3, you can see that for each personnel area, you also need to enter some basic address information.

Personnel areas must be assigned to a company code (you can assign more than one personnel area to the same company code, but a personnel area cannot be assigned to more than one company code). Based on what we've discussed so far, it should be clear that a personnel area can only be assigned to one company code, although you may want to assign multiple personnel areas to the same company code. In the United States, for example, there are different laws in each state, which may lead to the need for different personnel areas. The assignment of personnel areas to company codes is done in the following area of the IMG: SPRO • ENTERPRISE STRUCTURE • ASSIGNMENT • HUMAN RESOURCES MANAGEMENT.

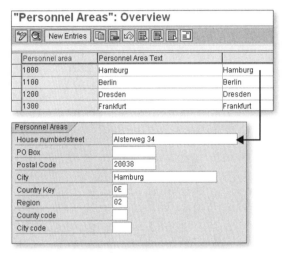

Figure 5.3 Personnel Areas

5.2.2 Employee Groups and SubGroups

Employees can be split into employee groups, usually on the basis of their relationship with their employer, but also based on how they are paid or on their contract status (employees, contractors, retired, etc.). Because you must have personnel data for all people being paid, most companies have to maintain data for former employees who still receive funds from the payroll.

For each employee group, you can set up default values and report on your selections. You can also further divide up the employees into subgroups. When we look further into the configuration, you'll see that some configuration settings can be made by subgroups, a functionality that has great value.

Employee groups and subgroups are completed in the following area of the IMG: SPRO • ENTERPRISE STRUCTURE • DEFINITION • HUMAN RESOURCES MANAGEMENT. Assignment of employees and subgroups are completed in the following area of the IMG: SPRO • ENTERPRISE STRUCTURE • ASSIGNMENT • HUMAN RESOURCES MANAGEMENT.

5.2.3 Payroll Area

As we discussed previously, separating employees into payroll groups requires setting up payroll areas, which controls when these employees are paid. In reality, a payroll function often requires running more than one payroll; for example, pensioners may have to be run separately and therefore have a different payment date.

> **Note**
>
> To make things easier, SAP ERP recommends setting up only those payroll areas that are absolutely necessary.

Define the payroll area in the following area of the IMG: SPRO • PERSONNEL MANAGEMENT • PERSONNEL ADMINISTRATION • ORGANIZATIONAL DATA • ORGANIZATIONAL ASSIGNMENT • CREATE PAYROLL AREA. Figure 5.4 shows the screen for setting up new payroll areas; make sure you select the PAYROLL FOR PA checkbox, which confirms that the payroll area is relevant for paying people.

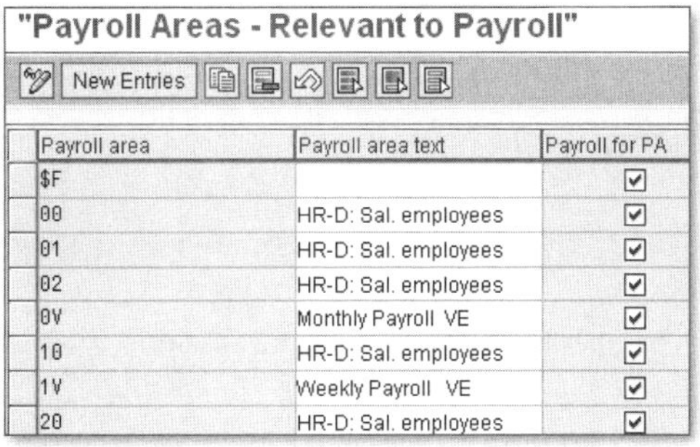

"Payroll Areas - Relevant to Payroll"		
Payroll area	Payroll area text	Payroll for PA
$F		☑
00	HR-D: Sal. employees	☑
01	HR-D: Sal. employees	☑
02	HR-D: Sal. employees	☑
0V	Monthly Payroll VE	☑
10	HR-D: Sal. employees	☑
1V	Weekly Payroll VE	☑
20	HR-D: Sal. employees	☑

Figure 5.4 Payroll Area

5.2.4 Payroll Control Record

The payroll control record controls the actually running of the payroll and retains an audit trail detailing when a payroll is run and which users are processing it. This is a very different concept from what we are used to seeing in the Financials areas; after the payroll run begins, the control record locks all personnel numbers, preventing any changes from being made to those records. When the process is complete and you have exited Payroll, the record is updated accordingly and releases the master records. If you want to see who last changed the payroll record, this is visible by looking at the record.

In Section 5.1.2, Payroll, we briefly discussed the three stages of the payroll process: the prerequisite stage (when the payroll area is released for the payroll run), the payroll run, and exiting Payroll. Looking at this from a payroll control record point of review, the following is what happens in each stage:

▶ **Prerequisite stage**
The control record is updated.

▶ **Run payroll**
The control record locks all data involved. The payroll run is checked to ensure that it is complete and accurate, and then the status to Check Payroll Results is changed manually. If necessary, a corrective run is performed.

▶ **Exit payroll**
The control records are released for processing.

This process is set up in the following area of the IMG: SPRO • PERSONNEL MANAGEMENT • PERSONNEL ADMINISTRATION • ORGANIZATIONAL DATA • ORGANIZATIONAL ASSIGNMENT • CREATE CONTROL RECORD. Figure 5.5 shows an example of a control record set up in the system.

Figure 5.5 Payroll Control Record

5.2.5 Payroll Calendar

Each company defines a *payroll calendar* that informs the pay dates for the year ahead. This could be a paper exercise, but you can also define a payroll calendar in the system and then use this calendar to automatically drive the payroll activities.

In practice, most companies tend to define the calendar and the payroll periods so that the Payroll Driver program can complete its calculation, but they still manually start the payroll process. In this discussion, we look at the configuration of several important elements that contribute to the payroll calendar.

You can access the payroll calendar (Figure 5.6) via the SAP Easy Access menu: HUMAN RESOURCES • PAYROLL • <YOUR COUNTRY> • TOOLS • PAYROLL CALENDAR.

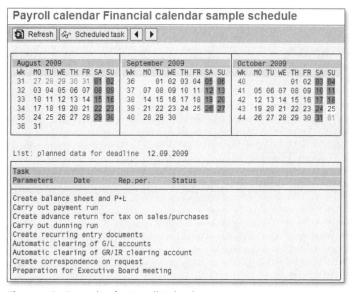

Figure 5.6 Example of a Payroll Calendar

You can view the calendar and also define job scheduling. Job scheduling is configured in the following area of the IMG: SPRO • PAYROLL • (COUNTRY) • PAYROLL CALENDAR • DEFINE SCHEDULE FOR PAYROLL CALENDAR. As you can see from Figure 5.7, this is a fairly straightforward piece of configuration.

You must assign a factory calendar and a holiday calendar to decide working days. The specific dates for the start and end of each payroll period are defined by the period parameters in the following area of the IMG: SPRO • PAYROLL • (COUNTRY) • BASIC SETTINGS • PAYROLL ORGANIZATION • DEFINE PERIOD MODIFIERS. Figure 5.8 shows a number of period parameters, which is common in large complex organizations.

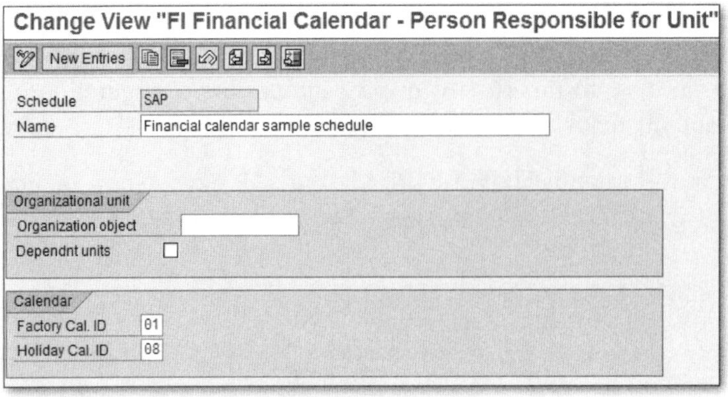

Change View "FI Financial Calendar - Person Responsible for Unit"

New Entries

Schedule	SAP
Name	Financial calendar sample schedule

Organizational unit
Organization object	
Dependnt units	☐

Calendar
Factory Cal. ID	01
Holiday Cal. ID	08

Figure 5.7 Setting Up a New Payroll Calendar

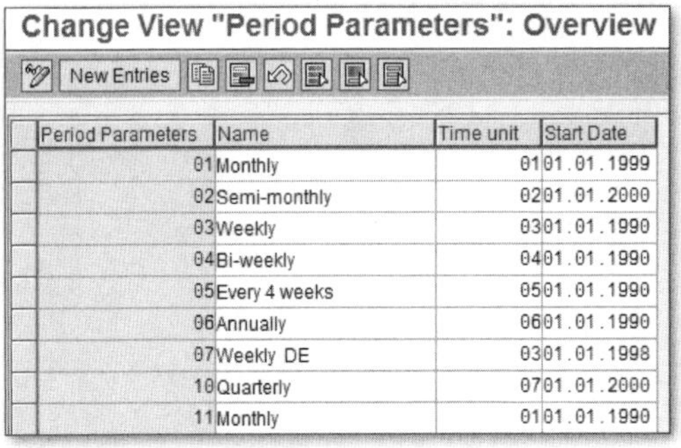

Change View "Period Parameters": Overview

New Entries

Period Parameters	Name	Time unit	Start Date
01	Monthly	01	01.01.1999
02	Semi-monthly	02	01.01.2000
03	Weekly	03	01.01.1990
04	Bi-weekly	04	01.01.1990
05	Every 4 weeks	05	01.01.1990
06	Annually	06	01.01.1990
07	Weekly DE	03	01.01.1998
10	Quarterly	07	01.01.2000
11	Monthly	01	01.01.1990

Figure 5.8 Payroll Period Parameters

The actual pay date needs to be defined within each payroll period. As we mentioned earlier, there can be more than one pay date in a month for each payroll run; this is shown in the example in Figure 5.9. These dates are configured as date modifiers in the following area of the IMG: SPRO • PAYROLL • (COUNTRY) • BASIC SETTINGS • PAYROLL ORGANIZATION • DEFINE DATE MODIFIERS.

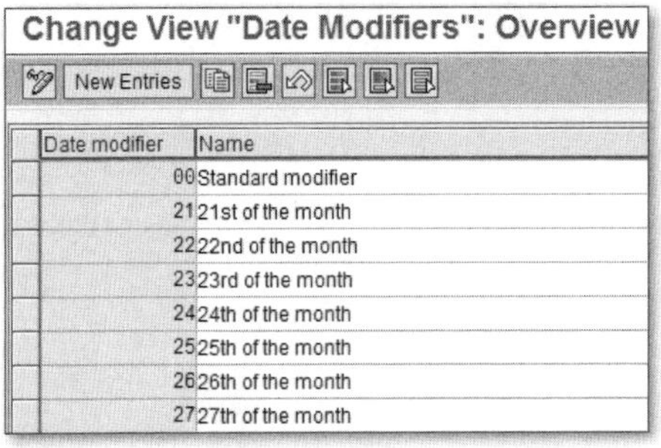

Change View "Date Modifiers": Overview

New Entries

Date modifier	Name
00	Standard modifier
21	21st of the month
22	22nd of the month
23	23rd of the month
24	24th of the month
25	25th of the month
26	26th of the month
27	27th of the month

Figure 5.9 Setting Up Date Modifiers

5.2.6 Organizational Structure

The central component in SAP ERP HCM is the organizational structure (org structure), which, as we mentioned, shows the relationships that different employees have within the organization and with each other. This is set up in a hierarchy structure, which should reflect the actual situation in the organization. After you understand the functions of the org structure, you will know which relationships can and cannot be set up. You define your org structure within the SAP Easy Access menu: HUMAN RESOURCES • ORGANIZATIONAL MANAGEMENT • ORGANIZATIONAL PLAN • ORGANIZATION AND STAFFING.

Figure 5.10 shows an example of an org structure. We saw this information earlier in the chapter, but we revisit it now to remind you what you're working with. After the structure is set up, you need to make sure it is always current because it drives many HR processes.

Staff Assignments (Structure)	ID	Chief
IDES AG	O 00000001	
IDES New Zealand Company	O 50003514	Managing Director
Compañía Modelo CO	O 50003776	Director General
Exec.directory - Germany	O 00000100	Dr. Herbert Braunstein
Executive Board - Italy	O 00000220	
IDES Nederland	O 50002925	
Executive Board - USA	O 00000300	Mrs Debbie Davis
Chief Executive Officer (US)	S 49999998	
Mrs Debbie Davis	P 00100135	
Executive Assistant to CEO (US)	S 49999999	
Operations - (US)	O 50000590	Mr. John Williams
Chief Operating Officer - (US)	S 50000046	
Executive Assistant to COO (US)	S 50000047	
Mrs Barbara Kent	P 00100113	
Operations (US)	O 50028929	
Vice President Operations (US)	S 50000050	
Mr. Jonathan Tyler	P 00100115	
Hospitality (US)	O 50028893	
Best Restaurant	O 50028894	
Production - (US)	O 50000600	Mr. Timothy Hayes
Director of Production	S 50011133	
Admin. Production	S 50011134	
New York Production Site	O 00003000	Mr. John Martin
Assembly Worker	S 50011147	
Mrs Victoria Gonzales	P 00100038	
Production Manager	S 50011148	
Assembly Worker	S 50011149	

Figure 5.10 Example of an HR Organizational Structure

5.3 Employee Master Record

The basic master data object in the SAP ERP HCM component is the employee master record, which must contain a significant amount of information to handle the diverse range of its subprocesses. As you'll recall from discussions in earlier chapters, material master records have a number of screens to store information; similarly, employee information is grouped together in *infotypes*, which is just another way of saying "screens" or "tabs." Although there are many infotypes (both standard and customized), our main focus in this chapter is integration with the payroll process, so we focus only on infotypes related to this subject.

SAP ERP uses personnel actions to control certain standard HR processes, such as when an employee is hired or leaves. For each action, the system can be advised as to the sequence in which data needs to be accessed or processed to ensure consistency and completeness in processing. In this section, we highlight the key infotypes in the payroll process. We restrict our discussion to generic infotypes related to integration with SAP ERP Financials; consult your local statutory settings to understand whether any local variations are applicable. Infotype configuration is completed in the following area of the IMG: SPRO • PERSONNEL MANAGEMENT • PERSONNEL ADMINISTRATION • CUSTOMIZING PROCEDURES • INFOTYPES.

When you first look at an employee's master record, you will see the screen shown in Figure 5.11. This shows all of the active infotypes (these have been ticked) and is accessed by Transaction PA30.

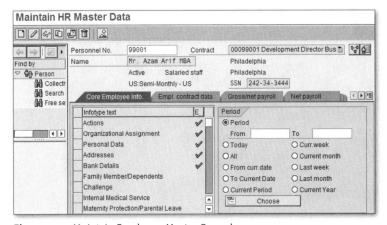

Figure 5.11 Maintain Employee Master Record

You can access all employee information from this front page. Select an infotype, and then click the CREATE/CHANGE/DISPLAY icons at the top of the screen.

Next we discuss the most important infotypes in detail. We have selected these infotypes carefully because you need to be aware of all of these infotypes to fully understand the payroll process.

5.3.1 Infotype 0000: Actions

The Actions infotype (Figure 5.12) is the first that we are concerned with because it records the actions an employee is involved in, starting with their hire. The business processes that an employee goes through during his entire career with the company are recorded in this infotype. It also records internal actions, such as performance appraisals and disciplinary actions.

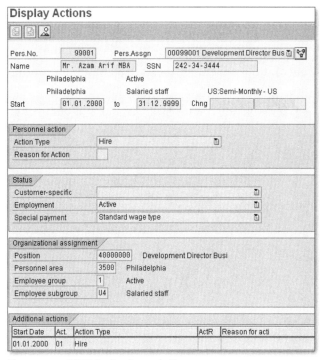

Figure 5.12 IT0000 - Employee Actions

One common use for the Action infotype is to record when an employee moves departments, which can affect retrospective postings (which we discussed earlier).

5.3.2   Infotype 0001: Organizational Assignment

The Organizational Assignment infotype (Figure 5.13) is key because it drives a number of processes and can also influence transaction code access (if you use structural authorizations) for an employee. In simple terms, it records where an employee exists in the organization. Looking at Figure 5.13, you can see a number of the concepts we have mentioned come into play.

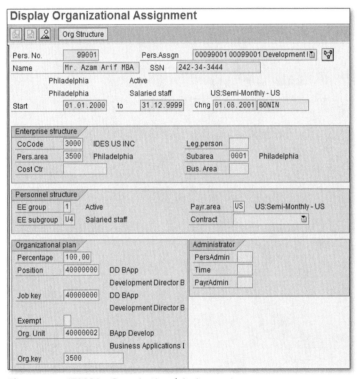

Figure 5.13   IT0001 - Organizational Assignment

It you look at the information in the header, you can see the basic information is recorded in relation to where this particular employee sits in the enterprise.

5.3.3 Infotype 0002: Personal Details

This infotype contains the personal data for an employee (Figure 5.14), such as time with the company and the different roles he has had within the company. It also holds basic information about marital status and dependents because this information may be relevant for payroll deductions.

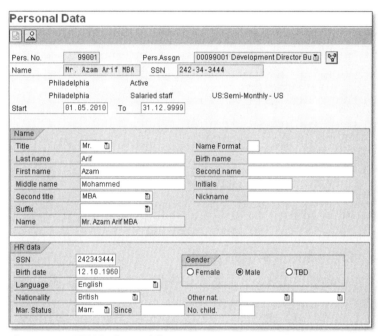

Figure 5.14 IT0002 - Personal Data

If you click the OVERVIEW button on this record, you can see the changes in this employee's history with the company.

5.3.4 Infotype 0006: Address

The Address infotype (Figure 5.15) holds information about an employee's address and contact details. This information may be required to send out correspondence for this person.

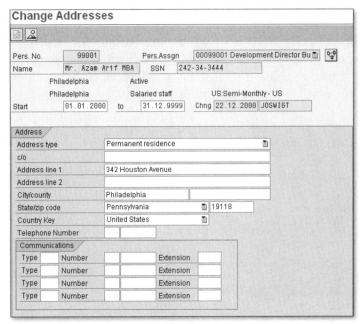

Figure 5.15 IT0006 - Employee Address

5.3.5 Infotype 0007: Planned Working Time

The Planned Working Time infotype (Figure 5.16) stores information about an employee's normal working hours. This information is relevant for work scheduling (which we don't cover in this chapter) and also for time recording (which we talk about later). Figure 5.16 shows the details contained on this screen.

5.3.6 Infotype 0008: Basic Pay

The main purpose of this infotype is to collect all of the elements that make up this employee's basic pay. These are represented in SAP ERP as wage types and are important configurable objects that we discuss in more detail later in this chapter.

Looking at the example in Figure 5.17, you can see three wage types for this employee: basic pay, bonuses, and premiums. This information helps the Payroll Driver program calculate a person's pay.

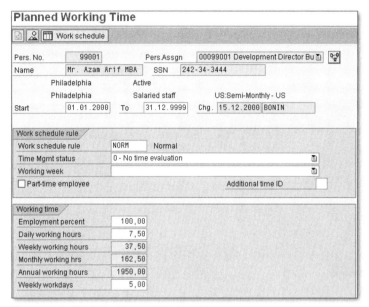

Figure 5.16 IT0007 - Planned Working Time

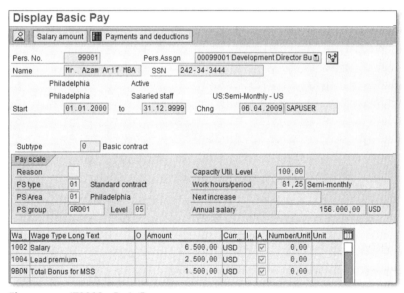

Figure 5.17 IT0008 - Basic Pay

You can find specific information about this person's salary and deductions by clicking the Salary Amount and Payments and Deductions buttons at the top of the screen. Figures 5.18 and 5.19 show the details contained on these screens.

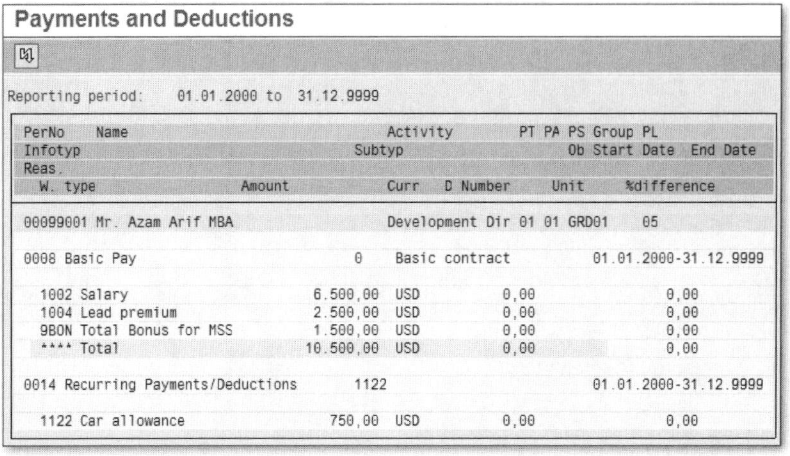

Figure 5.18 Payments and Deductions

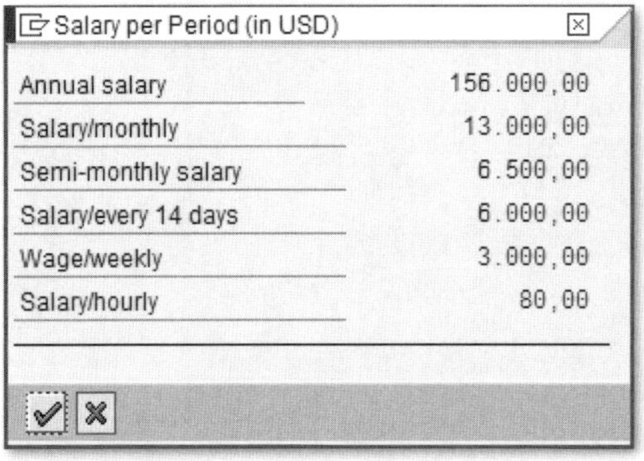

Figure 5.19 Salary Amount

5.3.7 Infotype 0009: Bank Details

In the Bank Details infotype screen, you see how an employee is to be paid; for example, in Figure 5.20, the employee is being paid by bank transfer. The payment method here is the same payment method defined in SAP ERP Financials. We recommend that you set up payroll-specific payment methods because this allows easy visibility and control over the different types of payment. For more information about this, see Chapter 4, Section 4.9.5.

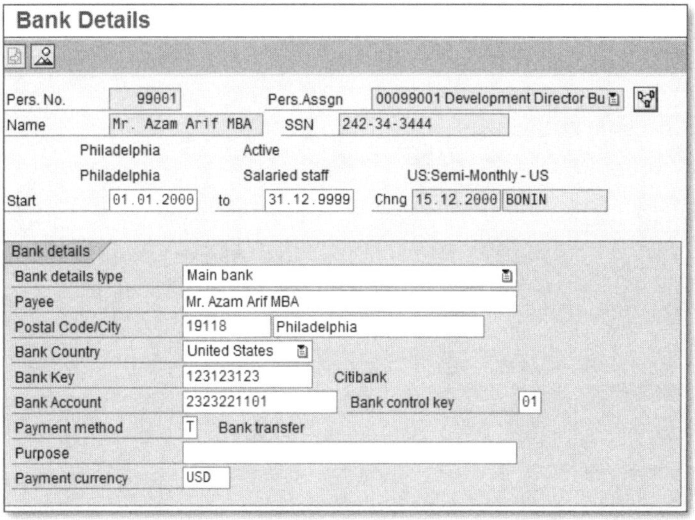

Figure 5.20 IT0009 - Employee Bank Details

5.3.8 Infotype 0014: Recurring Payments and Deductions

For every employee, there are a number of possibilities in terms of recurring payments and deductions that need to be subtracted from their salary. These can be for different things, such as union membership or a loan repayment. Figure 5.21 shows an example.

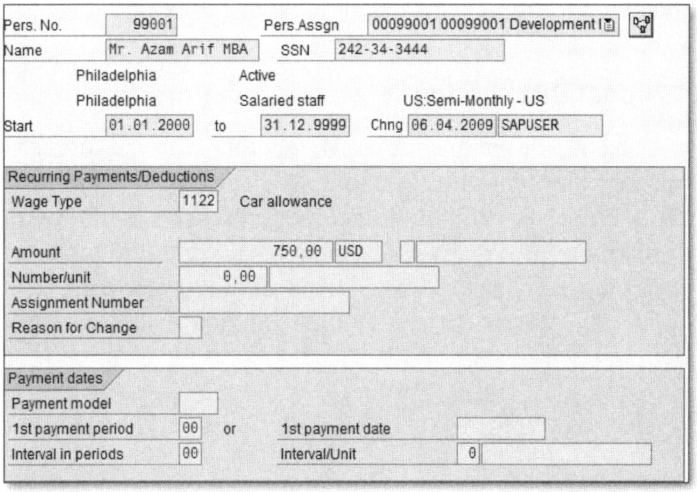

Figure 5.21 IT0014 - Pay Deduction

Again, clicking on the OVERVIEW button shows all of the deductions that are set up for this employee, as shown in Figure 5.22.

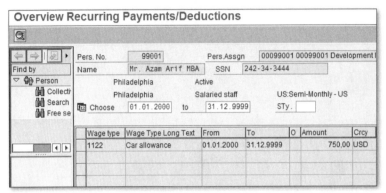

Figure 5.22 Overview of Recurring Payments/Deductions

For each of these deductions, the system allows you to set up limits for how much the deduction could be. These rules can be set up specifically for a group of employees and can vary from group to group.

5.3.9 Infotype 0016: Contract Elements

The details of employees contracts are stored in infotype 16. This infotype contains information such as the employee's contract type and any sick pay circumstances. This is also where you define the employee's and employer's notice periods.

5.3.10 Infotype 0027: Cost Distribution

An employee's costs may need to be assigned somewhere other than the cost center that is assigned to that employee. In this example, we have an employee who is spending time working on two specific projects. We could use the timesheet function to recharge costs from this employee's home cost center to the projects, but this would require a timesheet to be completed. Instead, this employee's time is simply recharged at a flat rate. We charge 10% and 25% of their costs to the two internal orders, as shown in Figure 5.23.

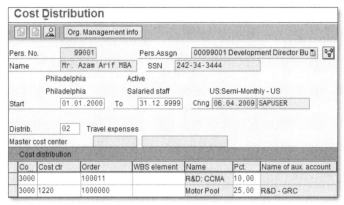

Figure 5.23 IT0027 - Cost Distribution for This Employee

The same can be done to recharge costs to WBS or to cost centers directly.

5.3.11 Infotypes 0207 and 0209: US-Specific Infotypes

U.S. tax code is different from other countries in that the tax is defined at the state level. For this reason, U.S. payroll systems use infotype 207 to record your resident data and thus which laws are applicable to you. All are subject to federal tax, but it is also necessary to deal with state tax.

Should an employee work in different states, some of their time may be subject to different state taxes. In this scenario, infotype 207 can be used to define allocations. You should also fill in infotype 209 to reflect an employee's unemployment state.

5.3.12 Infotype 2010: Employee Remuneration

Some U.S. implementations use this infotype to load up specific payment data for employees who may be working few or odd hours and thus do not fit into the general working of the rest of the organization, for example, ad hoc cleaners or drivers who are paid on a job-by-job basis. Figure 5.24 shows an example of someone who is called in to clean up hazardous waste; because this is done on an ad hoc basis, it's difficult to set up a regular payment scheme.

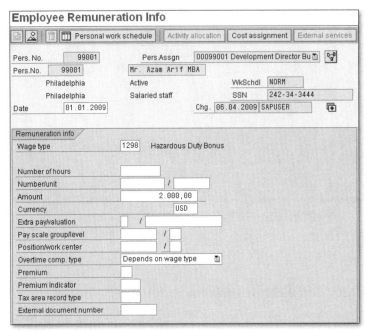

Figure 5.24 IT2010 - Employee Remuneration

If this sounds useful in your line of work, you can find more information from a dedicated U.S. payroll resource.

5.4 Configuration and Design of Payroll

The payroll process in SAP ERP depends on the configuration of the Payroll components of both SAP ERP HCM and SAP ERP Financials, as well as the setup of the employee master records in the system. In Section 5.1.2, Payroll, we talked about the basic payroll process, central to which is the Payroll Driver. This is basically the program that calculates and eventually posts the payroll results; it is dependent on the rules that we specify in the payroll schema.

In this section, we look at the configuration and design of Payroll, starting in HR and ending up in SAP ERP Financials. The following lists the areas we will cover:

- Wage types
- Symbolic accounts
- Account determination
- Vendor/customer account determination
- Payroll posting to Financial Accounting (FI)
- Payroll posting variants

5.4.1 Payroll Driver

SAP ERP provides a single program to do the payroll run for each country, known as the International Payroll Driver. For each country, the country-specific settings (variants) enable the country-specific rules to be used to calculate final pay correctly. Figure 5.25 shows how the country-specific variants are visible in the SAP Easy Access menu.

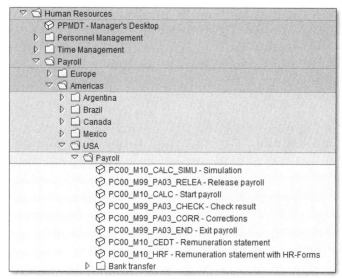

Figure 5.25 Country-Specific Payroll Menus

If you look at Figure 5.26, you can see that the PAYROLL DRIVER is a specific program for different countries, not just a different variant.

Figure 5.26 Country-Specific Payroll Drivers

The Payroll Driver can be run in simulation mode, which is always a good idea because it allows you to see if there are any errors. You can select which records to include in the run; the usual option is to run payroll by payroll area. If you have a specific issue with a selection of employee records, you can run payroll for that selection, as long as they are within the same payroll area. After you run the Payroll Driver, you will see a log produced to explain the results (Figure 5.27). Within the log, you get confirmation of successful processing, as well an indication of errors.

To run payroll, you have to specify the schema that you want to use to calculate the results. We discuss payroll schemas next.

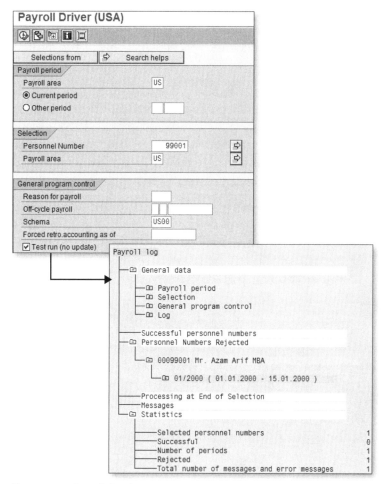

Figure 5.27 Payroll Results

5.4.2 Payroll Schema

In simple terms, a schema is a set of rules that determine how the payroll is calculated. It takes the program through a logical route to calculate results, taking into account the required statutory rules. SAP ERP comes loaded with a number of country-specific payroll schemas, but you will probably need to configure some elements of this to meet local company-specific requirements. Within a schema, you also find subschemas, which deal with the specific functionality and include the detailed rules.

In the previous section, we looked at a number of infotypes, many of which affect the final pay figure. The payroll schema controls how all this information is brought together and the order in which the information is accessed to ensure that the figure you end up with is correct. For example, determining how much tax is to be paid should be made after you've determined the total amount of basic pay, not before.

To see what's in the payroll schema, you can use Transactions PE01 and PE02. A deeper discussion of this topic goes beyond the scope of this book, but if this is important to your line of work, you should review these transactions to understand how payroll schemas are set up.

5.4.3 Wage Types

The wage type is where you actually determine the value or rate of an element of pay or deduction. There are wage types for all sorts of things, including basic pay, deductions, and bonuses. Standard SAP ERP systems are supplied with a complete list of standard wage types (contained in the Wage Type Catalogue), but you can also configure your own and therefore replicate any specific requirements you have within your organization. For example, you may have a specific bonus scheme or deduction requirement that is not reflected in the standard SAP ERP-supplied wage types.

Wage types reflect an important configuration step in the automatic account determination for payroll posting to SAP General Ledger. As you will see in the next sections, the combination of wage types and symbolic accounts is used to assign general ledger accounts to payroll postings. For this book, it's only important to understand what a wage type is and what it's used for, so we don't provide detailed explanations of the payroll rules and regulations.

Wage types are set up in different areas of the IMG; the menu paths shown in the following section relate to all countries (United States, Great Britain, etc.). SAP ERP provides specific IMG menu paths for each country, so you can configure your country-specific settings as required.

Types of Wage Types

There are three types of wage types in the system:

- ▸ Wage types entered directly into an employee's record in an infotype
- ▸ Wage types calculated in the background, as a result of configuration
- ▸ Wage types automatically generated during processing

Some of these are apparent by looking at infotype 0008, Basic Pay, but they can also be found elsewhere on the employee's master record. Deductions and bonuses are also wage types and are found on other infotypes (e.g., 0014, Recurring Payments/Deductions).

When setting up wage types, the configuration is done in the following area of the IMG: SPRO • Personnel Management • Personnel Administration • Customizing Procedures • Infotypes. After you access this area, there are different places for you to actually configure the wage type, depending on its type.

5.4.4 Symbolic Accounts

The main purpose of the symbolic account is to define the account assignment category, in other words, to define what SAP ERP Financials account assignment object must be supplied when making a posting. For example, for salary postings, we expect the posting to go to an expense account, and the standard object should be a cost center. In general, expenses require cost objects, and balance sheet postings require profit centers. Symbolic accounts are set up in the following area of the IMG: IMG • Payroll • Payroll GB • Reporting for Posting Payroll Results to Accounting • Activities in the HR System • Employee Grouping/Symbolic Account • Define Symbolic Accounts.

> **Note**
>
> It's important to understand the fundamentals of the SAP ERP Financials solution before completing this configuration activity. In general, we would make use of balance sheet codes (requiring a profit center) and expense codes (requiring a cost center), but this is an important integration step in this area of configuration, and you should ensure this configuration conforms to the Financials settings.

Figure 5.28 shows how we set up the account assignment category for each symbolic account. In this scenario, we set up a number of symbolic accounts, one per wage type. You don't have to do this, but as you'll see in the next section, it influences the account determination. Other options on this screen that you may select include the following:

▶ MOMAG
This setting enables account determination according to the employee grouping account determination.

▶ FIXED MOMAG
This setting is relevant for FM/GM-based (Funds Management/Grants Management) account determination.

▶ NEGATIVE POSTING indicator
This indicator enables negative postings to be made when making reversal postings. (Note: This should be reviewed in detail before being ticked.)

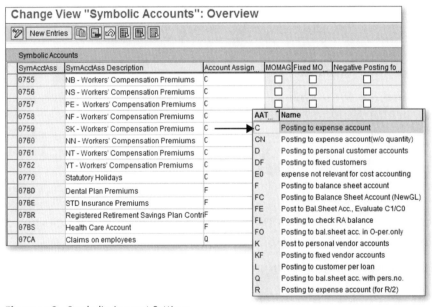

Figure 5.28 Symbolic Account Settings

Now that you've defined the symbolic accounts, you can link the wage type to a symbolic account using the following area of the IMG: IMG • PAYROLL • PAYROLL GB • REPORTING FOR POSTING PAYROLL RESULTS TO ACCOUNTING • ACTIVITIES IN THE HR SYSTEM • MAINTAIN WAGE TYPES • DEFINE POSTING CHARACTERISTICS OF THE WAGE TYPE.

Looking at Figure 5.29, you can see that in this configuration step, you set up posting settings for each wage type. Specifically, you indicate which symbolic account is relevant (in terms of account assignment), and also how the debits and credits are posted. As we said before, you can link multiple wage types to the same symbolic account.

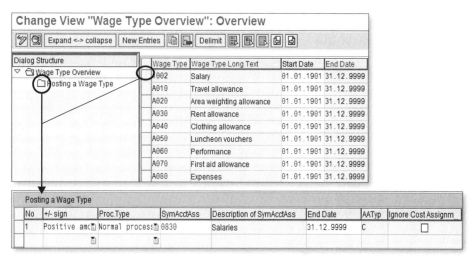

Figure 5.29 Linking Wage Type to Symbolic Account

The HR team usually completes this configuration activity because you are linking two HR objects together. This configuration shouldn't be done in isolation; be sure to think about the range of general ledger accounts you will eventually want to post to. Figuring this out now will make the next configuration activity easier.

> **Note**
>
> The setup of employee grouping specifically in relation to account determination is not the same as the employee groups we discussed at the start of this chapter (Section 5.2.2, Employee Groups and Subgroups).

5.4.5 Account Determination

At this point, you need to define the account determination rules at the chart of accounts level. This configuration is consistent with the settings we've already made for the MM-FI account determination, so if you've covered this section, you'll recognize the look of the screens.

Access the following area of the IMG: IMG • PAYROLL • PAYROLL GB • REPORTING FOR POSTING PAYROLL RESULTS TO ACCOUNTING • ACTIVITIES IN THE AC SYSTEM • ASSIGN ACCOUNTS. As you can see in Figure 5.30, there are a number of configuration options that you need to review and understand.

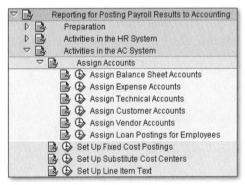

Figure 5.30 Account Determination

You need to understand some basic principles of where you expect postings to go, in terms of when payroll runs and posts to accounting. Payroll consultants usually concern themselves with running payroll and ensuring that payments reach the employees. Financials consultants, however, are very concerned with ensuring the right accounts are picked up. In Table 5.1, we summarize the key concepts for the posting of payroll to the ledger.

Type of Posting	Comment
Salary expense	In HR terms, the cost of employees is referred to as the *salary expense*. We expect this to be posted to expense general ledger accounts in the P&L. This is a summary posting by the general ledger account.
Vendors	In some circumstances, the employer needs to make deductions from an employee's salary. We make this association through a wage type link with the vendor number through account determination.

Table 5.1 Summary of Key Concepts for Financial Posting of Payroll

Type of Posting	Comment
Expenses	Employees may be eligible to be refunded for any business expenses they incur. The normal route approach here is to configure the SAP Travel Management component, although we do we not cover that component in this book.
Customers	If an employee has taken a loan, or you are making an advanced payment to an employee, this needs to be set up by configuring this relationship (not covered this in this book).
Technical	This setting is needed for when a payroll run (which could have thousands of lines) needs to post into many general ledger documents (which are limited to 999 lines).
	This is usually a control account through which all control postings go. A single gross pay control account is common here, or it's possible to set up control accounts by company code.

Table 5.1 Summary of Key Concepts for Financial Posting of Payroll (Cont.)

Let's first look at the expense accounts configuration because this is a good way to understand the other configuration settings. In Figure 5.31, you can see that, in the same way we defined the MM account determination settings, we have a transaction key against which we assign general ledger accounts. The system needs a symbolic account against which to assign a general ledger account, and, as we have seen already, the symbolic account is linked to the wage type. This is where we make the account assignment.

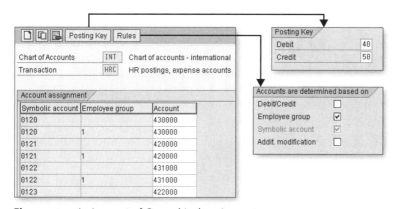

Figure 5.31 Assignment of General Ledger Accounts

When setting up expense postings, you expect to see symbolic accounts that enable the coding of salary, overtime, and perhaps expenses to the relevant general ledger accounts. This table might have a number of entries. You can also include employee groups, which we mentioned in our earlier discussion of symbolic accounts, to differentiate the account assignment for each symbolic account.

5.4.6 Vendor/Customer Account Determination

As part of the payroll process, there is usually a need to make postings against vendors and, sometimes, customers. Perhaps some of your deductions need to be paid to a specific organization on behalf of the employee; for example, sometimes courts order fines that must come out of an employee's salary. In such a situation (see Figure 5.32), if you set up the court as a vendor in your system, you can link the deduction directly to the vendor account and therefore enable Payroll to generate the deduction postings automatically.

Figure 5.32 Setting Deduction Vendors

5.4.7 Full Payroll Posting to Finance

The previous sections showed how the system determines the Financials postings that need to be made. We do physically need to process the posting-to-accounting activity because it is possible to make payments to employees without doing this step. This is to avoid situations where you're unable to pay employees due to a blocked cost center or some other Financials issue; because this isn't really a valid reason to hold back making the payroll payments to employees, the system segregates these two activities.

The volume of transactions in Payroll is a lot of information for posting to the general ledger, so SAP ERP recommends that the transactions be posted at a summary level (see Section 5.4.8, Payroll Posting Variant). Many organizations adopt this policy because they don't want the payroll information to be posted at the line level into the general ledger, which makes it too easy to get detailed information about a specific employee's pay. Thus, the general ledger generally contains only a summarized posting per general ledger account and cost object, with the detailed analysis of the employees who make up these figures contained in the payroll details.

Now that everything is configured, it's time to demonstrate a payroll run.

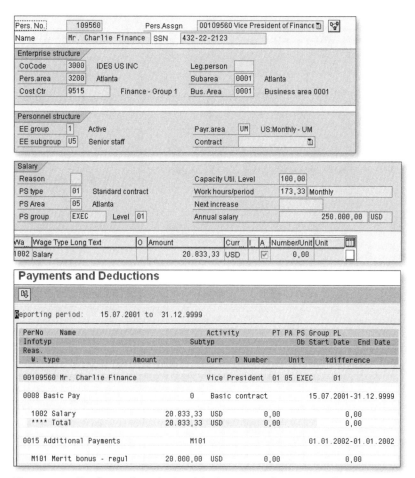

Figure 5.33 Employees Organizational Assignment and Basic Pay Information

Let's start by refreshing our memory and looking at an employee's organizational assignment and basic pay infotype (Figure 5.33). This shows both infotype 0008 and the payments and deductions information for this employee, which you should expect to see when you pay the employee.

After ensuring that all your employee's details are correct for this payroll period, you can run payroll in test mode. When you're satisfied that everything is correct, run the actual payroll, which checks the payroll log to ensure all records have processed correctly (Figure 5.34).

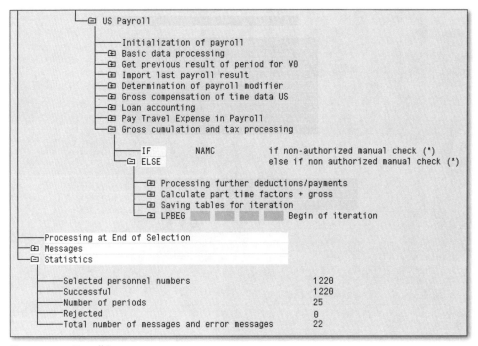

Figure 5.34 Payroll Log

For all payroll runs, you can use Transaction PCP0 to check the current status. Payroll has two purposes: first, to make payments out to employees, and, second, to update the ledger. Looking at Figure 5.35, you can see that the screen is split into two sections presenting the posting of payments to employees and the posting of the ledger entries to SAP General Ledger.

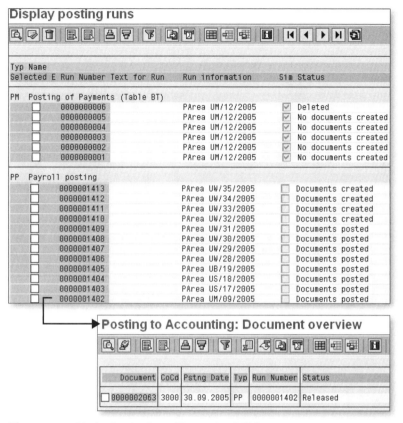

Figure 5.35 Display Posting Runs (Transaction PCP0)

You can look at your payroll posting run by double-clicking it (Figure 5.36). This view shows the payroll posting document (which is not the same view as the document that you will eventually see in SAP General Ledger). At this level, you see an entry made for each general ledger account and Controlling (CO) account assignment object being paid in this run; you can also see the posting to general ledger expense (salaries codes), taxes, and balance sheet clearing (control) accounts.

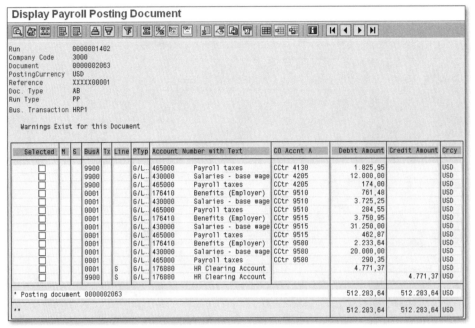

Figure 5.36 Payroll Posting Document

> **Note**
>
> Earlier, in Figure 5.34, warning messages appeared at the bottom of the posting. Because these messages were only warnings, it was still possible to process the payroll. These messages are shown in Figure 5.37.

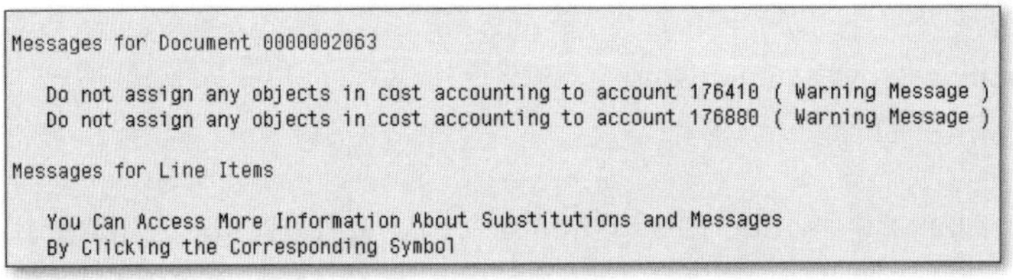

```
Messages for Document 0000002063

    Do not assign any objects in cost accounting to account 176410 ( Warning Message )
    Do not assign any objects in cost accounting to account 176880 ( Warning Message )

Messages for Line Items

    You Can Access More Information About Substitutions and Messages
    By Clicking the Corresponding Symbol
```

Figure 5.37 Messages Generated from Payroll Run

Because this is a posting per general ledger account and CO object combination, you can see the breakdown of this posting. Double-clicking the amount of $31,250.00 in Figure 5.36, you can see the breakdown of what makes this amount, as shown in Figure 5.38. This shows that there were two items making up this amount.

Display revision information for posting document

	Sele	Account with Text	G/L	CO Accnt	WT	Wage Type Long Text	Pers.No.	Debit Amount	Credit Amount	Exp.type	Crcy
	☐	430000 Salaries...	430000	CCtr 9515	1002	1002 Salary	109560	20.833,33			USD
	☐	430000 Salaries...	430000	CCtr 9515	1002	1002 Salary	109569	10.416,67			USD
*		430000 Salaries...		CCtr 9515		1002 Salary		31.250,00			USD
**								31.250,00			USD

Figure 5.38 Revision Information for Posting Document

Figure 5.38 is a summary report by employee. To see the details below the summary report, double-clicking on a line, which produces Figure 5.39. The first thing you should note here is that the line on the previous screen was per employee. The detail behind each line is quite lengthy; and here you can see a long list of wage types associated with this employee.

Display revision information for posting document

Only Posted Wage Types

25.08.2009 Employee's Payroll Results and Posted Amounts
         For a Period

Display of All Wage Types, Unsummarized

Pers.No.	Sequence Number	Status Ind	IN:Payroll Area	IN:Period	IN:PayTyp	IN:ID	IN:Date	FOR:Payroll Area
109560	00051	A	UM	09 2005				UM

Payroll Results (Table RT):

Wage Type	Wage Type Long Text	Amount	Crcy	Posted: Debit	Posted: Credit
/101	Total gross	20.833,33	USD	39,27	39,27
/102	401(k) Wages	20.833,33	USD	39,27	39,27
/104	NQP Eligible Earns	20.833,33	USD	39,27	39,27
/109	ER benefit contributions	1.014,44	USD	39,27	39,27
/110	Net payments/Deductions	68,60-	USD	39,27	39,27
/114	Base wage for BSI	20.833,33	USD	39,27	39,27
/301	TG Withholding Tax	41.666,66	USD	39,27	39,27
/303	TG EE Social Security Tax	20.833,33	USD	39,27	39,27
/304	TG ER Social Security Tax	20.833,33	USD	39,27	39,27
/305	TG EE Medicare Tax	20.833,33	USD	39,27	39,27
/306	TG ER Medicare Tax	20.833,33	USD	39,27	39,27
/310	TG ER Unemployment Tax	41.666,66	USD	39,27	39,27
/401	TX Withholding Tax	6.079,29	USD		6.079,29
/405	TX EE Medicare Tax	302,08	USD		302,08
/406	TX ER Medicare Tax	302,08	USD	302,08	302,08
/550	Statutory net	14.451,96	USD	302,08	302,08
/559	Payment	14.383,36	USD		14.383,36
/560	Amount to be paid	14.383,36	USD		14.383,36
/5PY	Good Money	20.833,33	USD		14.383,36
/5U0	Tot EE tax	6.381,37	USD		14.383,36
/5U1	Tot ER tax	302,08	USD		14.383,36

Figure 5.39 Detailed Information for Employee Payroll Posting

Not all of the wage types will post to the ledger for this employee; you should focus on only posted wage types. If you click the ONLY POSTED WAGE TYPES button (as shown in Figure 5.39), the screen shown in Figure 5.40 appears.

Payroll Results (Table RT):

Wage Type	Wage Type Long Text	Amount	Crcy	Posted: Debit	Posted: Credit
/401	TX Withholding Tax	6.079,29	USD		6.079,29
/405	TX EE Medicare Tax	302,08	USD		302,08
/406	TX ER Medicare Tax	302,08	USD	302,08	302,08
/559	Payment	14.383,36	USD		14.383,36
2110	Std Medical EE after-tax	36,83-	USD		36,83
2117	Dental EE after-tax	31,77-	USD		31,77
2310	Std Medical Employer	465,42	USD	465,42	465,42
2317	Dental Employer	7,50	USD	7,50	7,50
2410	Std Medical Provider	502,25	USD	502,25	502,25
2417	Dental Provider	39,27	USD	39,27	39,27

Figure 5.40 Posted Wage Types for This Employee Payroll Posting

Let's now revisit Figure 5.35, which shows Transaction PCP0, Display Posting Runs. Recall that it is from this screen that you can double-click a posting run to see the POST TO ACCOUNTING: DOCUMENT OVERVIEW screen. If you select this item, and then select GOTO • ACCOUNTING DOCUMENTS, you'll see the link to the accounting document from this payroll document, as shown in Figure 5.41.

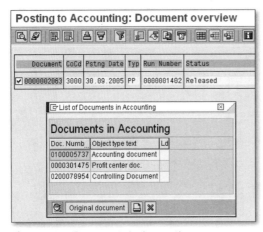

Figure 5.41 Documents in Accounting

The accounting document posted reflects the document we saw previously. If you look at the financial document it produces, you should be able to match line items to the Payroll document shown earlier in Figure 5.36.

5.4.8 Payroll Posting Variant

The final configuration activity we need to look at is the payroll posting variant. Although it actually comes into play earlier in the process (when you are running the Payroll Driver), we've deliberately included it here so that you can better understand the configuration.

The posting variant controls the posting to accounting settings, which we need to manage the document that is being posted. In Figure 5.42, the document type, reference information, and the way documents are structured are all controlled by the posting variant. The posting variant configuration path and screen are shown in Figure 5.43.

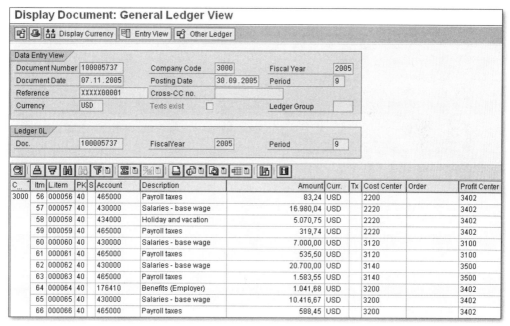

Figure 5.42 Accounting Document from Payroll

There are several important settings made in this configuration activity, but we focus on the following fields for the purposes of this discussion:

▶ DOCUMENT TYPE
This defines the Finance document type that is posted to.

▶ PREFIX FOR REFERENCE
If you look back at Figure 5.42, you can see that the REFERENCE field has a prefix in it. This is defined in this field.

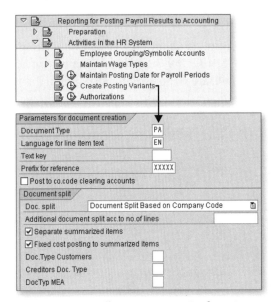

Figure 5.43 Payroll Posting Variant Configuration

▶ DOC. SPLIT
The document splitting settings here are not the SAP General Ledger document splitting settings. When you post payroll, there can be thousands of lines; here, you specify whether these documents are to be split up by company code or by account assignment object. This decision needs to be made based on practicality and business requirements. If you are posting to hundreds of account assignment objects, then this could generate hundreds of documents.

▶ SEPARATE SUMMARIZED ITEMS
As we mentioned earlier, the payroll generates separate documents for the expense and balance sheet items. The setting to request that is made here.

5.5 Summary

This chapter explained the integration of SAP ERP HCM with SAP ERP Financials. We did not cover every element of SAP ERP HCM but instead focused specifically on the configuration and design of the two key integration areas: Organizational Management and Payroll. This is a very interesting area because more and more organizations are implementing SAP Payroll and SAP ERP HCM. In the next chapter, we look at the complex subject of integrating Asset Accounting, Investment Management, and Project Systems.

This chapter looks at Investment Management through investment orders and projects, and explains the integration of these with Asset Accounting and SAP General Ledger. In doing so, we cover the full lifecycle of an asset from the creation of the master record to retirement.

6   Integrating Asset Accounting, Investment Management, and Project Systems

In this chapter, we explain three complex processes: Asset Accounting (AA), Investment Management, and Project Systems (PS). We look at the business processes of investment orders and PS, which are used by different organizations as a way of capitalizing spending. Both these processes end with the creation of an asset for the organization, which is represented by a fixed asset in the AA component in SAP ERP. We also talk about the processes related to fixed assets, from their creation to retirement, by building on the coverage we gave AA in our previous book, *SAP ERP Financials: Configuration and Design*.

AA is a complex area, and it is vital for SAP ERP consultants to fully understand all of the relevant integration points to ensure that they are able to configure a system that meets the client's requirements. For this reason, our focus is on the integration points; however, we have structured the chapter so that it covers not only the organizational structure and integration points but also the whole process as well. The following main areas are covered in this chapter:

- The asset lifecycle
- The configuration of AA and Investment Management
- Account determination in AA
- Master data
- Asset acquisition through investment order
- Posting values to assets using external acquisition

- ▸ Posting transfers to assets
- ▸ Posting depreciation runs
- ▸ Posting retirement with scrapping
- ▸ PS

The chapter begins with a brief overview of the asset lifecycle process and then explains in detail the main organizational elements within AA. We then discuss the configuration steps required in Investment Management and highlight the key integration points that should be configured to run processes such as asset acquisition, transfers, depreciations, and retirements. At the end of the chapter, we explain the configuration and settings in PS.

6.1 Overview of the Asset Lifecycle

In this section, we briefly explain the most common asset-based postings that occur during an asset's life cycle (Figure 6.1). During this process, the system transfers the cost from assets under construction to the final asset, and then posts depreciations, transfers, and retirements based on the settings made in the system. It also calculates appropriate depreciation values to be posted to the general ledger using the account determination settings (as will be explained in detail later in this chapter). After discussing the lifecycle, we explain the relevant integration points involved in this lifecycle.

6.1.1 Assets Acquisition Through External Vendor/Investment Order/ Projects

Assets can be acquired in many different ways, such as through external vendor purchases or through capitalization as part of the asset under construction (AuC) process (which involves investment order or project system functionality). During this process, the costs related to an AuC are accumulated on an investment order/ project and then settled every month to the AuC, so that it is properly represented in the balance sheet. After the AuC is complete, it is settled to the final asset, and, from that point on, it starts its life; in other words, the asset will have depreciation, transfers, and retirements postings made to it. During this process, the account determination settings that determine what general ledger accounts are posted to for each asset transaction also come into play.

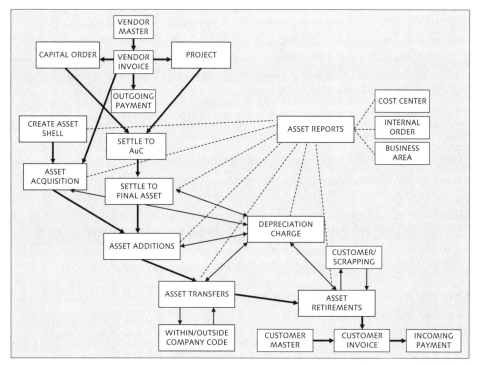

Figure 6.1 Asset Lifecycle

6.1.2 Asset Transfers

During its lifecycle, an asset can be transferred from one department to another department or from one company code to another company code. Based on the account determination settings, the system posts the correct entries and transfers important information such as the capitalization dates, depreciation terms, and so on, to the new asset.

6.1.3 Depreciation Posting

Depreciation is a method used in accounting and finance whereby you spread the cost of an asset over the span of its useful life. A depreciation posting is one of the most important steps in an asset's life. The relevant depreciation amount is based on either your company's group requirements or the legal statutory requirements. Whatever the case, the important thing to note is that when you perform the depreciation run at month-end, the system automatically calculates the correct depreciation amounts and posts them to the relevant general ledger accounts. This calculation is posted to the general ledger based on the account determination settings made as part of the configuration.

6.1.4 Asset Retirement

Based on the condition of an asset, it can be retired by either selling it to an external customer or by scrapping it for no revenue. In both these cases, the system calculates profit or loss at the time of the asset retirement by looking at the total cost of acquisition, including transfers to this asset during its lifetime, and then reduces it by the total depreciation already posted to date, as well as transfers out from this asset. The profit or loss is posted to the respective general ledger accounts based on account determination settings, which are explained later in this chapter.

After explaining briefly the asset lifecycle, we will look at the core configuration steps for both AA and Investment Management in the next section.

6.2 Core Configuration of Asset Accounting and Investment Management

In Chapter 2, SAP Enterprise Structure, we explained the enterprise structure for our SAP ERP solution design, which outlined the basic building blocks needed to build our solution. This section provides you with details for all of the necessary organizational elements and related settings that are required for the integration of AA with Investment Management and SAP General Ledger. We begin by discussing the core configuration of AA and then move on to the core configuration of Investment Management.

> **Note**
>
> At this point, you might also expect to read about the configuration and design of projects as investment objects (i.e., PS). However, we will follow through the discussion to the asset's processes so as not to disturb the flow of our explanation of investment orders. The configuration and design relevant to the integration of projects is discussed later in Section 6.10, Project Systems.

6.2.1 Core Configuration of Asset Accounting

Let's discuss the most important configuration steps from an AA point of view, which are as follows:

► Copy the reference chart of depreciation.

► Assign the chart of depreciation to company codes.

► Specify the number assignment across company codes.

► Specify account determination.

► Create screen layout rules.

► Define asset number range intervals.

► Define asset classes.

► Define depreciation areas.

► Specify the transfer of APC (acquisition and production costs) values.

► Specify the transfer of depreciation terms.

► Determine depreciation areas in asset classes.

► Define how depreciation areas post to the general ledger.

► Activate account assignment objects.

► Specify account assignment types for account assignment objects.

Copy Reference Chart of Depreciation

The chart of depreciation is the organizational element used to manage various legal requirements, as well as your company's group or internal controlling requirements for the depreciation and valuation of assets. Your chart of depreciation is a directory of depreciation areas arranged according to your business and legal requirements. A chart of depreciation can be used for all of the company codes in a given country.

To define your chart of depreciation, you copy a reference chart of depreciation, including all of the depreciation areas from the reference chart. You can use the chart of depreciation to manage all different types of valuation rules for your assets in a specific country or economic region. If necessary, you can delete any depreciation areas that you do not need in your copied chart of depreciation and add any new depreciation areas if you need them to meet your requirements.

The IMG path for this configuration step is SPRO • FINANCIAL ACCOUNTING (NEW) • ASSET ACCOUNTING • ORGANIZATIONAL STRUCTURES • COPY REFERENCE CHART OF DEPRECIATION/DEPRECIATION AREAS. A screen with activities, including COPY REFERENCE CHART OF DEPRECIATION, appears, as shown in Figure 6.2.

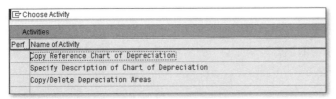

Figure 6.2 Copy Reference Chart of Depreciation

If you're creating a chart of depreciation for a country for which SAP ERP has not delivered a standard country-specific chart of depreciation, the easiest method is to copy a chart of depreciation with similar depreciation parameters and then make changes to it. To copy a chart of depreciation, double-click the COPY REFERENCE CHART OF DEPRECIATION activity, and then, in the next screen, click the COPY icon (as shown in Figure 6.3). In the COPY dialog box that appears, specify the chart of depreciation you want to copy from and the chart of depreciation you want to copy to (the latter is a number you assign). Click the checkmark icon.

Figure 6.3 Copy Chart of Depreciation

The system returns a message related to the transport of number ranges and addresses. Click the checkmark icon to manually maintain the number ranges and addresses in the system.

After the chart of depreciation has been copied, go back into the activity screen shown in Figure 6.2, and double-click the SPECIFY DESCRIPTION OF CHART OF DEPRE-CIATION activity. Change the name of your chart of depreciation, as shown in Figure 6.4.

Change View "Chart of depreciation: Specify name"

ChDep	Description
1TH	Sample chart of depreciation: Thailand
1TW	Sample chart of depreciation: Taiwan
1US	Sample chart of depreciation: USA
1VE	Sample chart of depreciation: Venezuela

Figure 6.4 Example Chart of Depreciations

Go back to the activity screen shown in Figure 6.2, and select the COPY/DELETE DEPRECIATION AREAS activity. Behind each chart, you will find the valid depreciation areas for it, as shown in Figure 6.5. Delete the depreciation areas that are not needed from your new chart of depreciation, or add new depreciation areas by copying them.

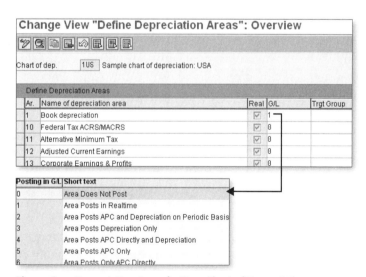

Change View "Define Depreciation Areas": Overview

Chart of dep. 1US Sample chart of depreciation: USA

Define Depreciation Areas

Ar.	Name of depreciation area	Real	G/L	Trgt Group
1	Book depreciation	☑	1	
10	Federal Tax ACRS/MACRS	☑	0	
11	Alternative Minimum Tax	☑	0	
12	Adjusted Current Earnings	☑	0	
13	Corporate Earnings & Profits	☑	0	

Posting in G/L	Short text
0	Area Does Not Post
1	Area Posts in Realtime
2	Area Posts APC and Depreciation on Periodic Basis
3	Area Posts Depreciation Only
4	Area Posts APC Directly and Depreciation
5	Area Posts APC Only
6	Area Posts Only APC Directly

Figure 6.5 Depreciation Areas for Your Chart of Depreciation

Now that your chart of depreciation is configured, let's look at assigning the chart of depreciation to a company code.

Assign a Chart of Depreciation to a Company Code

In this configuration step, you assign your chart of depreciation to your company code. The IMG path for this configuration step is SPRO • FINANCIAL ACCOUNTING (NEW) • ASSET ACCOUNTING • ORGANIZATIONAL STRUCTURES • ASSIGN CHART OF DEPRECIATION TO COMPANY CODE (Transaction OAOB). In the MAINTAIN COMPANY CODE IN ASSET ACCOUNTING: OVERVIEW screen, shown in Figure 6.6, enter the relevant chart of depreciation in the CHRT DEP column.

Change View "Maintain company code in Asset Accounting"

CoCd	Company Name	Chrt dep	Description
2000	IDES UK	1GB	Sample chart of depreciation: Great Britain
3000	IDES US INC	1US	Sample chart of depreciation: USA
3010	Euro Subsidiary - Belgium	1DE	Sample chart of depreciation: Germany
UK	SAFA UK	1GB	Sample chart of depreciation: Great Britain
US	SAFA US	1US	Sample chart of depreciation: USA

Figure 6.6 Assignment of Chart of Depreciation to Your Company Code

The next step is to look at specifying a number assignment across company codes.

Specify Number Assignment Across Company Codes

In this configuration step, you define a cross-company code assignment of the main asset number. This step is required only if you want a cross-company code number assignment; otherwise, you can skip this step and go to the next step. In AA, you can allocate the main asset number across different company codes, so for every company code, you can determine from which other company code the number assignment should be carried out.

The IMG path for this configuration step is SPRO • FINANCIAL ACCOUNTING (NEW) • ASSET ACCOUNTING • ORGANIZATIONAL STRUCTURES • SPECIFY NUMBER ASSIGNMENT ACROSS COMPANY CODES (Transaction AO11).

In the screen that appears, shown in Figure 6.7, use the No. CoCd column to specify which company code you want to use for the cross-company code number assignment for your company codes.

Based on the settings in this screen, the system assigns the main asset number from the number range of the assigning company code to these company codes. If a cross-company code number assignment is not required, you must enter your company code key in the No. CoCd column.

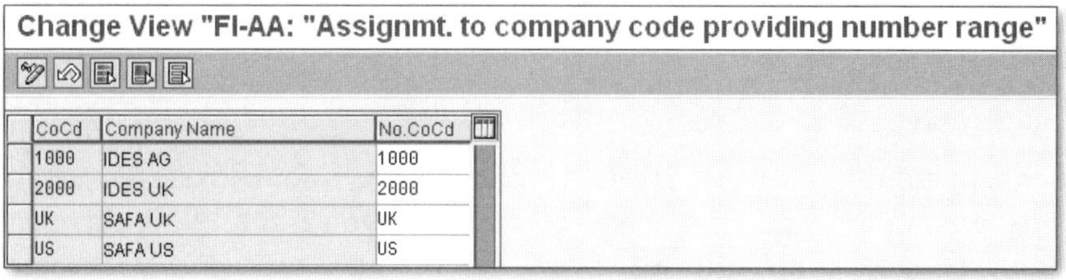

CoCd	Company Name	No.CoCd
1000	IDES AG	1000
2000	IDES UK	2000
UK	SAFA UK	UK
US	SAFA US	US

Figure 6.7 Assignment of Number Range to Company Code

Specify Account Determination

From an integration point of view, this configuration step is essential because it serves as a basis for establishing a link between AA and SAP General Ledger. It does this by defining the account determination keys and description, which will be used later in this chapter to include the general ledger accounts to which postings are made.

The key of an account determination must be stored in the asset class. By doing this, the account determination links an asset master record to the general ledger accounts that will be posted for an accounting transaction using the asset class.

We recommend that you create at least the same number of account determinations as your fixed asset balance sheet reconciliation accounts in SAP General Ledger. As a standard, SAP ERP supplies a number of account determinations that can be used if they meet your specific requirements.

The IMG path to configure settings for account determination is SPRO • Financial Accounting (New) • Asset Accounting • Organizational StructureS • Asset classes • Specify Account Determination. Figure 6.8 shows the screen where you can configure the required settings. Select the New Entries button, and enter the account determination key and its description.

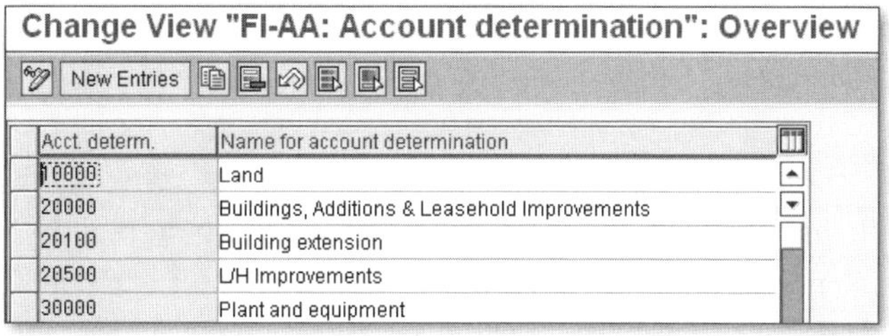

Acct. determ.	Name for account determination
10000	Land
20000	Buildings, Additions & Leasehold Improvements
20100	Building extension
20500	L/H Improvements
30000	Plant and equipment

Figure 6.8 Define Account Determination

Next, let's look at creating screen layout rules.

Create Screen Layout Rules

In this configuration step, you can create screen layout rules for each screen layout key you have created; by defining screen layout rules, you control the fields that appear in the asset master record. Specifically, you use these settings to determine whether fields should appear as required, optional, or suppressed during the creation of an asset master record. There are two steps in creating the screen layout rules:

1. Create the keys and descriptions of the screen layout controls using the following IMG path: SPRO • FINANCIAL ACCOUNTING (NEW) • ASSET ACCOUNTING • ORGANIZATIONAL STRUCTURE • ASSET CLASSES • CREATE SCREEN LAYOUT RULES. The rules you define in the screen shown in Figure 6.9 define the field status when you create a new asset master record for the selected account determination.

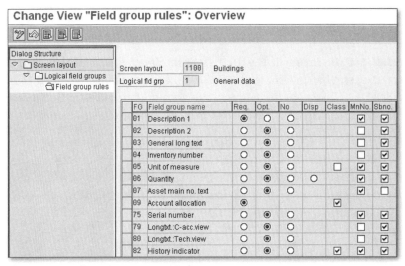

Figure 6.9 Defining Screen Layout Rules

2. Define the details of the screen layout control for asset master data, which controls the settings for the field groups in the asset master record. This step allows you to structure the asset master record individually for each asset class. For each field group you define, specify the following:

   ▶ The characteristics of the master record screen, that is, whether the fields are going to be required, optional, displayed, or suppressed

▶ The maintenance level, that is, the main asset number or subasset number

▶ A copy option at the time of creating a new master record, using another master record as a reference

Use the following IMG path: SPRO • FINANCIAL ACCOUNTING (NEW) • ASSET ACCOUNTING • MASTER DATA • SCREEN LAYOUT • DEFINE SCREEN LAYOUT FOR ASSET MASTER DATA.

The screen layout is defined for each key that was created in step 1, and for each screen of an asset master record, as shown in Figure 6.10.

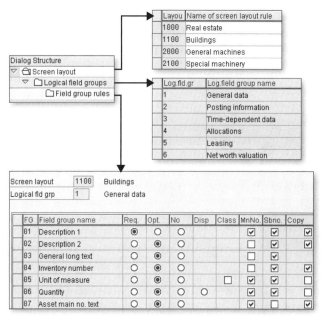

Figure 6.10 Defining Screen Layout for Asset Master Records

Next, we'll look at defining asset number range intervals.

Define Asset Number Range Intervals

In this configuration step, you define the number ranges for assigning the main asset number for your company code. Many companies use their asset numbering convention to categorize their asset portfolio. In the asset class definition, you can specify the number range for the assignment of numbers for that asset class. You have an option to create number ranges using internal as well as external assignments.

To keep the administration needed for the number assignment to a minimum, we recommend that you use number ranges with internal assignment for creating your assets. SAP ERP provides standard number ranges that can be used, or you can create your own number ranges, if required.

The IMG path for defining the number range intervals is SPRO • FINANCIAL ACCOUNTING (NEW) • ASSET ACCOUNTING • ORGANIZATIONAL STRUCTURES • ASSET CLASSES • DEFINE NUMBER RANGE INTERVAL (Transaction AS08). From the MAINTAIN NUMBER RANGE INTERVALS screen that displays as shown in Figure 6.11, you can either copy number ranges from a template company code, or you can create your own numbers in line with your business requirements. Figure 6.11 shows the creation of custom number ranges. If you want to specify an asset number manually at the time of creating an asset master record, you should define a number range that is externally defined by selecting the external (EXT) box for the appropriate number range.

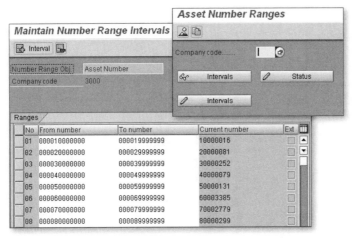

Figure 6.11 Creating Custom Asset Number Range Intervals

You' have now completed all of the necessary steps to define asset classes, which is one of the main organizational elements from an AA point of view. In the next step, we use the previously configured steps to define the asset classes.

Define Asset Classes

In AA, you can structure your assets by using the concept of *asset classes*. Asset classes represent a group of assets that are similar in nature and investment objective. You can define as many asset classes as you require in accordance with your company's group or statutory requirements. The asset classes are defined at the client level, and they apply to all company codes available in that SAP ERP system. (This is true even for company codes that have different charts of depreciation and therefore different depreciation areas.)

The configuration of asset classes is completed by following the IMG path SPRO • FINANCIAL ACCOUNTING (NEW) • ASSET ACCOUNTING • ORGANIZATIONAL STRUCTURES • ASSET CLASSES • DEFINE ASSET CLASSES (Transaction OAOA). As shown in Figure 6.12, there is an underlying configuration screen for each asset class that contains the settings for that asset class. These settings include the following:

▶ Account determination

▶ Screen layout rules for maintaining the asset master record

▶ The number range assignment for assigning the main asset numbers

We discussed each of these settings earlier in this section.

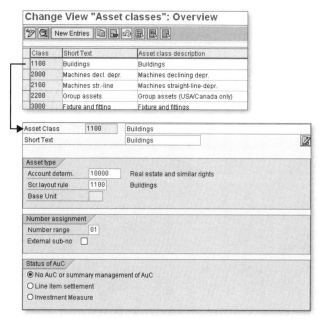

Figure 6.12 Asset Class Configuration

Define Depreciation Areas

In this step, you define your depreciation areas according to your legal or business requirements. Depreciation areas are identified by two-digit numeric keys. You can enter the different depreciation terms (a combination of depreciation keys, useful life, and screen layout) in the asset class or directly in the asset master record of the particular asset. This enables you, for example, to use straight-line depreciation for your internal accounting and declining-balance depreciation for external reporting.

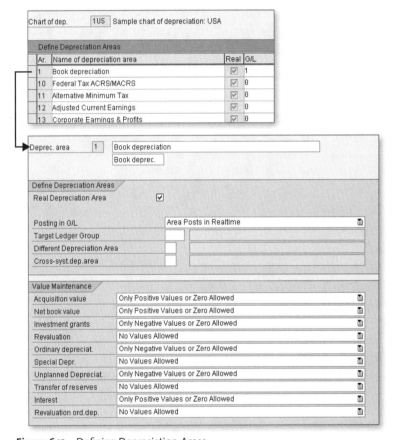

Figure 6.13 Defining Depreciation Areas

You can go to the configuration screen, shown in Figure 6.13, for defining depreciation areas using the following IMG path: SPRO • FINANCIAL ACCOUNTING (NEW) • ASSET ACCOUNTING • VALUATION • DEPRECIATION AREAS • DEFINE DEPRECIATION AREAS.

You must determine whether the transfer of asset values or depreciation from a depreciation area should be automatically posted to the general ledger. In the VALUE MAINTENANCE section, define the type of value management that is allowed for acquisition value and net book value. The standard setting is ONLY POSITIVE VALUES OR ZERO ALLOWED in all areas in which you want to depreciate your asset.

Next, we'll configure the transfer of acquisition and production costs (APC) values.

Specify Transfer of APC Values

In this step, you define the transfer rules for posting values from one depreciation area to another. These settings allow you to ensure that certain depreciation areas have identical asset values posted to them. You can configure the settings for the transfer of APC values through the following IMG path: SPRO • FINANCIAL ACCOUNTING (NEW) • ASSET ACCOUNTING • VALUATION • DEPRECIATION AREAS • SPECIFY TRANSFER OF APC VALUES (Transaction OABC). Either way, you'll see the screen displayed in Figure 6.14.

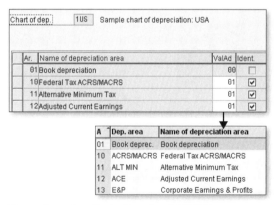

Figure 6.14 Specify the Transfer of APC Values

Select the depreciation area that should be used for transferring values to your selected depreciation areas. The standard system setting copies the asset balance sheet values from depreciation area 01 to all other depreciation areas during postings. Note, however, that you need only carry out this step if you want to copy posting values from a depreciation area other than 01.

Next we look at specifying the transfer of depreciation terms.

Specify Transfer of Depreciation Terms

In this configuration step, you set up rules for transferring depreciation terms from one depreciation area to another, to ensure that certain depreciation areas are uniformly depreciated. The IMG path for configuring this step is SPRO • FINANCIAL ACCOUNTING (NEW) • ASSET ACCOUNTING • VALUATION • DEPRECIATION AREAS • SPECIFY TRANSFER OF DEPRECIATION TERMS (Transaction OABD). In the screen that appears, shown in Figure 6.15, use the TTR column to specify the depreciation area from which the depreciation terms should be copied for the dependent depreciation areas.

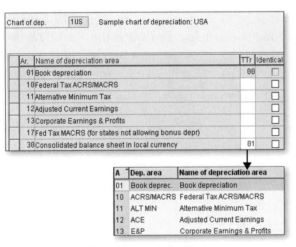

Figure 6.15 Transferring Depreciation Terms

Next we look at determining depreciation areas in the asset classes.

Determine Depreciation Areas in the Asset Classes

In this step, you configure the settings to determine the depreciation terms that should be used in your asset classes. The assets in an asset class normally use the same depreciation terms, that is, depreciation key, useful life, and screen layout. When creating new assets in the system, you don't have to maintain the depreciation terms because these values are defaulted from the settings in the asset classes.

You can configure these settings by either using the IMG path SPRO • FINANCIAL ACCOUNTING (NEW) • ASSET ACCOUNTING • VALUATION • DETERMINE DEPRECIATION AREAS IN THE ASSET CLASSES or by using Transaction OAYZ, as shown in Figure 6.16.

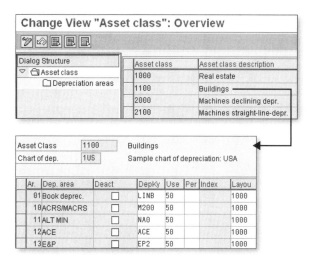

Figure 6.16 Define Depreciation Areas in Asset Classes

In the area specifications of your asset class, enter the depreciation key, useful life, and screen layout rule, as shown in Figure 6.16.

> **Note**
>
> As already discussed, we won't go into details on how to configure the depreciation keys and their related settings, If you are interested in understanding these settings, refer to our first book: *SAP ERP Financials: Configuration and Design*.

Now, let's define how depreciation areas post to SAP General Ledger.

Define How Depreciation Areas Post to SAP General Ledger

In this configuration step, you define how your depreciation areas post depreciations to SAP General Ledger. If you look at the standard depreciation areas in the reference chart of depreciation provided by the system, you can see that they are set up so that book depreciation area 01 automatically posts APC transactions to SAP General Ledger online. You can automatically post transactions from other depreciation areas to SAP General Ledger using periodic processing. (You must always use periodic processing to post depreciations to SAP General Ledger.)

The menu path for this configuration step is SPRO • Financial Accounting (New) • Asset Accounting • Integration with the General Ledger • Define How Depreciation Areas Post to General Ledger.

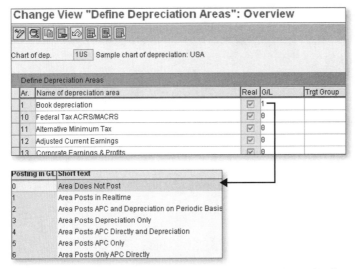

Figure 6.17 Define How Depreciation Areas Post to SAP General Ledger

As shown in Figure 6.17, you need to specify how your depreciation areas should post to SAP General Ledger by selecting from these options:

- ▶ 0 - Area Does Not Post
  No values are posted to SAP General Ledger.

- ▶ 1 - Area Posts in Realtime
  Assets are posted in SAP General Ledger in real time.

- ▶ 2 - Area Posts APC and Depreciation on Periodic Basis
  Assets are periodically posted to SAP General Ledger.

- ▶ 3 - Area Posts Depreciation Only
  Only depreciations are posted to SAP General Ledger.

- ▶ 4 – Area Posts APC Directly and Depreciation
  APC values are directly posted with depreciation to SAP General Ledger.

- 5 – Area Posts APC Only
  APC values are only posted to SAP General Ledger.
- 6 – Area Posts only APC Directly
  APC values are only posted directly to SAP General Ledger.

Next, we examine another important concept from an integration point of view: activating account assignment objects.

Activate Account Assignment Objects

In this step, you configure settings for additional account assignment objects (e.g., cost center, fund centers, internal orders, etc.) during posting in AA. This setting makes postings to the account assignment objects, such as cost centers, during the depreciation posting run every month (for example). If this setting isn't completed, the system displays an error message during the depreciation posting run saying that this assignment setting is missing.

The IMG path for activating the account assignment objects is SPRO • Financial Accounting (New) • Asset Accounting • Integration with GL • Additional Account Assignment Objects • Activate Account Assignment Objects, which leads you to the screen shown in Figure 6.18.

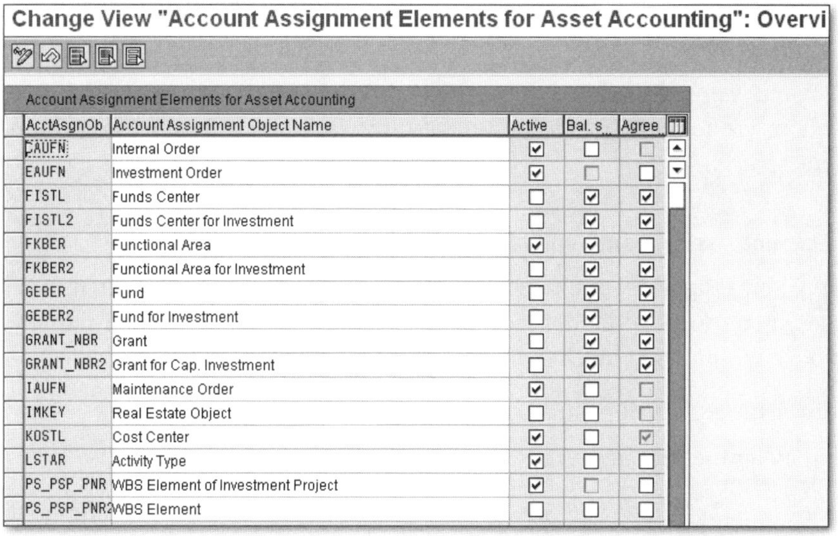
Change View "Account Assignment Elements for Asset Accounting": Overvi

Account Assignment Elements for Asset Accounting

AcctAsgnOb	Account Assignment Object Name	Active	Bal. s	Agree
CAUFN	Internal Order	☑	☐	☐
EAUFN	Investment Order	☑	☐	☐
FISTL	Funds Center	☐	☑	☑
FISTL2	Funds Center for Investment	☐	☑	☑
FKBER	Functional Area	☑	☑	☐
FKBER2	Functional Area for Investment	☐	☑	☑
GEBER	Fund	☐	☑	☑
GEBER2	Fund for Investment	☐	☑	☑
GRANT_NBR	Grant	☐	☑	☑
GRANT_NBR2	Grant for Cap. Investment	☐	☑	☑
IAUFN	Maintenance Order	☑	☐	☐
IMKEY	Real Estate Object	☐	☐	☐
KOSTL	Cost Center	☑	☐	☑
LSTAR	Activity Type	☑	☐	☐
PS_PSP_PNR	WBS Element of Investment Project	☑	☐	☐
PS_PSP_PNR2	WBS Element	☐	☐	☐

Figure 6.18 Activate Account Assignment Elements for Asset Accounting

For each account assignment object, you can make the following selections:

▶ ACTIVE
Activate the account assignment objects you need for AA.

▶ BALANCE SHEET
Indicate whether the account assignment object is relevant to the balance sheet. If you have specified this, you can no longer change the account assignment object directly in the asset master record once the asset has been capitalized; you must create a new asset and transfer that asset to the new one to make this change.

▶ AGREEMENT
Specify whether the account assignment object you entered at the time of posting should match the account assignment object entered in the asset master record. If you set this indicator, you cannot change the account assignment object when posting.

Note that to allow the posting of transactions to SAP General Ledger, you have to ensure that the account assignment objects you want to use are available for input by using the field status of posting keys 70 (debit asset) and 75 (credit asset). You must also ensure that the field status group of the posted accounts are consistent. You can configure the field status settings of posting keys using menu path SPRO • FINANCIAL ACCOUNTING • ASSET ACCOUNTING • INTEGRATION WITH THE GENERAL LEDGER • CHANGE THE FIELD STATUS VARIANT OF THE ASSET G/L ACCOUNTS.

In the previous step, we defined the settings to activate the account assignment objects. Next, we look at specifying the account assignment types for account assignment objects.

Specify Account Assignment Types for Account Assignment Objects

In this step, you assign account assignment types to the following account assignment objects: company code, depreciation area, and transaction type. These are the possible account assignment types for account assignment objects:

▶ Periodic postings (for all postings other than depreciation)

▶ Account assignment of depreciation

If you want to assign both account assignment types to an account assignment object, you have to create at least two table entries for the account assignment object, as shown in Figure 6.19.

The IMG path to complete this configuration is SPRO • FINANCIAL ACCOUNTING (NEW) • ASSET ACCOUNTING • INTEGRATION WITH GENERAL LEDGER • ADDITIONAL ACCOUNT ASSIGNMENT OBJECTS • SPECIFY ACCOUNT ASSIGNMENT TYPES FOR ACCOUNT ASSIGNMENT OBJECTS, or you can use Transaction ACSET.

You should create a generic entry using an asterisk (*) for the transaction type because the system uses the account assignment type you entered for all transaction types for that account assignment object in both the company code and the depreciation area.

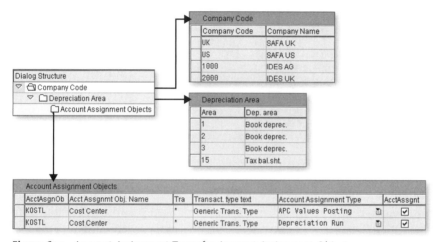

Figure 6.19 Account Assignment Types for Account Assignment Objects

In this configuration activity, you should activate all of the account assignment types you need, although cost center is usually sufficient for most solutions. You don't have to delete the ones you don't need; you can deactivate them and activate them again later if you need them. As mentioned before, it's important that you complete the configuration of activating account assignment objects and specify account assignment types for account assignment objects before you can run the new depreciation program RAPOST2000. Otherwise, the system gives you error messages related to missing cost centers or internal orders assignments at the time of the depreciation run.

Up to this point, we've completed the main configuration of all organizational elements and settings related to AA. Next, we complete the configuration settings from an Investment Management point of view, which enables us to use capital investment orders and project systems for capitalizing assets.

6.2.2 Core Configuration of Investment Management

In this section, we discuss the settings that enable us to use internal orders as investment measures, including the following:

- Define asset classes for AuC.
- Define order types.
- Define an investment profile.
- Define a budget profile.
- Define tolerance limits for availability controls.
- Maintain an allocation structure.
- Maintain a settlement profile.

Let's begin with the definition of asset classes for AuC.

Define Asset Classes for AuC

In this configuration step, we look at the specific settings for the asset class for assets under construction (AuC) (The settings for the rest of the asset classes were covered in previous sections.) *Assets under construction* are special tangible assets that need to be categorized separately in the balance sheet during their construction or assembly phase. After they are ready to be used by your company, you transfer them to the final asset so that depreciation can be charged to them for the span of their useful life.

To create an asset class for AuC, use the following IMG path: SPRO • INVESTMENT MANAGEMENT • INTERNAL ORDERS AS INVESTMENT MEASURES • MASTER DATA • ASSETS UNDER CONSTRUCTION • DEFINE ASSET CLASSES. In the CHANGE VIEW "ASSET CLASSES": OVERVIEW screen, click the NEW ENTRIES button. The system takes you to the CHANGE VIEW "ASSET CLASSES": DETAILS screen, as shown in Figure 6.20.

From an Investment Management point of view, the most important field here is the INVESTMENT MEASURE filed in the STATUS OF AUC section. After you have selected this button, the system then recognizes all of the assets created under this asset class as related to Investment Management, and no direct postings, such as vendor invoices or transfers, are allowed; for example, you could not post a vendor invoice using Transaction 100 (External Asset Acquisition).

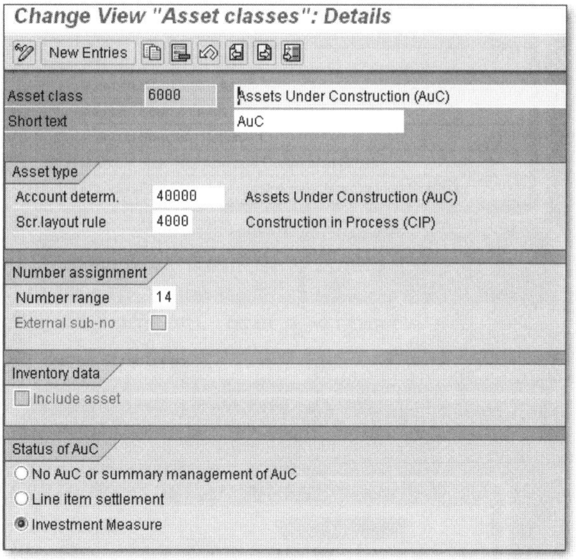

Figure 6.20 Define Assets Under Construction Asset Class

We also recommend that you use a separate number range for AuC classes, so that you can easily distinguish AuC assets from normal assets. The process for creating account determination for AuC — which must be linked to the respective balance sheet accounts and screen layout — is exactly the same as those of other asset classes, explained in the previous sections.

In the next step, you must define a unique order type for capital investment orders. Note that we don't cover the complete internal order accounting configuration here because the assumption is that all of the related settings will already have been completed; we are just creating another order type for the investment orders to explain our process.

> **Note**
>
> If you need information about the complete configuration for internal order accounting, refer our first book: *SAP ERP Financials: Configuration and Design*.

Define Order Types

One of the most important concepts in internal order accounting is the *order type*; you always create an internal order with reference to an order type. Order types pass on certain settings to the internal orders that are created with reference to that order type. They are created at the client level and are available to any controlling area within that client. In general, there are four types of orders:

▶ **Overhead cost order**
These monitor costs related to internal activities settled to cost centers.

▶ **Investment order**
These monitor costs related to internal activities settled to fixed assets. (This is the relevant order type for our discussion, so we cover only this type in detail.)

▶ **Accrual order**
These offset postings for accrued costs calculated in the Controlling (CO) component.

▶ **Orders with revenues**
These capture revenue that is not part of the core business of the company's operations.

To define order types, use the following IMG path: SPRO • Investment Manage-ment • Internal Orders as Investment Measures • Master Data • Orders • Define Order Types (Transaction KOT2). The Change View "Order Types": Over-view screen appears. To create a new order type, click the New Entries button.

In the next screen, enter the "01" order category (for internal orders), and press Enter. The Display View "Order Types": Details screen appears, as shown in Figure 6.21. Enter the information in the respective sections, as outlined in the following list.

▶ Settlement Prof.
Enter the settlement profile ID, which controls the settlement logic and origin structures. We look into creating a unique settlement profile for this order type later in this section.

▶ Planning Profile
Enter the planning profile ID that should be the default setting for this order type. This controls the settings for planning with internal orders associated with this order type.

▶ Budget Profile
Enter the budget profile ID for this order type, which controls the budgeting-related settings within orders. You use this to activate the budget availability

control settings for your orders. We look into creating the budget profile for this order type later in this section.

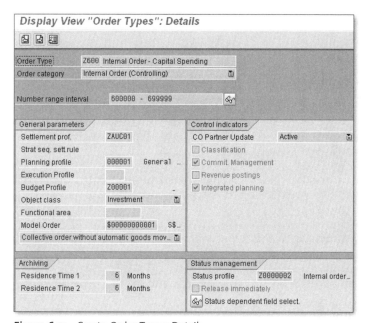

Figure 6.21 Create Order Types: Details

▶ OBJECT CLASS
Object classes help you categorize your controlling objects according to their respective business function so that you can analyze them from different business perspectives. Four object classes are available: OVERHEAD, PRODUCTION, INVESTMENT, and PROFITABILITY ANALYSIS AND SALES. For our order type, the relevant class is INVESTMENT.

▶ CO PARTNER UPDATE
You configure this field for updating orders during CO cost allocations. You have three options: ACTIVE, SEMI-ACTIVE, and NOT ACTIVE.

The standard system setting is SEMI-ACTIVE, which means that during settlements between orders, both records are updated; however, during settlement between cost centers and internal orders, cost center records are not updated with the order details.

▶ COMMIT. MANAGEMENT
If you want to activate commitment management, set this flag. This lets you track commitments at the time of purchase requisitions, purchase orders (POs), and so on. For capital investment orders, we set this flag so that commitments can be tracked.

▶ REVENUE POSTINGS
If you want to post revenues to your orders, set this flag.

▶ INTEGRATED PLANNING
Set this flag if you want Profit Center Accounting (PCA) to be updated with internal order planning.

▶ STATUS PROFILE
If you have activated general status management, you must enter the status profile ID.

▶ RELEASE IMMEDIATELY
If you set this flag, orders with this type will be released immediately upon creation.

After you've entered all of the details, click the SAVE button, and the system creates your order type.

Next, we look at the important setting involved in maintaining an investment profile. This is a prerequisite for using the investment orders as capital investment measures.

Define Investment Profile

When you create the capital investment measure, the investment profile controls the following activities:

▶ Creation of an AuC related to the capital investment measure
▶ Creation of master data for the depreciation simulation and forecast

To create your own investment profile, use the following menu path: SPRO • INVESTMENT MANAGEMENT • INTERNAL ORDERS AS INVESTMENT MEASURES • MASTER DATA • DEFINE INVESTMENT PROFILE (Transaction OITA).

In the CHANGE VIEW "INVESTMENT PROFILE": OVERVIEW screen, click the NEW ENTRIES button. In the next screen, shown in Figure 6.22, enter the information shown in the following list. Note that this list covers only the most important fields.

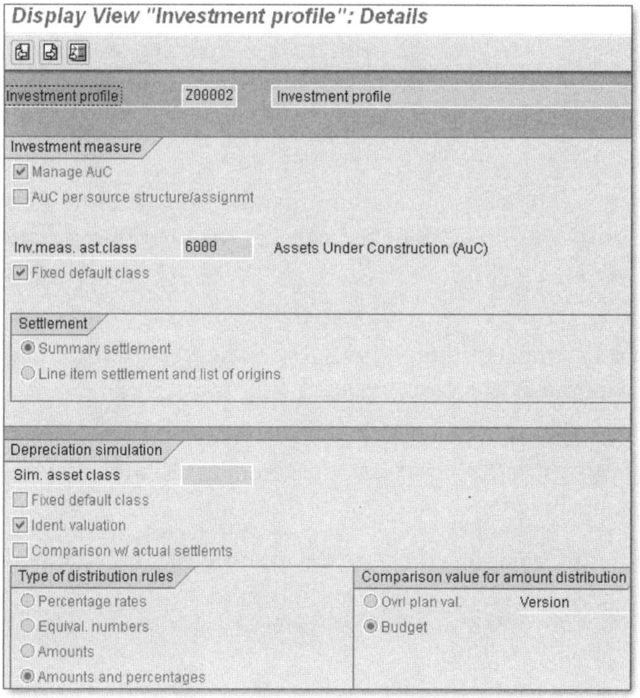

Figure 6.22 Creating an Investment Profile

- ▶ INVESTMENT PROFILE
  Enter the investment profile ID and its description.

- ▶ MANAGE AUC
  Set this indicator if you want the system to automatically create an AuC for each assigned order or WBS element (this is covered during the project-related process explained later in this chapter). In our case, we set this flag so that the AuC is automatically created when a new investment order is created.

- ▶ INV.MEAS.AST.CLASS
  Enter the asset class that should be used by the system to provide default values for the AuC linked to the investment measure. (You can change this when you create the investment measure.)

- ▶ FIXED DEFAULT CLASS
  By setting this flag, you cannot manually enter the asset class when you create the investment measure. The system then uses the asset class entered in the investment profile as a default value.

▶ SUMMARY SETTLEMENT
Select this button if you want to settle costs to either all debits or to certain cost elements in summary form to various receivers. For our investment profile, we choose the SUMMARY SETTLEMENT option.

▶ IDENT. VALUATION
Set this indicator if you want the system to ensure that the same depreciation start date and depreciation terms for each of the parts of the distributions are used. For our example, we set this flag.

▶ AMOUNTS AND PERCENTAGES
Set this indicator if you want the distribution rules for the depreciation simulation to be in the form of amounts and percentages.

▶ BUDGET
If you select this indicator, the system compares the total depreciation simulation amounts to the budgeted amounts.

After entering the preceding information, click the SAVE button, and the system generates your investment profile.

Next, we look at the budget profile settings.

Define Budget Profile

In this configuration step, you create budget profiles to allocate budgets to your investment orders. You can create your own budget profiles or use the standard ones offered with the system.

To create an investment profile, use the following menu path: SPRO • INVESTMENT MANAGEMENT • INTERNAL ORDERS AS INVESTMENT MEASURES • PLANNING AND BUDGETING • MAINTAIN BUDGET PROFILE (Transaction OKOB). In the CHANGE VIEW "BUDGET PROFILE FOR CO ORDERS": OVERVIEW screen, click the NEW ENTRIES button. In the next screen, shown in Figure 6.23, enter the information shown in the following list.

▶ BUDGET PROFILE
Enter the budget profile ID in this field.

▶ TEXT
Enter a description of your budget profile in this field.

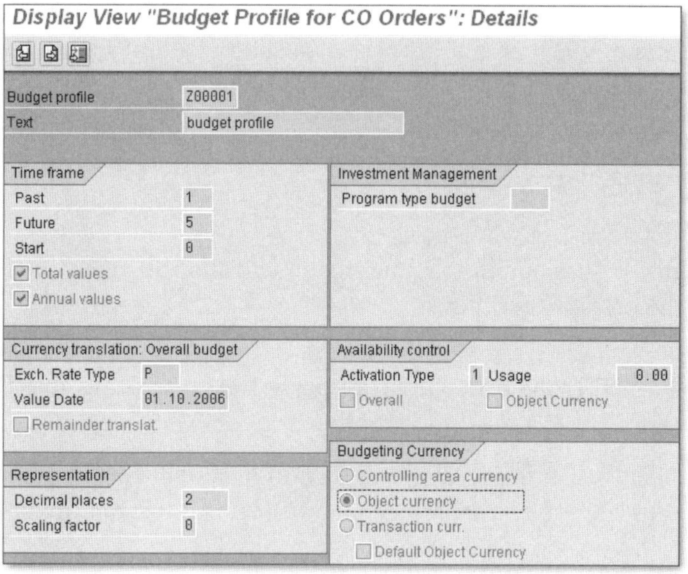

Figure 6.23 Maintain Budget Profile Details

▶ PAST
In this field, enter the value that represents how far in the past you want to plan/budget, using the start year (discussed later in this list) as the reference point.

▶ FUTURE
In this field, enter the value that represents how far in the future you want to plan/budget, using the start year (discussed later in this list) as the reference point.

▶ START
This value determines the start year for planning and budgeting, and also acts as a reference value for calculating the current, past, and future fiscal years (discussed in the previous list items).

▶ TOTAL VALUES
This setting controls whether the budgeting can be done for total values.

▶ ANNUAL VALUES
This setting controls whether the budgeting can be done for annual values.

▶ EXCH.RATE TYPE
Enter the exchange rate type that should be used to convert the budgets in a foreign currency into the local currency.

▶ ACTIVATION TYPE
This indicator determines whether and how the availability control should be activated. There are three options:

  ▶ 0: Cannot be activated.

  ▶ 1: Automatic activation during budget allocation.

  ▶ 2: Background activation.

For our budget profile, we use option 1, for automatic activation as soon as you enter a budget for the investment order.

▶ OBJECT CURRENCY
This option controls whether the budgeting currency is the same as the object currency, which, in our case, is an investment order.

After entering these details, click the SAVE button, and the system creates your budget profile. We do this later in the chapter to enter a budget against our investment order.

Next, we look at defining settings for tolerance limits for budget availability control.

Define Tolerance Limits for Availability Control

In this configuration activity, you define the controls that will help you identify the possibility of a budget being overspent, which automatically triggers either a warning or error message, depending on the settings you make. To define the tolerances, use the following menu path SPRO • INVESTMENT MANAGEMENT • INTERNAL ORDERS AS INVESTMENT MEASURES • PLANNING AND BUDGETING • DEFINE TOLERANCE LIMITS FOR AVAILABILITY CONTROL. The initial screen is shown in Figure 6.24.

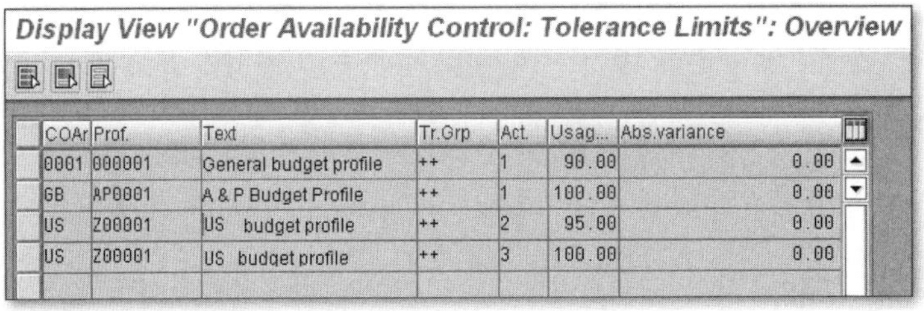

COAr	Prof.	Text	Tr.Grp	Act.	Usag...	Abs.variance	
0001	000001	General budget profile	++	1	90.00	0.00	
GB	AP0001	A & P Budget Profile	++	1	100.00	0.00	
US	Z00001	US budget profile	++	2	95.00	0.00	
US	Z00001	US budget profile	++	3	100.00	0.00	

Display View "Order Availability Control: Tolerance Limits": Overview

Figure 6.24 Define Tolerance Limits for Availability Control

In the screen shown in Figure 6.24, enter the information provided in the following list:

- COAr
  Enter the controlling area in this column.

- Prof.
  Enter the budget profile ID.

- Text
  Enter the budget profile text.

- TrGrp
  Enter the activity group for which you are defining the availability control. We enter ++, that is, All Activity Types.

- Act.
  This indicator controls the type of action that should be taken after the defined tolerance limit is exceeded. Depending on your requirements, you can enter one of the three options:

  - 1: Warning.

  - 2: Warning with mail to person responsible.

  - 3: Error message.

- Usage in %
  This is a percentage value that represents the fund commitments to the overall budget in the form of a ratio. If this percentage value is exceeded, the system triggers the action explained in the preceding list item.

- Abs.Variance
  If you enter an amount here, the system checks whether the difference between the assigned funds and the budgeted amount exceeds this amount, and triggers the availability control using one of the actions explained previously.

In the next section, we look at some of the settings related to the settlement process. Settlement is a process where costs entered on an object (such as a cost center or internal order) are allocated to another object (such as a different cost center or an asset) as part of the month-end process. The former object in this process is called the *sender* object, and the latter object is called the *receiver* object. Now that you understand the basic definition of settlement, we can move on to understand the maintenance of the allocation structure, which helps in the settlement process.

Maintain the Allocation Structure

As part of the settlement process, you allocate the costs incurred on sender objects using primary and secondary cost elements to the receiver objects. An allocation structure is comprised of one or more settlement assignments that define which costs (entered through cost elements) are to be settled to which receivers (cost centers, assets, internal orders, etc.).

To define an allocation structure, use the following menu path: SPRO • INVESTMENT MANAGEMENT • INTERNAL ORDERS AS INVESTMENT MEASURES • SETTLEMENT • MAINTAIN ALLOCATION STRUCTURES. The initial screen is shown in Figure 6.25.

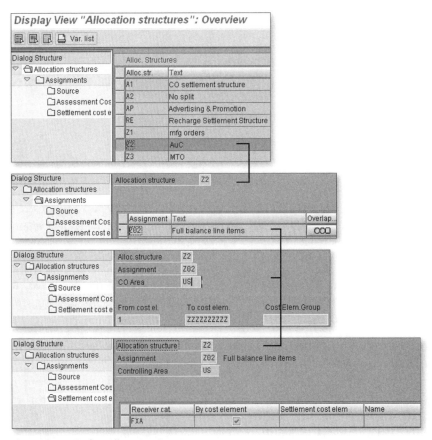

Figure 6.25 Define Allocation Structure

After you access this screen, follow these steps:

1. Click the New Entries button, and enter the allocation structure ID with a brief description in the Text field. Press `Enter`.

2. Click the allocation structure to select it, and then, from the Dialog Structure area, double-click the Assignment field. Enter the assignment ID and text, and press `Enter`. You can see an orange radio button in the Overlapping status column, which confirms that the cost element data is entered as a source in your structure.

3. Click the Assignment line created in the previous step. From the Dialog Structure area, double-click the Source field. Enter the range of cost elements in the From Cost El. and To Cost Elem. fields, or enter a cost element group ID in the Cost Elem.Group field. Press `Enter`.

4. From the Dialog Structure area, double-click the Settlement Cost Elements field and select FXA (fixed assets) in the Receiver Cat. column. Set the flag in the By Cost Element column. By setting this flag, you are saying that the debit cost element will also be the credit cost element during the settlement process.

5. From the Dialog Structure area, double-click the Assignments field. This time you can see that the Overlapping check status is green, which means that it is okay to save your allocation structure settings.

You have now successfully completed the definition of an allocation structure.

Next, let's look at the definition of a settlement profile itself, which uses the already-configured allocation structure in its definition.

Maintain Settlement Profiles

In this configuration activity, you define different control parameters for carrying out settlements. Note that you need to define the settlement profile first and then enter the settlement rule in the sender object. Also note that the settlement parameters cannot be maintained during the settlement to the receiver objects, so you must save the settlement profile in your order type defined in the previous steps.

To define a settlement profile, use the following menu path: SPRO • INVESTMENT MANAGEMENT • INTERNAL ORDERS AS INVESTMENT MEASURES • SETTLEMENT • MAINTAIN SETTLEMENT PROFILES.

In the screen shown in Figure 6.26, click the NEW ENTRIES button. In the resulting screen, enter the information from the following list.

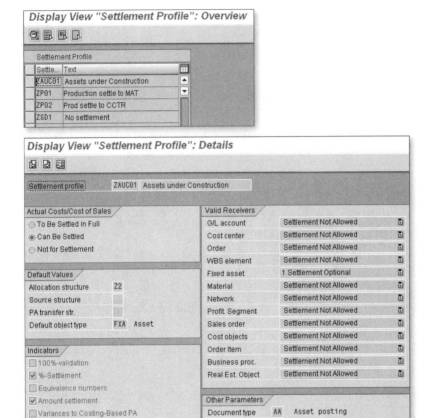

Figure 6.26 Maintain Settlement Profile

- SETTLEMENT PROFILE
  Enter the settlement profile ID and a brief description.

- ACTUAL COSTS/COST OF SALES
  Define the settings for settling the actual costs or cost of sales. You have three options:

  - TO BE SETTLED IN FULL: Select this option if you want to ensure that there is a zero balance at the time of closing; otherwise, the system gives an error message.

  - CAN BE SETTLED: Select this option if a zero balance isn't mandatory.

▶ NOT FOR SETTLEMENT: Select this option if you don't want the actual costs to be settled from this object.

▶ ALLOCATION STRUCTURE
Enter the allocation structure created in the previous steps in this field.

▶ SOURCE STRUCTURE
This structure is used when you want to settle the costs incurred on the sender to multiple receivers — which is split by cost elements — thereby retaining the source information.

▶ DEFAULT OBJECT TYPE
You can maintain a default receiver object such as a fixed asset (FXA) in this settlement profile.

▶ 100%-VALIDATION
Set this flag if you want to ensure that the percentage entered in the settlement rules total to 100%. In this case, the system issues a warning message if the total is not equal to 100%.

▶ %-SETTLEMENT
Set this flag if you want the settlement rule to determine the percentage costs to be settled for distributing costs.

▶ AMOUNT SETTLEMENT
Setting this flag allows you to define certain amounts to be settled to a specific cost object, such as an internal order or cost center.

▶ VALID RECEIVERS
Here you define the valid receivers for this settlement profile. For all options, as you can see in Figure 6.26, there are three settings allowed:

  ▶ SETTLEMENT OPTIONAL: Select this setting if you want to allow settlement to one of the receivers.

  ▶ SETTLEMENT REQUIRED: Select this setting if you want at least one of the settlement rules to have that receiver (G/L account, fixed asset, etc.).

  ▶ SETTLEMENT NOT ALLOWED: Select this setting if you do not want to allow settlement to a specific receiver.

Now that you've successfully completed the configuration settings for the AA organizational elements and related settings from an Investment Management point of view, let's discuss the account determination settings that link AA with SAP General Ledger in real time.

6.3   FI-AA Account Determination

From an integration point of view, the account determination setting is the key concept for this chapter. In this section, we look into how the settings in the organizational element section, together with the master data section (explained later), affect account determination settings. We also briefly cover the concept of parallel accounting in SAP General Ledger (the New General Ledger) from an AA point of view (to see how it impacts integration).

> **Note**
>
> We explain the account determination concept and configuration settings before going into any processes so that you will be familiar with the settings discussed in each step.

6.3.1   Define Accounts in Account Determination Settings

As previously discussed, account determination is used to link AA with SAP General Ledger by assigning SAP General Ledger accounts (the balance sheet accounts, special reserve accounts, and depreciation accounts) for AA postings (see Figure 6.27). To configure these settings, use the following menu path: SPRO • FINANCIAL ACCOUNTING (NEW) • ASSET ACCOUNTING • INTEGRATION WITH GENERAL LEDGER • ASSIGN G/L ACCOUNTS (Transaction AO90).

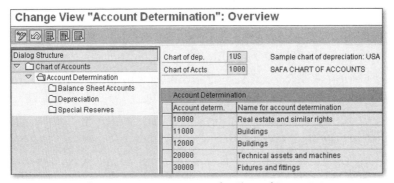

Figure 6.27   Define Account Determination for Chart of Depreciation

For each account determination and depreciation area combination you defined (refer to Section 6.2, Core Configuration of Asset Accounting and Investment Management), you need to specify the SAP General Ledger accounts that are posted for transactions related to acquisition (balance sheet), depreciation, and revaluation, as we'll see in detail next.

Balance Sheet Accounts

In the left pane, select BALANCE SHEET ACCOUNTS in the DIALOG STRUCTURE area. As shown in Figure 6.28, enter the SAP General Ledger accounts to which you want to post the acquisition and production costs, down payment accounts, gain and loss accounts on sale of fixed assets, and so on.

Chart of dep.	1US	Sample chart of depreciation: USA
Chart of Accts	CAUS	Chart of accounts - United States
Account determ.	30000	Fixtures and fittings
Deprec. area	1	Book depreciation

Acquisition account assignment

Acquisition:Acquis. and production costs	21000	Office equipment
Acquisition: down payments		
Contra account: Acquisition value	199990	Acquisition - dispos
Down-payments clearing account		
Acquisition from affiliated company	199991	Clear- Affil.Com. FA
Revenue frm post-capitaliz:	251000	Extraordinary Income

Retirement account assignment

Loss made on asset retirement w/o reven.	200010	Loss on assets scrap
Clearing acct. revenue from asset sale	825000	Suspense a/c - dispo
Gain from asset sale	250000	Profits on disposal/
Loss from asset sale	200000	Loss on disposal/sal
Clear.revenue sale to affil.company	825000	Suspense a/c - dispo

Figure 6.28 Balance Sheet Accounts for Acquisition

Depreciation Accounts

Next, select DEPRECIATION in the DIALOG STRUCTURE, and the screen shown in Figure 6.29 appears. In the fields on the right, define the accumulated depreciation account, depreciation expense account, unplanned depreciation accounts, and so on.

Ordinary depreciation account assignment		
Acc.dep. accnt.for ordinary depreciation	21010	Accumulated deprecia
Expense account for ordinary depreciat.	481000	Depreciation Expense
Expense account for ord. dep. below zero	481000	Depreciation Expense
Revenue from write-up on ord.deprec.	253000	Income from asset wr

Special depreciation account assignment		
Accumulated dep. account special dep.		
Expense account for special depreciation		
Expense account for spec.dep.below zero		
Revenue from write-up on special deprec.		

Unplanned depreciation account assignment		
Accumulated dep. account unpl. deprec.	21010	Accumulated deprecia
Expense account for unplanned deprec.	481000	Depreciation Expense
P&L act.unpl.dep.below 0	481000	Depreciation Expense
Revenue from write-up on unplnd. deprec.	253000	Income from asset wr

Figure 6.29 Accounts for Depreciation Postings

For special reserves, you need to select the depreciation area for which the calculation applies. In our scenario, we do not define this setting, but the configuration screen is the same as the two examples we looked at in Figures 6.28 and Figure 6.29.

Now let's look at another important integration setting: specifying the document type for posting depreciation.

6.3.2 Specify Document Type for Posting Depreciation

In this step, you assign the document type to the company code that should be used for posting depreciation in the system. The standard document type provided by SAP ERP is AF. The menu path to complete this configuration step is SPRO • FINANCIAL ACCOUNTING (NEW) • ASSET ACCOUNTING • INTEGRATION WITH GENERAL LEDGER • POST DEPRECIATION TO THE GENERAL LEDGER • SPECIFY DOCUMENT TYPE FOR POSTING OF DEPRECIATION (Transaction AO71). From the screen shown in Figure 6.30, enter a new document type, if it was created by you. If an appropriate document type exists, you can assign it by company code.

To post depreciation successfully using the new depreciation program RAPOST2000, you need to remove the BATCH INPUT ONLY flag in the document type AF because this new program doesn't create a batch session, and the depreciation run will fail with this setting active.

CoCo	Company Name	Doc.type	Description	
UK	SAFA UK	AF	Dep. postings	▲
US	SAFA US	AF	Dep. postings	▼
2000	IDES UK	AF	Dep. postings	
2200	IDES France	AF	Dep. postings	
2201	IDES France affiliate	AF	Dep. postings	
2700	IDES Schweiz	AF	Dep. postings	
3000	IDES US INC	AF	Dep. postings	

Figure 6.30 Assign Document Type for Posting Depreciation

6.3.3 Parallel Ledgers in SAP General Ledger and Integration with Asset Accounting

In this section, we briefly explain the concept of parallel ledgers in SAP General Ledger from an AA perspective. We don't go into great detail about the SAP General Ledger functionalities, which include the concepts of leading ledger, document splitting, and parallel ledgers; the idea here is to explain the parallel ledger concept from an AA point of view, so that you can see how integration has changed within SAP General Ledger.

> **Note**
>
> If you want to understand more about the SAP General Ledger functionalities, refer to our first book: SAP ERP Financials: Configuration and Design.

Many international companies are now required to generate multiple financial statements based on various accounting standards because they are subject to different sets of laws. For example, publicly listed companies in Europe are required to submit their consolidated financial statements according to not only their country-specific local legal accounting standards but also per the International Financial Reporting Standards (IFRS). The same is the case with companies in the United States because they are required to comply with U.S. Generally Accepted Accounting Principles (GAAP) accounting standards, as well as IFRS. The parallel accounting concept helps companies achieve this objective because postings and financial statement reports are made separately but simultaneously in accordance with all required accounting standards.

SAP General Ledger enables you to simultaneously maintain parallel ledgers per different accounting standards, a functionality not available in older releases. This new method is called *the ledger solution*. The concept is based on the fact that there is a leading ledger, 0L, which is the main general ledger (provided as a standard). Each company has exactly one leading ledger that uses the local currency, fiscal year variant, and posting variant assigned to your company code. In addition to the leading ledger, you can also define nonleading ledgers to simultaneously maintain information for different accounting standards. The leading ledger is the only ledger that updates CO, and you can only define one leading ledger in the system.

You keep parallel ledgers for all your groups, as well as local postings to meet different accounting standards. Each ledger represents one of the accounting standards you need to maintain in the system. As a standard functionality, the system posts to all ledgers simultaneously, unless you have configured the system differently or would like to post to a specific ledger at the time of data entry itself (which means that postings specific to accounting standards are made to specified ledgers only). All accounting transactions — customer invoices, vendor invoices, journal vouchers, and so on — are posted to all ledgers at the same time. (Some month-end processes, such as foreign currency valuation and asset depreciation, are affected by different accounting principles and are posted only to the necessary ledgers.)

After you activate SAP General Ledger, the system automatically creates the leading ledger (0L). To set up parallel accounting with the ledger solution, you need to create the nonleading ledgers for each of the accounting standards you plan to use for reporting. To define and activate the nonleading ledgers required for the ledger solution, use the following menu path: SPRO • FINANCIAL ACCOUNTING (NEW) • FINANCIAL ACCOUNTING BASIC SETTINGS (NEW) • LEDGERS • LEDGER • DEFINE LEDGERS FOR GENERAL LEDGER ACCOUNTING.

You create the ledgers at the client level and then activate and assign them to your relevant company codes. You must specify the local currency defined in the leading ledger as the local currency in the nonleading ledgers as well. The same is true for the second and third currencies. In other words, you can use multiple currencies in the nonleading ledgers as long as the leading ledger has them too.

When you create a ledger, the system automatically creates a ledger group with the same name. You can change the name of the ledger group, or you can combine any number of ledgers in a ledger group. Ledgers in the ledger group are combined for joint processing while performing a specific function.

In SAP General Ledger, AA can be configured to comply with various accounting standards, such as U.S. GAAP, IFRS, and local GAAP. Valuation differences arise due to different and diverse Asset Accounting treatments, normally at the time of asset acquisitions, depreciation, and retirement. SAP ERP uses the concept of depreciation areas (as explained earlier in this chapter) to reflect these valuation differences. You assign each depreciation area to a ledger group; for each depreciation area, you define the depreciation terms, useful life, and other parameters. The system then determines depreciation value for each depreciation area using the rules you've specified there. The system posts depreciation and the acquisition and production cost (APC) values separately for each depreciation area to the assigned ledgers.

In SAP General Ledger, you can use a wizard to help set up parallel valuation in AA. You can find the wizard by using the following menu path: SPRO • FINANCIAL ACCOUNTING (NEW) • ASSET ACCOUNTING • VALUATION • DEPRECIATION AREAS • SET UP AREAS FOR PARALLEL VALUATION.

To set up parallel accounting in AA, you are required to create the relevant depreciation areas and ledger groups. Depreciation area 01 is the master depreciation area, and you post the depreciation values of depreciation area 01 to all ledgers. The first step in parallel accounting is to assign the master depreciation area to the ledger group. In this step, you assign the master depreciation area 01 to the ledger group 0L. The ledger group of the master depreciation area 01 should contain the leading ledger 0L; this ensures that the values are updated in CO, so you can see the depreciation values by cost center. For the sake of simplicity, assume that your master depreciation area (01) valuates according to your local accounting principles, and depreciation area 25 uses valuation according to IFRS. Create a new depreciation area called *delta depreciation area, 60,* that will contain the difference between areas 25 and area 01. By using this new area, 60, you can post the APC differences to the ledger group that you use for IFRS valuation. Area 25 will post depreciation to the same ledger group as well.

> **Note**
>
> FI accounts that are posted in the ledger solution in SAP General Ledger are exactly the same ones in each depreciation area, which means you don't need to adjust the account determination settings explained earlier in this chapter.

With the necessary settings for the organizational elements and account determination in place, let's focus on the key master data elements from an integration point of view.

6.4 Master Data

In this section, our main focus is on the asset master record because master records related to investment orders and projects are covered as part of their related processes in the next sections. In this section, we are talking about standard fixed asset master records, not AuC (although AuC will also become final assets when they are completed) because the creation of AuC will be better explained as part of that process, rather than in this section.

Let's start with the creation of a standard asset master record.

Create Asset Master Record

An asset master record contains all of the necessary entries that highlight the properties of a specific asset: its name, capitalization date, cost center assignment, manufacturer's details, depreciation-related settings, and so on. The whole idea of an asset master record is to ensure that all of the important information about the asset is stored in this place, which will be used during postings to this asset.

The menu path to create an asset master record is SAP EASY ACCESS • ACCOUNTING • FINANCIAL ACCOUNTING • FIXED ASSETS • ASSET • CREATE • ASSET (Transaction AS01). In the CREATE ASSET: INITIAL SCREEN that appears, shown in Figure 6.31, select the asset class, company code, and number of similar assets. If you're creating multiple assets that are similar to each other, you can use the NUMBER OF SIMILAR ASSETS field to state the total number of similar assets you want created at the same time, and the system creates that many asset master records. You can use the REFERENCE fields by entering an existing ASSET number in the COMPANY CODE to create an asset quickly.

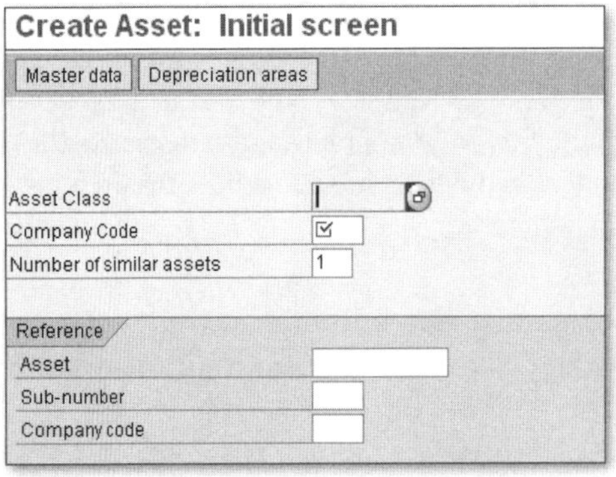

Figure 6.31 Create Asset: Initial Screen

Figure 6.32, Figure 6.33, and Figure 6.34 contain important integration fields, as outlined in the following list.

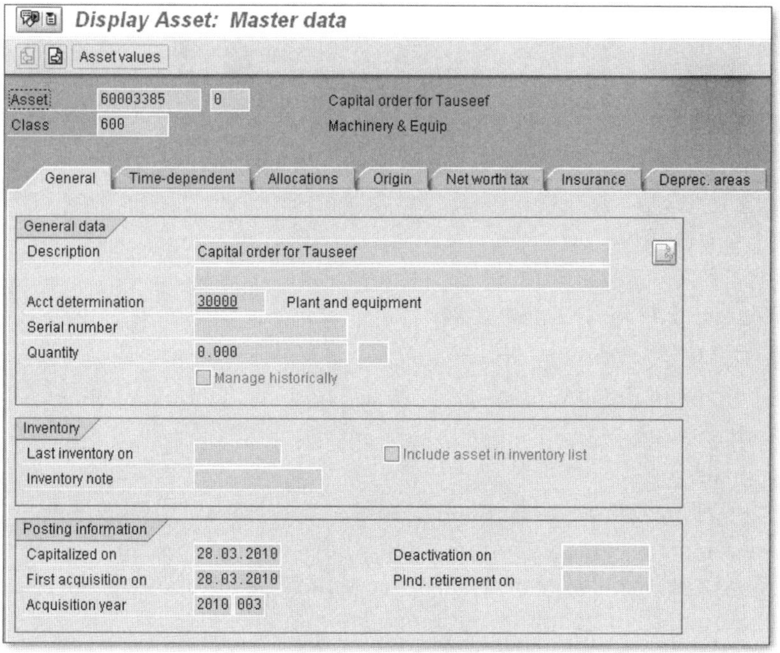

Figure 6.32 Create New Asset Master Data: General Tab

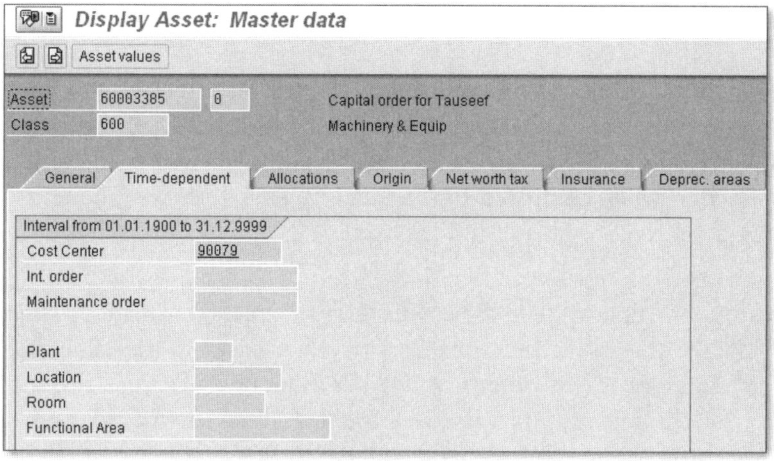

Figure 6.33 Create New Asset Master Data: Time-Dependent Tab

299

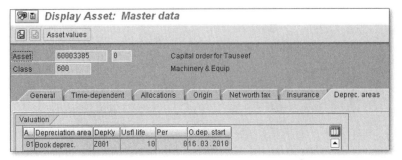

Figure 6.34 Create New Asset Master Data: Deprec. Areas Tab

► GENERAL tab
Holds the general data for the new asset.

   ► DESCRIPTION
   This is the name of the new asset. You can use both of the available lines for your description.

   ► ACCT DETERMINATION
   This is taken from the asset class entered in the first screen. This is an important field from an integration point of view; the system will use this account determination to link the general ledger accounts that are posted when an asset transaction is entered in the system.

   ► SERIAL NUMBER
   Enter the manufacturer's serial number because it will help you enquire about this asset from the manufacturer.

   ► QUANTITY
   Enter the quantity of the asset in this field. This QUANTITY field is used, for example, at the time of partial retirement, whereby the system will retire the proportionate value of the asset based on the quantity entered in the retirement transaction when compared to the quantity entered here. (The retirement transaction is covered later in the chapter.)

   ► CAPITALIZED ON
   When postings are first made to the asset, the system uses this field to assign the value date to the asset. The capitalization date is basically the value date of the asset. This date is very important because other postings, such as transfers, depreciations, and retirements, use this date to calculate the values that are posted for this asset in SAP General Ledger.

▶ Deactivation On

The system posts the value date of the retirement in this field when the asset is completely retired.

▶ First Acquisition On

This field is automatically set with the asset value date of the first acquisition posting.

▶ Time-Dependent tab

Holds important information about assignments to objects, such as cost centers, internal orders, and so on.

▶ Cost Center

Enter the cost center to which the postings are made for this asset. This is an important field from an integration point of view because it links an asset to the CCA component.

▶ Int. Order

You can allocate an internal order using this field. Again, just like the cost center assignment, this field is important because it assists with the flow of asset-related information to the internal order component within CO.

▶ Plant

Use this field to enter the plant assignment for this asset. This information can be used in AA for further analysis.

▶ Location

Enter the location of the asset in this field.

▶ Origin tab

Holds information about the origin of this asset (not shown in the figures).

▶ Vendor

Enter the vendor number from which the asset was purchased.

▶ Manufacturer

Enter the manufacturer details in this field, which help in making inquiries about the asset.

▶ Original Asset

Enter the legacy asset number to create a link with the SAP ERP asset number for reconciliation and audit trail purposes. After the AuC is settled, the system populates this field with the AuC number for future reference.

- ▶ DEPREC. AREAS tab
  Displays information about different depreciation areas and settings within depreciation areas.

  - ▶ VALUATION
    This displays settings for different depreciation areas, such as the depreciation keys, useful life in years and period, ordinary depreciation start date (which is provided by default from the capitalization date entered in the GENERAL tab), and so on. These are important fields because they are used to calculate depreciation values for monthly depreciation postings and also to keep track of the useful life and expired useful life when determining the profit or loss at the time of retirements.

After you entered the information, click the SAVE button, and the system generates an asset number from the number range assigned to the asset class for this newly created asset.

You have now created the asset master record and can move on to the individual steps in the asset lifecycle explained earlier in this chapter.

The next section first explains the process of asset acquisition through investment order and then takes it through the process where it will be settled to a final asset.

6.5 Asset Acquisition Through Investment Order

As explained earlier, you can acquire an asset using internal orders as investment measures and then accumulate the costs on that investment order, which is settled to an AuC on a periodic basis. After the asset is completed, the costs are transferred to the final asset. To understand this process, consider the following subprocesses:

- ▶ Create an investment order and AuC.
- ▶ Maintain budgets for investment orders.
- ▶ Post a vendor invoice.
- ▶ Perform a settlement of investment order to AuC.
- ▶ Perform a settlement of AuC to final asset.
- ▶ Change the investment order status to complete.

6.5.1 Create an Investment Order and Asset Under Construction (AuC)

In this step, we create the master record for an investment order using the order type that we configured in the previous sections. Because of the settings explained earlier, the system creates an AuC at the same time an investment order master record is created.

> **Note**
>
> We don't go into the details of every screen while creating the investment order but instead focus on the fields that are relevant for integration.

You can create an investment order using the following menu path: SAP MENU • ACCOUNTING • CONTROLLING • INTERNAL ORDERS • MASTER DATA • SPECIAL FUNCTIONS • ORDER • CREATE (Transaction KO01). The initial screen is shown in Figure 6.35.

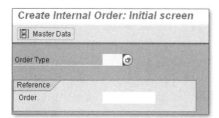

Figure 6.35 Create Internal Order: Initial Screen

In the CREATE INTERNAL ORDER: INITIAL SCREEN, enter the order type that we created earlier for investment orders in the ORDER TYPE field. Press ⎡Enter⎤. In the next screen, CREATE INTERNAL ORDER: MASTER DATA, enter the short description of the investment order in the SHORT TEXT field.

On the ASSIGNMENTS tab, shown in Figure 6.36, enter the company code, profit center, and responsible CCtr (cost center) in the relevant fields. The OBJECT CLASS field is automatically filled with INVESTMENT because of the settings we chose when creating the order type.

In the STATUS section of the CONTROL DATA tab, shown in Figure 6.37, the system provides the system status as CRTD (created) and the user status as IPRO (in process). In the CONTROL DATA section, the system automatically provides the currency of the company code, and the ORDER CATEGORY is set to 1, based on the order type settings configured earlier. We leave the STATISTICAL ORDER and PLAN-

INTEGRATED ORDER checkboxes unflagged because this is a real order that will need to be settled later; if you set the STATISTICAL ORDER flag, you will then be unable to settle it to AuC or final asset.

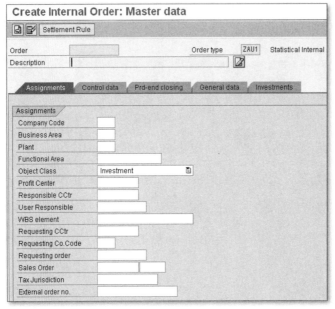

Figure 6.36　Create Internal Order: Assignments Tab

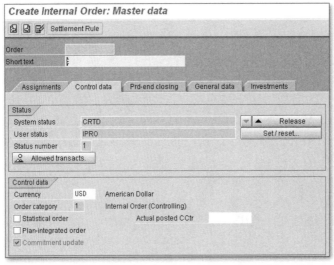

Figure 6.37　Create Internal Order: Master Data, Control Data Tab

On the INVESTMENTS tab, shown in Figure 6.38, the investment profile ID appears under the INVESTMENT MANAGEMENT section. The system automatically provides this information based on the settings made during configuration.

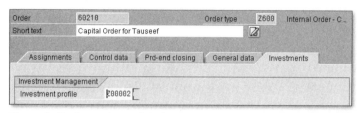

Figure 6.38 Create Internal Order: Master Data Investment, Measures Tab

After entering this information, click the SAVE button, and the system creates an investment order number from the number range assigned to the order type. Next, you should check whether the system automatically created the AuC based on prior configuration. To do this, go back to the investment order master record using Transaction KO02. Click the CONTROL DATA tab, and you should see the system status changed to CRTD AUC, as shown in Figure 6.39.

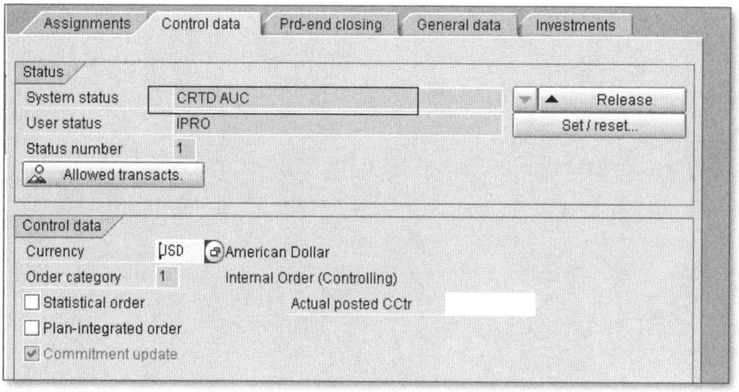

Figure 6.39 Investment Order: System Status Changes

From the menu bar, click EXTRAS • ASSET UNDER CONSTRUCTION, and the system shows the created AuC master data (Figure 6.40) but without the actual asset number. After you post the vendor invoice to this investment order, the system automatically creates the AuC number from the range assigned to the AuC asset class.

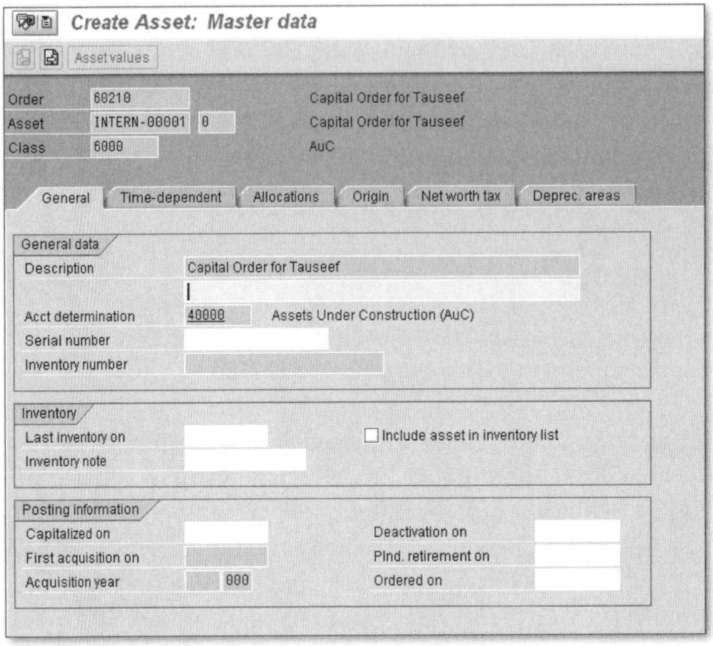

Figure 6.40 AuC Created with Investment Order

We have now completed the master data for both the investment order and AuC, meaning that we can now post an invoice. However, first we must change the status of the investment order to RELEASED, which is done by clicking the RELEASE button next to the SYSTEM STATUS field. The status changes to REL AUC, as shown in Figure 6.41. Vendor invoices can now be posted to this investment order.

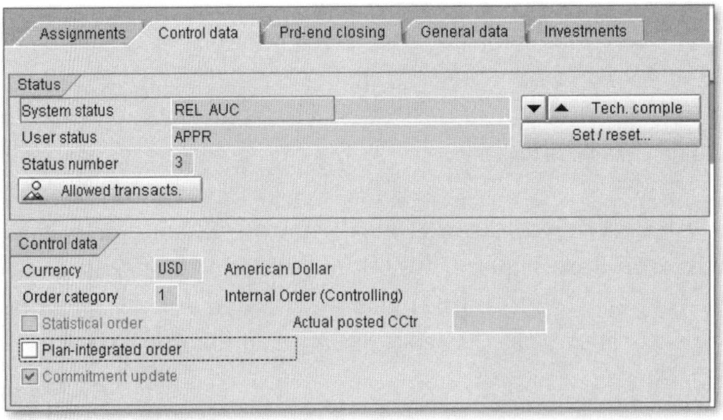

Figure 6.41 Investment Order: System Status Changes

Next, let's discuss the process of maintaining a specific budget on the investment order, which is important for controlling the availability of the budgeted amount to spend against that investment order.

6.5.2 Maintaining Budgets for Investment Orders

To maintain budgets on your investment order, use the following menu path: SAP EASY ACCESS • ACCOUNTING • CONTROLLING • INTERNAL ORDERS • BUDGETING • ORIGINAL BUDGET • CHANGE (Transaction KO22). In the resulting screen, shown in Figure 6.42, enter the investment order number in the ORDER field, and click the ORIGINAL BUDGET button.

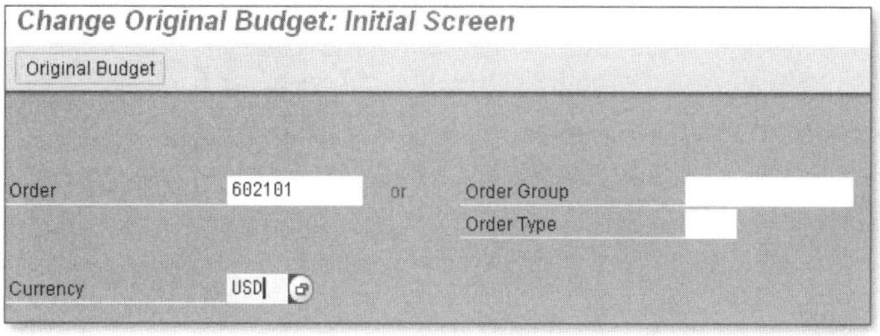

Figure 6.42 Maintain Budget for Investment Order

In the CHANGE ORIGINAL BUDGET: ANNUAL OVERVIEW screen, enter the total annual amount for the respective years in their respective rows. The total of all of these annual years should be equal to the Overall row, shown in Figure 6.43.

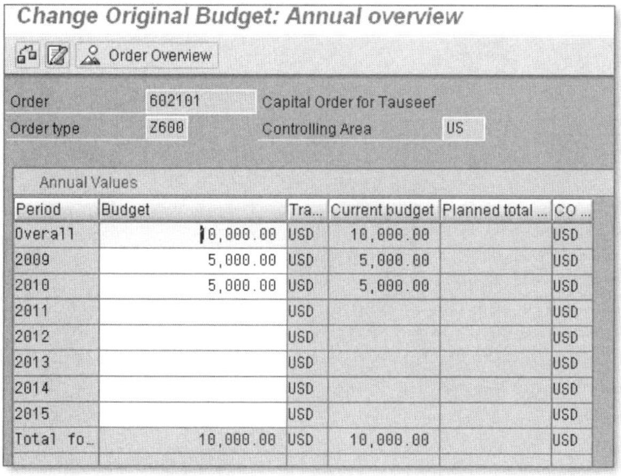

Figure 6.43 Maintain Budget for Investment Order: Annual Values

Click the SAVE button, and your budget is saved for the investment order. Recall that the way we set the budget profile and its settings, you will get a warning message when the budget reaches 95% and an error message when the budget reaches 100%, ensuring that no amount over and above the investment order's approved budget is posted.

In the next section, we post a vendor invoice to this investment order so that we can then settle it to AuC as part of the month-end process.

6.5.3 Posting a Vendor Invoice

Vendor invoices can be posted to the investment order either through the purchase order (PO) process or by using the direct vendor invoice through Accounts Payable (AP). We covered the process of vendor invoices through a PO in detail in Chapter 4, Integrating the Purchase-Order-to-Payment Process, so, for this example, we enter a direct vendor invoice through AP using SAP MENU • ACCOUNTING • FINANCIAL ACCOUNTING • VENDORS • DOCUMENT ENTRY • INVOICE or by using Transaction FB60 (Figure 6.44).

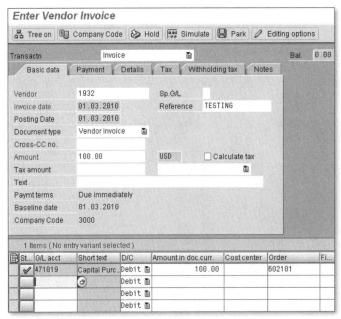

Figure 6.44 Entering a Vendor Invoice

In the ENTER VENDOR INVOICE screen, enter the information given in the following list:

▶ VENDOR
Enter the SAP ERP vendor number in this field.

▶ INVOICE DATE
Enter the invoice date here.

▶ REFERENCE
Enter some meaningful information in this field. This is a freely definable field; most of the time, companies use it to enter the invoice number received from the vendor.

▶ POSTING DATE
Enter the posting date here.

▶ DOCUMENT TYPE
This is automatically entered as VENDOR INVOICE.

▶ AMOUNT
Enter the amount of the invoice here.

▶ CURRENCY
Enter the invoice currency here.

▶ CALCULATE TAX
Set this flag if you want the system to calculate tax for you based on the code selected from the dropdown option available under this field.

▶ TEXT
This is also a freely definable field and can be used to enter a specific reference to this asset.

▶ G/L ACCT
Enter the general ledger account to which the expense should be posted. Normally, special general ledger accounts are created for this process, whereby they act as a control account and have different field status controls from the normal expense accounts. After the settlement to the AuC, these control accounts should be equal to zero.

▶ D/C
Select the DEBIT option here.

▶ AMOUNT IN DOC. CURR.
Enter the amount that should be charged to this general ledger account.

▶ ORDER
Enter the investment order we created earlier.

After entering this information, you can click the POST button. The system creates a vendor invoice document and posts values to the investment order, provided the invoice amount doesn't exceed the budget amount entered on this investment order. Actual costs related to this investment order are collected over a given period, and, at the end of the month, the costs that have accumulated on the investment order are posted to the AuC, as explained in the next section.

The first settlement of the investment order results in the creation of the AuC, and all subsequent settlements are also posted to this same AuC, until it is complete.

Let's now look at the settlement process, from investment order to the AuC.

6.5.4 Settlement of Investment Order to AuC

After postings have been made to the investment order, you need to settle the accumulated costs to the AuC to ensure that the values are reflected in the balance sheet account for part of the work done on this asset. When the settlement is made to the AuC, the system not only creates the AuC itself but also uses the account determination settings explained earlier to determine which account to post the values to in SAP General Ledger.

Before we explain the settlement process, note that, up to this point, the settlement profile for the investment order is blank, and no entries appear there. The system automatically creates the entry after the successful settlement.

You can settle the investment order using SAP MENU • ACCOUNTING • CONTROLLING • INTERNAL ORDERS • PERIOD-END CLOSING • SINGLE FUNCTIONS • SETTLEMENT • INDIVIDUAL PROCESSING or by using Transaction KO88 (Figure 6.45).

You must enter the investment order number in the ORDER field, and fill in the SETTLEMENT PERIOD, FISCAL YEAR, and PROCESSING TYPE fields. (The PROCESSING TYPE should be set to AUTOMATIC.) We recommend that you carry out a test run by setting the flag on the TEST RUN option.

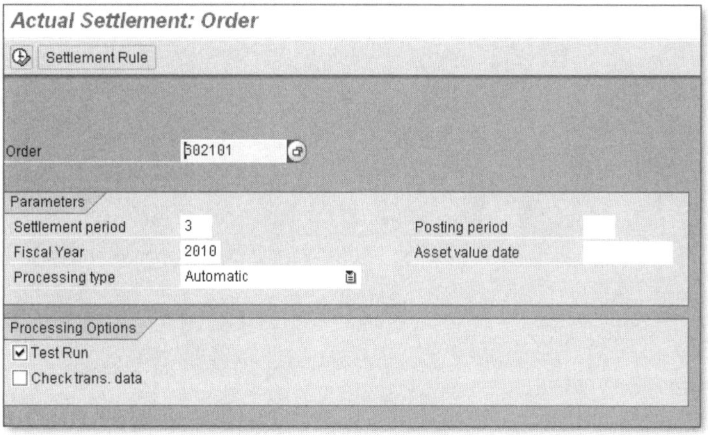

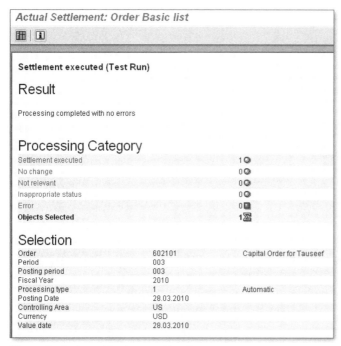

Figure 6.45 Actual Settlement: Order Screen

Click EXECUTE, and the next screen appears (Figure 6.46). This screen shows you the results of the test run. There shouldn't be any errors in the run, or the live run will fail.

Figure 6.46 Actual Settlement: Test Run

If there are no errors, deselect the TEST RUN flag, and click the EXECUTE button again. The system brings you to the screen shown in Figure 6.47, which shows you that the settlement has been executed.

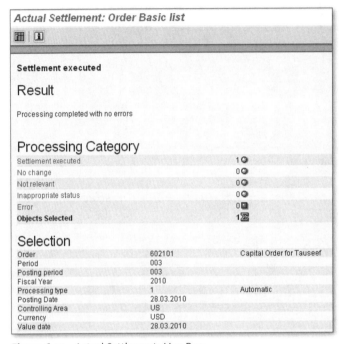

Figure 6.47 Actual Settlement: Live Run

Click the DETAILS list icon on the top-left of the screen, and the screen shown in Figure 6.48 appears.

This is an important screen that explains the following:

▶ The relationship between the senders and receivers, and the value that has been settled.

▶ The set of accounting documents posted after the settlement. In our example, the system posted a FI document, a CO document, a profit center document, and an asset transaction to reflect the effects of settlement in FI, CO, and AA, respectively. The system used the account determination settings to post the values to the right general ledger account during this process.

▶ The system automatically created the settlement profile with the correct asset number and settlement percentage.

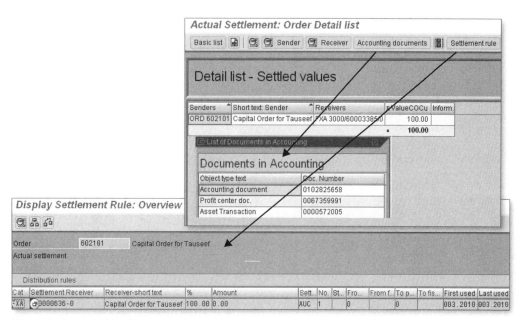

Figure 6.48 Actual Settlement: Accounting Documents and Settlement Profile Views

We have now successfully settled our costs to the AuC at the end of the month, and we are ready to look at the next step: transferring the AuC to a final asset after its completion.

> **Note**
>
> Depending on the nature of the AuC, you might have several settlements from the order before the AuC is complete and ready to be settled to the final asset.

6.5.5 Transfer of the AuC to Final Fixed Asset

In this process step, we have reached the completion of the AuC and now need to move it to the final asset stage so that depreciation can start. To complete this transfer, you must create master data (also known as the *asset shell*) in AA and then carry out the settlement process to move the accumulated costs to the final asset. The creation of the final asset master record is exactly the same as explained in Section 6.4, Master Data, so refer to that section to remind yourself of the important points. After the asset is created, you are ready to settle the AuC to a final asset.

After the successful creation of the master record, enter the asset number in the settlement profile of the investment order. To do this, use Transaction KO02, and click the SETTLEMENT RULE button, as shown in Figure 6.49.

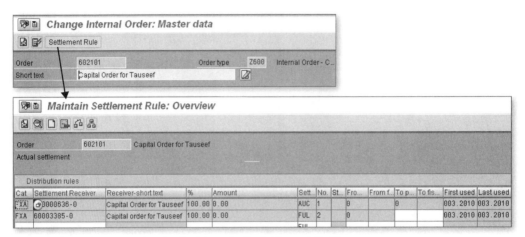

Figure 6.49 Entering the Final Asset in the Settlement Profile

Enter the category (CAT) as "FXA" (fixed asset), and enter the final asset number generated previously in the SETTLEMENT RECEIVER column. In the % column, enter "100", and in the SETTLEMENT TYPE, enter "FUL" for full settlement. Click SAVE.

Execute Transaction KO88 again, but this time the purpose is to settle the cost from the AuC to the final asset. Apart from the information you entered the first time you settled the costs to AuC, enter the asset value date because this is the date that is used by the system to calculate the start of the depreciation. The settlement process works exactly the same way as to the process of settling an investment order to the AuC, whereby the settlement senders and receivers are represented by different posted documents, such as accounting documents, profit center documents, asset transactions, and so on. The difference is that, this time, the receiver is the final asset, not the AuC. The system again uses the account determination settings explained earlier to post to the correct general ledger accounts, and the right values are reflected in the balance sheet.

Figure 6.50 and Figure 6.51 show the ASSET EXPLORER screens for the final asset after the settlement. These show that the values have been transferred successfully, and the system is now calculating planned depreciation values that will be posted when the next depreciation run takes place.

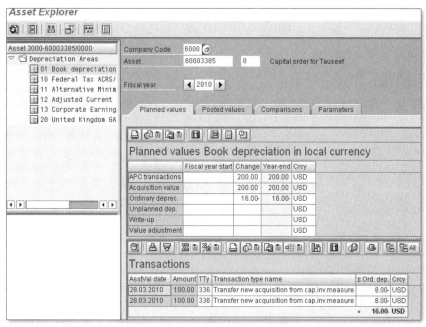

Figure 6.50 Asset Explorer: Final Asset – Planned Values

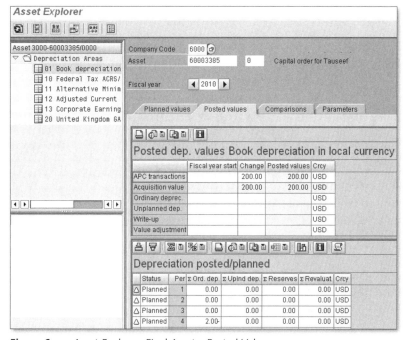

Figure 6.51 Asset Explorer: Final Asset – Posted Values

We have now completed the process of creating the final asset from the investment order. The next step is to close the order so that no more costs can be charged to it.

6.5.6 Change the Investment Order Status to Complete

The last step is to change the status of the investment order to complete so that no costs can be charged to it in coming periods. Execute Transaction KO02; in the Control Data tab, shown in Figure 6.52, click the System Status button to change it to a closed status (CLSD AUC) to ensure that no FI postings are made to this order in the future.

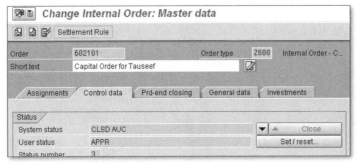

Figure 6.52 Investment Order Status Complete

This completes the process for acquiring assets through investment orders. We now move on to the process of posting values to assets using external acquisition.

6.6 Posting Values to Assets Using External Acquisition

In the previous sections, we looked at the process of acquiring assets through investment orders. In this section, we look at the steps involved in posting values to an asset using external acquisition, that is, through a vendor invoice. We posted a vendor invoice to the investment order in the previous section, which was then settled to the AuC — but here we are posting a vendor invoice directly to a fixed asset. To do this, you must have completed the asset master data, which is very similar to creating the asset shell for the final asset (which we discussed in the previous section). After you've created an asset shell, you now have to post values to it by following these steps:

1. Use the following menu path for posting values to an asset using external acquisition with vendors: SAP Easy Access • Accounting • Financial Accounting • Fixed Assets • Posting • Acquisition • External Acquisitions • With Vendor (Transaction F-90).

2. Enter the information given in the following list in the screen shown in Figure 6.53.

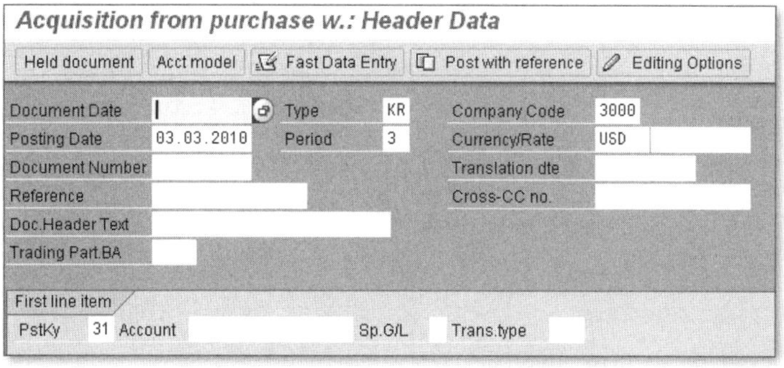

Figure 6.53 Acquisition of Asset with Vendor: First Screen

▶ Document Date
  Enter the document date.

▶ Type
  Enter the document type, which, in our case, is "KR" (vendor invoice) because we are posting an external acquisition with vendor.

▶ Company Code
  Enter your company code.

▶ Posting Date
  Enter the posting date.

▶ Period
  Enter the posting period. The system automatically provides this field when you enter the posting date.

▶ Currency/Rate
  Enter the currency in which the invoice will be created.

▶ Reference
  This is a freely definable field and can, for example, be used to enter the vendor invoice number for future reference.

▶ Doc. Header Text
This is also a freely definable field and can be used to enter a specific reference to this asset.

▶ PstKy
Enter the posting key for Credit Vendor (e.g., "31").

▶ Account
Enter the SAP ERP vendor account number from which the asset is purchased.

▶ Trans.Type
Leave this field blank.

3. After entering the information in the preceding list, press ⟨Enter⟩, and then use the following list to complete the Enter Vendor Invoice: Add Vendor Item screen, as shown in Figure 6.54.

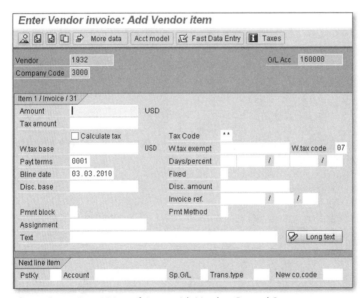

Figure 6.54 Acquisition of Asset with Vendor: Second Screen

▶ Amount
Enter the amount of the invoice.

▶ Calculate tax
If the invoice is tax-related, select this checkbox, and the system calculates the tax accordingly.

▶ PAYT TERMS

The system automatically provides the payment terms from the vendor master record in this field.

▶ BLINE DATE

The system automatically provides the baseline date from the payment terms settings.

▶ TEXT

Enter any useful information in this field that would help you identify this transaction in the future.

▶ PSTKY

Enter the posting key "70", which is debit asset, because we are posting values to the asset.

▶ ACCOUNT

Enter the asset number you created in the previous step.

▶ TRANS.TYPE

Enter transaction type "100", which is external acquisitions. SAP ERP has provided standard transaction types that can be used and are more than sufficient to meet your requirements.

4. Use the following list to complete the fields in the Enter Vendor invoice: Add Asset Item screen shown in Figure 6.55.

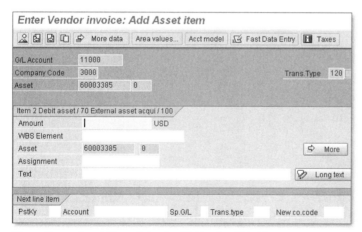

Figure 6.55 Acquisition of Asset with Vendor: Third Screen

▶ AMOUNT
Enter the amount that should be posted to the asset.

▶ TEXT
Enter any useful information in this field that would help you identify this transaction in the future.

5. Simulate the transaction, and you'll see that the system has generated another line with the tax amount. Post your document, and a document number is generated. You have now successfully posted values to your asset.

From this point on, the final asset completes its lifecycle like any other asset acquired through investment order or PS (covered later, in Section 6.10, Project Systems). We will cover the rest of the steps in the asset lifecycle in subsequent sections.

6.7 Post Transfers to Other Assets

In this transaction, we transfer one asset to another asset in AA. The example we'll look at is within a company code, but the same logic can be used to transfer assets between two company codes, provided the configuration of intercompany accounts is completed.

1. Use the menu path SAP EASY ACCESS • ACCOUNTING • FINANCIAL ACCOUNTING • FIXED ASSETS • POSTING • TRANSFER • TRANSFER WITHIN COMPANY CODE (Transaction ABUMN).

2. Use the following list of fields to complete the first tab, Transaction Data, as shown in Figure 6.56.

▶ DOCUMENT DATE
Enter the document date.

▶ POSTING DATE
Enter the posting date.

▶ ASSET VAL. DATE
This is the value date for this asset in AA. The system uses this date to calculate the amount of depreciation for this transferred asset.

▶ TEXT
Enter any useful information in this field.

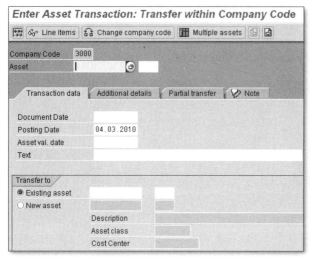

Figure 6.56 Asset Transfer within Company Code: Transaction Data Tab

▶ EXISTING ASSET
  If you want to transfer this asset to an existing asset number, enter the asset number.

▶ NEW ASSET
  If you want to create a new asset and transfer values to it, enter the description of the new asset, the asset class in which it should be created, and the cost center.

3. If you post your document at this stage, the system completely transfers the relevant values of this asset to the new or existing asset.

4. If you want to partially transfer the asset, use the following list to complete the Partial Transfer tab, as shown in Figure 6.57.

▶ AMOUNT POSTED
  Enter the partial amount in this field, and the system will only transfer this value to the new asset.

▶ PERCENTAGE RATE
  If you want to transfer a certain percentage to the new asset, enter the percentage amount to be transferred.

▶ QUANTITY
  If you have maintained the QUANTITY field in the asset master record, you have the option here to transfer an amount using quantity as the basis for calculating the transfer values.

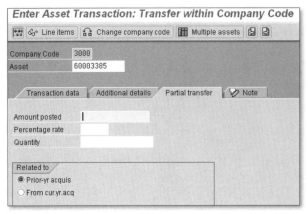

Figure 6.57 Asset Transfer Within Company Code: Partial Transfer Tab

▶ RELATED TO

Select the relevant option, depending on whether the transaction is related to prior or current year acquisitions.

5. Post your document, and the system generates not only the transfer document but also a new asset number (if you are transferring the values to a new asset).

Note

Total transfer of values from the old asset to the new asset will result in the deactivation of the old asset.

6.8   Post Depreciation Run

To post depreciation in the system, you need to execute a depreciation run on a periodic basis for the assets within your company code. The menu path is as follows: SAP EASY ACCESS • ACCOUNTING • FINANCIAL ACCOUNTING • FIXED ASSETS • PERIODIC PROCESSING • DEPRECIATION RUN • EXECUTE (Transaction AFAB). Follow these steps:

1. In the Depreciation Posting Run screen shown in Figure 6.58, enter the Company Code, Fiscal Year, and Posting Period information for the depreciation you wan to run.

2. Select Planned Posting Run from the options for Reasons for Posting Run. (This is the most common selection, but you can use the Repeat option if you've made corrections to manual depreciation or depreciation terms and want to complete the postings. In this case, the system only posts changes to the depreciation.) You must execute the depreciation run in the background because the system does not let you run it in the foreground (except in the test run, where it's restricted to approximately 1,000 assets). We also strongly recommend that you use the Test Run option first, to identify any problems before you do the live run.

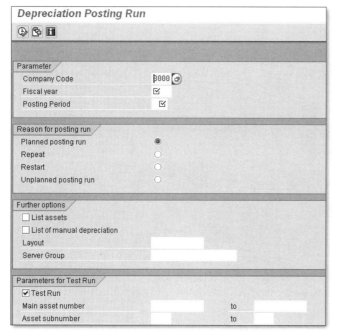

Figure 6.58 Depreciation Run

3. After you've checked that the depreciation run was complete using Transaction SM37, go to the Asset Explorer, and check the asset you created in the previous steps. On the Posted Values tab, the depreciation is posted for the period for which you have executed the depreciation run, with a green signal to indicate that the depreciation run was successful.

6.9 Post Retirements with Scrapping

So far, we've created the asset master record, entered values into it, posted transfers within a single company code, and posted depreciation. Now we are ready for posting retirements to an asset using the scrapping transaction. You also can retire assets to a customer, when the asset is sold to an outside customer for a given price. We discuss the scrapping transaction here because retiring an asset with a customer is very similar to creating a customer invoice. Follow these step to use the scrapping transaction to post retirements:

1. Access the menu path via SAP Easy Access • Accounting • Financial Accounting • Fixed Assets • Posting • Retirement • Asset Retirement by Scrapping, or by using Transaction ABAVN.

2. Use the following list to complete the information on the Transaction Data tab, as shown in Figure 6.59.

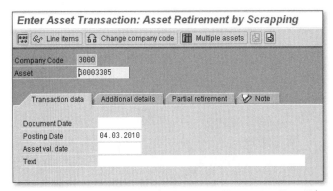

Figure 6.59 Asset Retirement by Scrapping: Transaction Data Tab

- ▶ Document Date
  Enter the document date.

- ▶ Posting Date
  Enter the posting date.

- ▶ Asset Val. Date
  This is the value date for this asset in AA. The system uses this date to calculate the amount of depreciation for this retiring asset.

- ▶ Text
  Enter any useful information in this field.

3. If you post your document at this stage, the system completely retires, deactivates the asset, posts the net book value (NBV) of the asset as a loss to the P&L account (maintained in the configuration step Assign GL Accounts), and also offsets the APC values and accumulated depreciation for the retired asset.

4. If you want to partially retire the asset (with partial retirement, deactivation of the asset does not take place because the asset still has a balance), use the following list to populate the Partial Retirement tab, shown in Figure 6.60.

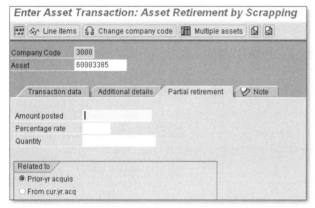

Figure 6.60 Asset Retirement by Scrapping: Partial Retirement Tab

▶ AMOUNT POSTED
Enter the partial amount, and the system will only retire this value of the asset.

▶ PERCENTAGE RATE
If you want to retire a certain percentage of this asset, enter the percentage amount to be retired.

▶ QUANTITY
If you've maintained the Quantity field in the asset master record, you can retire a partial amount using quantity as the basis for calculating the values to be retired.

▶ RELATED TO
Select the relevant option depending on whether the transaction is related to prior or current year acquisitions.

5. Post your document, and the retiring document is generated.

In the next section, we look at the complete process from a PS point of view.

6.10 Project Systems

In previous sections, we covered the configuration and design of the investment-order-to-asset business process. In this section, we look at the situation from another point of view: projects instead of investment orders. Much of the process remain the same, but the Project Systems (PS) component has some additional functionality that you'll learn about in this section. The SAP ERP solution for PS does not merely focus on the capitalization processes but also looks to provide some tools to enable an organization to manage the delivery of a project. The project can be broken down into work breakdown structures (WBS), which are used to manage the individual activities within the project. The component also provides milestones and Gantt charts to assist in the management and delivery of a project, which we also discuss in some detail to explain the full range of functionality. This discussion should help you understand why some organizations choose investment orders or projects.

First, let's recall where we are in the process and have another look at the asset lifecycle, with a particular focus on the project side (Figure 6.61).

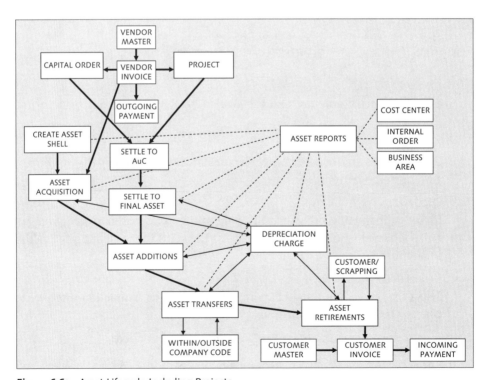

Figure 6.61 Asset Lifecycle Including Projects

In this section, we focus on the business process while also explaining the configuration and design. The basic principles of this process — such as the use of AuC and the settlement process — are the same as when an acquisition value is transferred to the asset from an investment order.

Next, we look at the following from a PS point of view:

- Enterprise structure
- Core configuration for creating a project
- Field status for WBS and projects
- Project milestones
- Project creation
- Project posting lifecycle
- Additional functionality

6.10.1 Enterprise Structure

Projects need to be activated as an object within your controlling area so that they can be selected as account assignment objects when posting any document in SAP ERP. We recall this configuration in Figure 6.62.

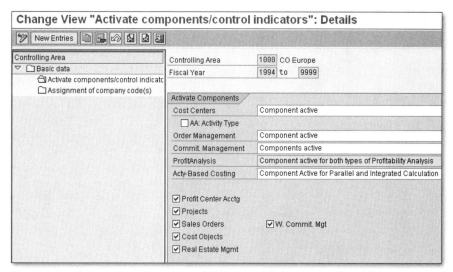

Figure 6.62 Activate Projects as Account Assignment Objects in the Controlling Area

This configuration was completed in the following area of the IMG: SPRO • CONTROLLING • GENERAL CONTROLLING • ORGANIZATION • MAINTAIN CONTROLLING AREA. This can also be accessed from: PROJECT SYSTEM • COSTS • ACTIVATE PROJECT MANAGEMENT IN CONTROLLING.

By activating projects in the controlling area, you are enabling the update of the WBS (and networks) as an additional account assignment object. This setting is made early during configuration, when you are setting up your enterprise structure. You can make this setting later, if you decide to use projects.

Because projects are account assignment objects, they are posted to when the CO document is created. The configuration of the CO document is necessary for this.

6.10.2 Core Configuration for Creating a Project

Let's examine the process of setting up a project; at each stage, we dip into the configuration to understand the requirements. PS has its own area within the application, and it offers quite an extensive range of functionality. In Figure 6.63, we can see the SAP Easy Access Menu for PS.

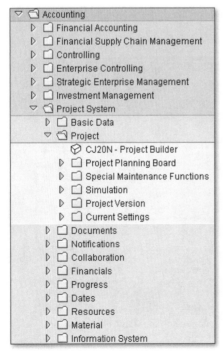

Figure 6.63 Project Systems Easy Access Menu

Transaction CJ20N is used for setting up a new project. Next, we start to look at the configuration and design steps involved in setting up a new project.

Project Numbering Conventions

The first thing to do when setting up PS is to determine the numbering convention for your projects. With master data, objects are numbered in a sequential order from number 1 onward; this goes against SAP's golden rule to not build intelligence into coding structures. However, you can treat projects as an exception to this rule because a good numbering convention can be used to link them with WBS. For this reason, a lot of time will be spent determining a good numbering convention, or *coding mask*. This configuration is done in the following area of the IMG: SPRO • PROJECT SYSTEM • STRUCTURES • OPERATIVE STRUCTURES • WORK BREAKDOWN STRUCTURE (WBS) • PROJECT CODING MASK • DEFINE PROJECT CODING MASK. The initial screen is shown in Figure 6.64.

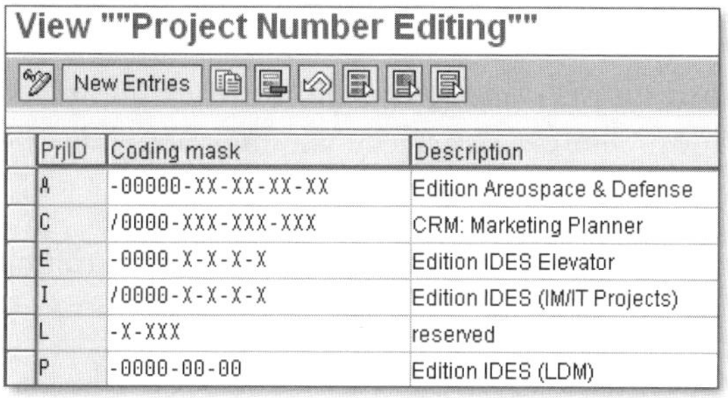

PrjID	Coding mask	Description
A	-00000-XX-XX-XX-XX	Edition Areospace & Defense
C	/0000-XXX-XXX-XXX	CRM: Marketing Planner
E	-0000-X-X-X-X	Edition IDES Elevator
I	/0000-X-X-X-X	Edition IDES (IM/IT Projects)
L	-X-XXX	reserved
P	-0000-00-00	Edition IDES (LDM)

Figure 6.64 Coding Masks for Projects

Project Status

Projects in real life move through stages where they are approved, set up, delivered, tested, closed, and so on. The stages are dependent on different things, such as the type of project or the size of the project. SAP ERP offers complete flexibility here, and lets you set up statuses that you can use to define the stages of the project. To set up a status profile, access the following area of the IMG: PROJECT SYSTEM • STRUCTURES • OPERATIVE STRUCTURES • WORK BREAKDOWN STRUCTURE (WBS) • WBS USER STATUS • CREATE STATUS PROFILE.

Figure 6.65 shows the setup of an example status profile. As mentioned already, the details of your setup really depend on a number of factors.

Status Profile		ZCAP	Major Capital Project					
Maintenance Language		EN	English					

User Status

Statu	Status	Short Text	Long	Init. st	Lowest	Highest	Posit	Priority
1	Init	Initiate Project	☐	☑	1	8	1	1
2	Aprv	For Approval	☐	☐	1	8	1	1
3	Live	Delivery	☐	☐	2	8	1	1
4	Depl	Final Deployment	☐	☐	2	8	1	1
5	Clos	Closure	☐	☐	2	8	1	1
6	rejt	Rejected	☐	☐	2	8	1	1
7	Deff	Deferred	☐	☐	2	8	1	1
8	Hold	On hold	☐	☐	2	8	1	1

Figure 6.65 Project Status Profile

Project Profiles

Naturally, different organizations need different categories/types of projects. To handle this, you can set up project profiles for each type you work with. The project profile is set up to bring together a number of configuration objects and allows you to control which are necessary for the different types of projects. For example, in terms of settlement, on a capital project, you want to ensure there is a settlement to AuC, whereas for a normal revenue project, you may not want any settlement at all. Profiles can help you control the following functionality:

▶ Organizational objects for your organization (e.g., company code, controlling area, profit center, plant, business area, and so on)

▶ WBS status profiles

▶ WBS scheduling profiles

▶ Settlement settings

In our simple example, we only look at a single profile for capital projects because this relates to the Investment Management scenario. In reality, organizations may have many profiles defined to deal with variations of both capital and revenue projects (PS is there to help with the management of projects and does not exist solely for Investment Management).

To create a project profile, you access the following area of the IMG: SPRO • PROJECT SYSTEM • STRUCTURES • OPERATIVE STRUCTURES • WORK BREAKDOWN STRUCTURE (WBS) • CREATE PROJECT PROFILE. There are a number of fields on the project profile, but we focus on those relating to the basic use of projects and integration with SAP ERP Financials.

In Figure 6.66, the first thing you should notice is that in this specific example, the project type (PROJ.TYPE) (which is basically a way projects are grouped together, e.g., building projects, etc.) is not being used, which you can tell from the blank field.

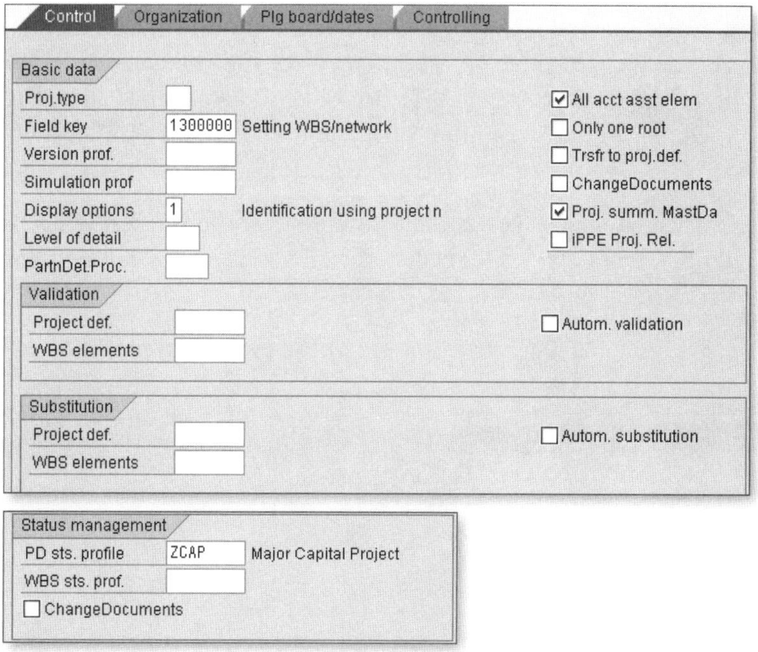

Figure 6.66 Project Profile – Control Settings

The FIELD KEY field relates to user-defined fields that can be set up to meet customer-specific needs. We talk about these later in this section.

As we have mentioned, projects (and WBS) can be real account assignment elements, which means that you can post actual costs to them. With this in mind, you must decide whether the project itself and all of the WBS below it should be treated as account assignment objects, or whether you will only post to lower-level WBS and not directly to the project (or some combination of both). Selecting the ALL ACCT ASST ELEM indicator makes all levels account assignment objects.

> **Note**
>
> In our experience, allowing users to post to each level causes confusion; they often don't know which level is correct and just post to the project itself instead.

In the middle of Figure 6.66, you can assign validations and substitutions to this profile. In PS, you can define project-specific validations and substitutions that can be set up to control the way in which you set up projects and WBS elements. We don't cover this here, but Chapter 7, Special Topics, talks about general validations and substitutions, which should be of interest to you if you are not familiar with this configuration.

The last thing to discuss in Figure 6.66 is the STATUS MANAGEMENT area, which is where you assign the statuses that we looked at earlier. Statuses are set at both the WBS and the project levels.

In Figure 6.67, you can see the ORGANIZATION tab of the project profile.

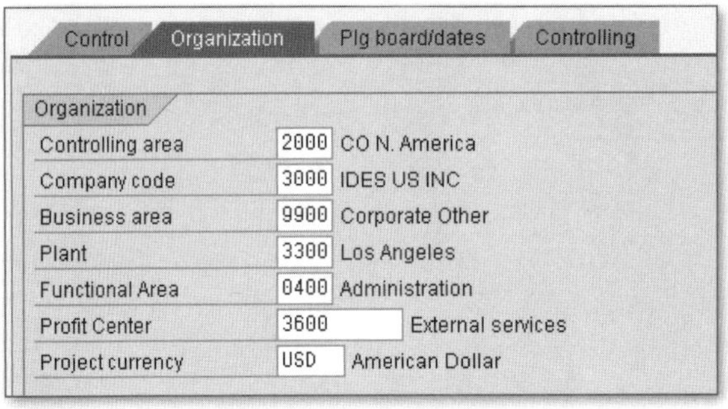

Control	Organization	Plg board/dates	Controlling

Organization		
Controlling area	2000	CO N. America
Company code	3000	IDES US INC
Business area	9900	Corporate Other
Plant	3300	Los Angeles
Functional Area	0400	Administration
Profit Center	3600	External services
Project currency	USD	American Dollar

Figure 6.67 Project Profile – Organization Tab

On the ORGANIZATION tab of the profile, you can see that it's possible to define a series of values for account assignment objects. Whatever values you define here become the default settings for each new project that is created in this profile. The values on this tab are all optional, so you can choose to define only those you want to define.

On Figure 6.68, you can see the settings made in relation to the scheduling and planning aspects of projects. We don't cover these in detail, but the only integration object worth noting here is the factory calendar, which is used to determine working days for planning and scheduling when work can be done.

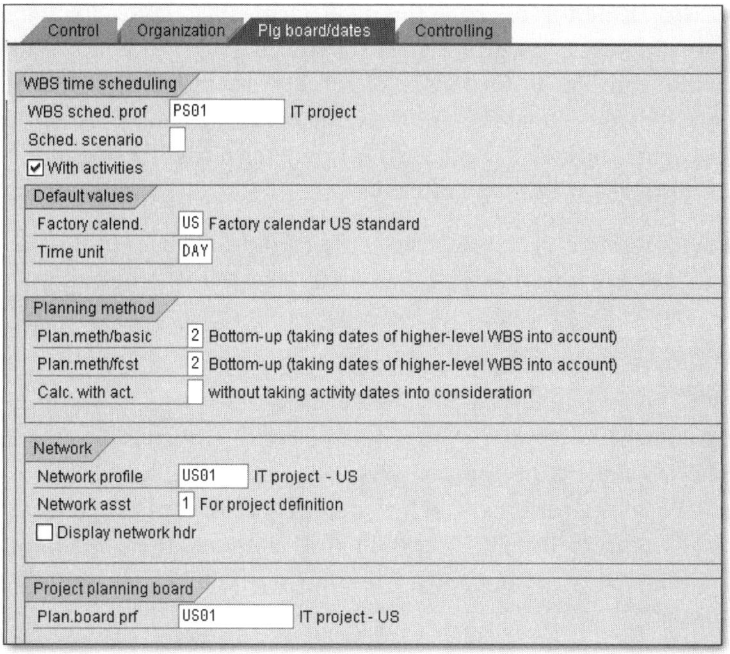

Figure 6.68 Project Profile – Planning Board

The final tab of the project profile (Figure 6.69) shows the integration with CO.

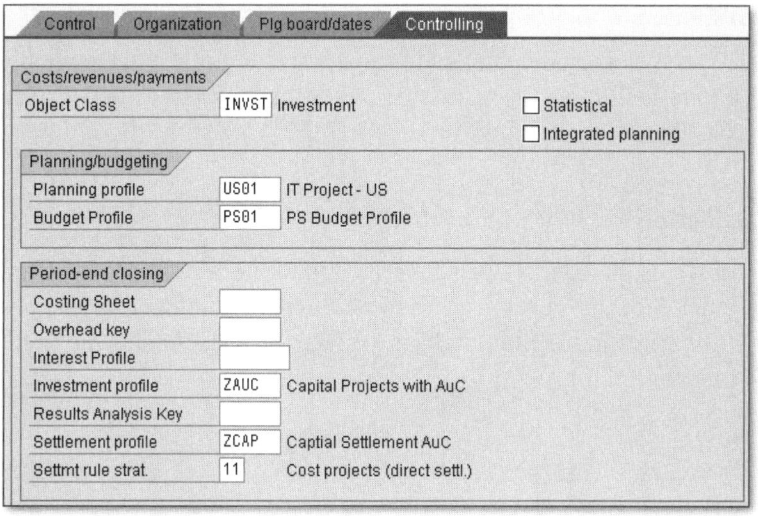

Figure 6.69 Project Profile – Controlling Tab

The OBJECT CLASS field at the top refers to the investment object, which is what we would expect to see for capital projects. There is also an investment profile assigned, which is the real link to the AuC. (We look at investment profiles in the next section, but remember that this is where they are assigned.) Finally, the SETTLEMENT PROFILE field is important because this is where you assign your settlement configuration settings for this type of project.

We look at both the investment profile and the settlement profile later in this section (see Sections 6.10.5, Creating a Project, and 6.10.6, Project Posting Lifecycle, respectively).

Person Responsible

On the WBS, we assign what is known as the *person responsible,* which is the person who can be assigned responsibilities for this WBS. This can be simply an administrative appointment, or you can use the field for other purposes, such as approvals. In such a situation, you can add SAP ERP user IDs to this table, and then, whenever a posting is made to the WBS, you can build a workflow that will involve notifying the person responsible.

To set this up, access the following area of the IMG: SPRO • PROJECT SYSTEM • STRUCTURES • OPERATIVE STRUCTURES • WORK BREAKDOWN STRUCTURE (WBS) • SPECIFY PERSONS RESPONSIBLE FOR WBS ELEMENTS.

Requesting Cost Centers

The requesting cost center should be linked to the department that will eventually own the asset you are building. For this reason, the value you put in here is also updated as the cost center for the AuC.

6.10.3 Field Selection for WBS and Projects

In this configuration step, you define the field selection for both WBS and projects. The approach is much the same as for other field status configuration tasks we have seen: For each of the fields in the provided list, you decide if the field is required, hidden, display only, and so on.

If PS is a new area for you, use the standard layouts that are supplied as much as possible; however, test them to make sure they work with your company. This activity is configured in the following area of the IMG: SPRO • PROJECT SYSTEM • STRUCTURES • OPERATIVE STRUCTURES • WORK BREAKDOWN STRUCTURE (WBS) • USER INTERFACE SETTINGS.

If you want to add custom fields to your WBS, SAP ERP offers an easy way to do this without the need for developers to build screen variants. In the example in Figure 6.70, you can see some custom fields that were set up for use in the pharmaceutical industry.

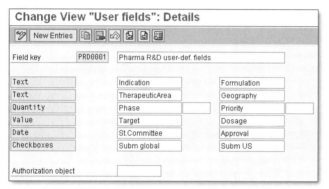

Figure 6.70 Creating User-Defined Fields for WBS

Your own custom fields can be seen on the WBS under the USER FIELDS tab, and they are configured within the same area of the IMG: SPRO • PROJECT SYSTEM • STRUCTURES • OPERATIVE STRUCTURES • WORK BREAKDOWN STRUCTURE (WBS) • USER INTERFACE SETTINGS.

6.10.4 Project Milestones

The PS component offers other functionality as well; for example, you can set up project milestones that can be used in project management. Milestones can be set up in the following area of the IMG: PROJECT SYSTEM • STRUCTURES • OPERATIVE STRUCTURES • MILESTONES • DEFINE MILESTONE USAGE. We don't go into any detail here because there is no link to the scope of our topic.

6.10.5 Creating a Project

Now that the base configuration is complete, we can set up our project. We're using an actual construction project, in which a company is building a new research facility, as an example for this section. Naturally, this type of project involves considerable investment, and the company wants to capitalize this investment at the end of the project. To begin, create the project header (Transaction CJ20N), which is based on the project profile we built earlier. As you can see, the default data we configured appears (Figure 6.71).

Figure 6.71 Set Up the Project

In the bottom-left corner, we inserted the dates we want to run the project, which is important during project management. If you look at the CONTROL DATA tab (Figure 6.72), you can see the other default settings we created in the project profile.

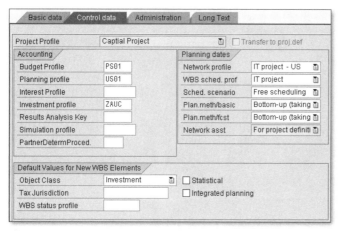

Figure 6.72 Setup Project – Control Data

Next we look at the settings for the investment profile and project structure.

Investment Profile

Investment profiles are set up in the following area of the IMG: SPRO • INVESTMENT MANAGEMENT • PROJECTS AS INVESTMENT MEASURES • MASTER DATA • DEFINE INVESTMENT PROFILE. The key job of the investment profile is to provide the link to the AuC, not only forcing the AuC process but also specifying the asset class that will be used. Figure 6.73 shows the configuration settings that should be made.

The other thing you see here is the definition of the settlement approach, either as a summary settlement or a line item settlement.

Project Structures

In the left-hand side of the screen shown in Figure 6.74, you can see the project structure. The project structure is created via the setup of WBS elements in relation to the individual tasks that are completed in the project's lifecycle. In our example in Figure 6.74, we decide at the start of the project that we want to capitalize all costs associated with the project, and we also want to manage actual spend against the plan. For these reasons, we set up WBSs to represent the project structure (Figure 6.74). We refer to each level as a phase of the overall project.

Investment profile	ZAUC	Capital Projects with AuC

Investment measure
- ☑ Manage AuC
- ☐ AuC per source structure/assignmt

Inv.meas. ast.class	4001	Assets under construction in investment measures
- ☐ Fixed default class

Settlement
- ◉ Summary settlement
- ○ Line item settlement and list of origins

Depreciation simulation

Sim. asset class		
- ☐ Fixed default class
- ☑ Ident. valuation
- ☐ Comparison w/ actual settlemts

Type of distribution rules	Comparison value for amount distribution
◉ Percentage rates	◉ Ovrl plan val. Version _____
○ Equival. numbers	○ Budget
○ Amounts	
○ Amounts and percentages	
○ Amounts and equiv. numbers	

Figure 6.73 Investment Profile

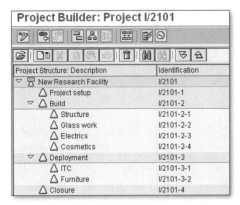

Figure 6.74 Project Structure

From this figure, we can see that the system uses a numbering convention to help explain the level of the WBS. The overall project code is I/2101, and levels below are I/2101-2, I/2101-3, and I/2101-4. We refer to these as Level 1 WBS. (This convention may be confusing at first, but when you understand the logic, you should find it easy to follow.) Below these are Level 2 WBS, and so on, as the situation demands.

> **Note**
>
> It is common to predefine the way this structure should be set up for a type of project. For this reason, organizations tend to use the project template functionality, which can be used as a default in the project profile, as well as in the levels or phases that the project should adopt.

As mentioned before, it's good practice to post costs to the lowest level WBS. Thus, for example, when you are in the building phase of a project, you want the postings to go to the levels below that. We control this by making only the lower levels account assignment elements. Similarly, in this example, we don't make the WBS I/2101-2 an account assignment element because we don't want people to post at this level.

Figure 6.75 shows the basic data screen for WBS I/2101-2-1. This is the build phase, which involves work specifically relating to the structure of the new facility.

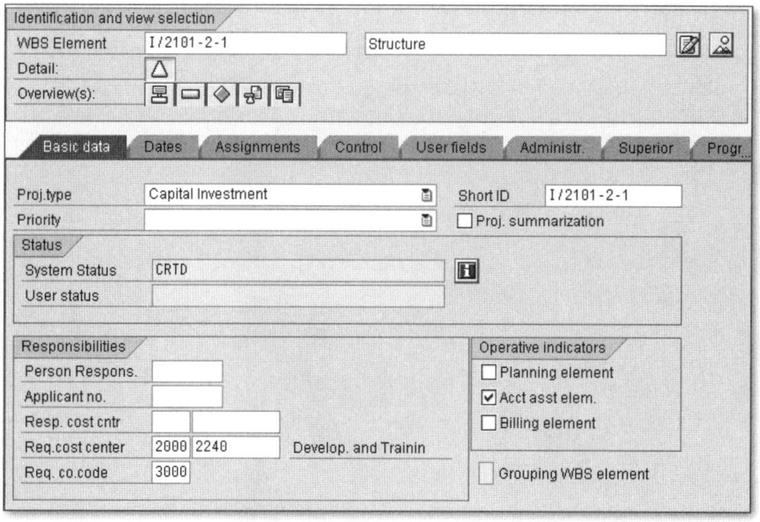

Figure 6.75 WBS Basic Data

We initially entered some dates for the overall project in Figure 6.71, which represented the dates for the overall work. For each WBS, you can manage its actual delivery. On the DATES tab (Figure 6.76), you can forecast dates and also capture actual start and end dates. (This all relates to the project management functionality, which is outside the scope of this chapter, so we won't discuss it further.)

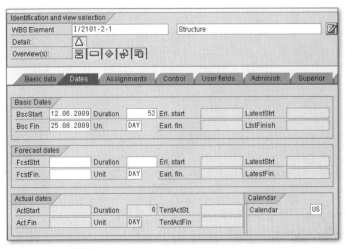

Figure 6.76 WBS Dates

On the ASSIGNMENTS tab, you can see that the same organizational assignments that were defined on the project profile are brought through (see Figure 6.77). If needed, we can make changes here that are specific to the WBS.

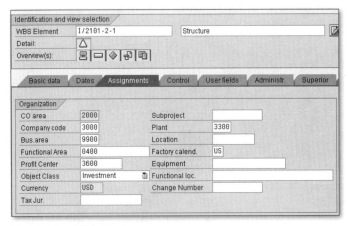

Figure 6.77 WBS Assignments

When you are ready for postings to be made about this WBS, you must release it by selecting EDIT • STATUS • RELEASE.

6.10.6 Project Posting Lifecycle

Purely from an Investment Management point of view, we now review the process by which a project is converted into an asset. Because there is significant overlap between the processes we covered earlier in this chapter, here we simply make reference to the previous text to show the commonality between the two processes.

With the project set up, you post your actual costs to the project through a variety of sources, for example, supplier invoices or internal recharging from a journal. You can also post to the WBS using timesheets, and thus use CO activities to recharge costs to the WBS.

The ongoing process is similar to the internal order process we saw earlier, in that there needs to be a process of periodic settlement. On a monthly basis, this settlement takes the costs from the WBS to an AuC. The system creates an AuC shell based on the settings you make in the investment profile (as we saw earlier in Figure 6.73). This was brought into the project profile, as we saw in Figure 6.72, and this was where we linked the project class to the investment profile and ultimately to the asset class.

In Figures 6.45 and 6.46, we saw the settlement transactions. For projects, we use Transaction CJ88, which looks and works exactly the same way. Looking back at the actual WBS in Transaction CJ20N, we view the settlement rules via EDIT • COSTS • SETTLEMENT RULES.

Before you do any settlement for a WBS, you will see the blank screen shown in Figure 6.78.

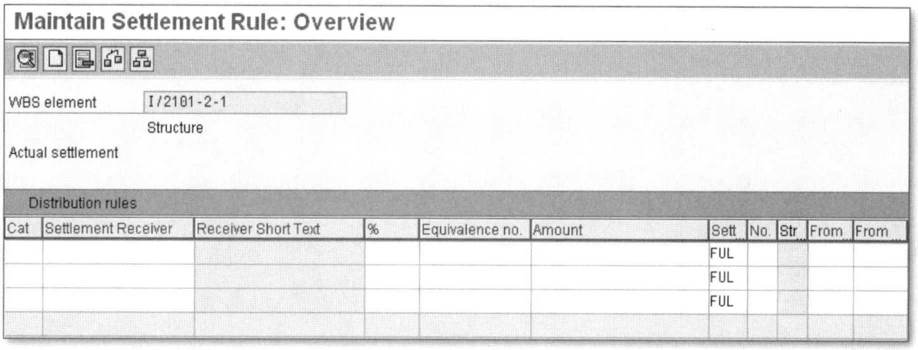

Maintain Settlement Rule: Overview										
WBS element	I / 2101-2-1									
	Structure									
Actual settlement										
Distribution rules										
Cat	Settlement Receiver	Receiver Short Text	%	Equivalence no.	Amount		Sett	No.	Str	From	From
							FUL				
							FUL				
							FUL				

Figure 6.78 No Settlement Rules Entered Manually

After you start periodic settlement, the system automatically creates an AuC and updates the settlement rules with its number (under a rule called "AuC"). When you want to run your final settlement, you need to create a fixed asset and manually enter it into this screen as the FUL settlement rule. If you remember when we defined settlement profiles, you will recall that you defined which objects could be used as valid receivers (Figure 6.79).

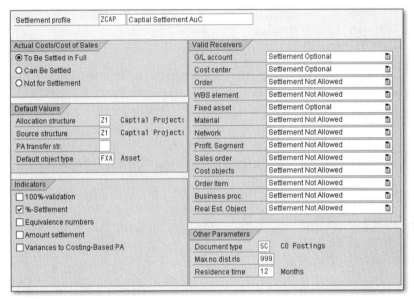

Figure 6.79 Capital Settlement Profile

6.10.7 Additional Functionality

Although PS is never going to be a complete project-management solution, what you do have is a tool that is already integrated into your overall business processes and that enables you to run and manage projects to some extent. To conclude our PS discussion, let's look at some additional functionality offered by the component.

Figure 6.80 shows the Gantt chart function.

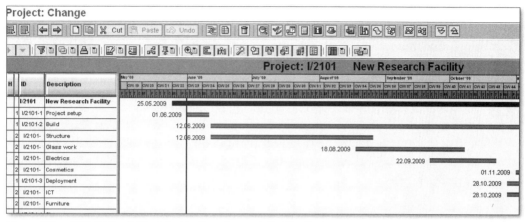

Figure 6.80 SAP PS Gantt Chart for the New Research Facility Project

Within each WBS, you can also define milestones. If it is a large piece of work, you may want to make use of milestone planning to monitor progress, as shown in Figure 6.81.

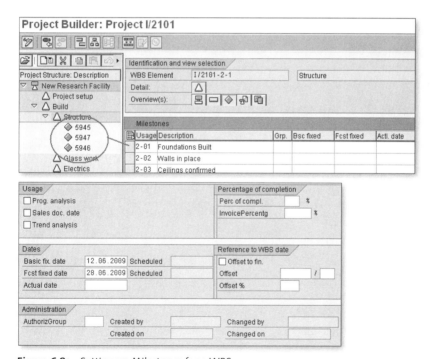

Figure 6.81 Setting up Milestones for a WBS

After you've set up milestones, you can define percentages to report on the progress of these milestones. The percentages are based on *activities* that you define. To go into more detail about activities is beyond the scope of the book, but they are similar to the Plant Maintenance (PM) approach of defining operations and then defining internal and external resources for these operations.

Finally, let's briefly talk about the document overview option, which allows you to load non-SAP ERP documents and attach them to the project. For example, if you maintain an issue and risks register in Excel, you can save it locally and attach it to the WBS. You can do the same with design documents, blueprints, business cases, and so on.

6.10.8 Conclusion

The important thing to take away from all this is that projects work in a similar way to investment orders, in that they operate in the same way as investment objects — but there is additional functionality available to help manage a project. If this additional functionality is relevant to your organization, you may want to use projects instead of investment orders.

6.11 Summary

In this chapter, we looked at two options for Investment Management, both ending with the creation of an asset for the organization. In doing so, we looked at the main transactions within Asset Accounting that you may need to process.

Simply understanding Asset Accounting represents a sufficiently advanced level of knowledge in the SAP ERP Financials area; if you are also able to understand its integration with investment orders and projects, you have mastered a complex area of functionality that few consultants truly grasp. In the next chapter, we cover a few useful special topics.

This bonus chapter should be a treat for anyone who has gotten this far. Master these topics to gain valuable skills that go beyond the Financials area.

7   Special Topics

We conclude the book with a chapter that puts together a selection of important topics applicable across the entire finance area. We struggled to restrict this chapter to a sensible size, and we chose those topics that will deliver the greatest benefit to the most readers.

The objective of this chapter is to cover special topics that are important not only for consultant implementations but also for users who deal with SAP ERP on a daily basis. In this chapter, we cover these topics in detail:

▸ Interrogating SAP ERP Tables with the Data Browser (Transaction SE16)

▸ Easing Data Migration with the Legacy System Migration Workbench

▸ Making Your Vendor/Customer Line Item Reports Work for You

▸ Enforcing Additional Organization Checks by Configuring Your own Validations

▸ Using Substitutions to Allocate Default Account Assignment Objects

In the sections that follow, we discuss each topic in enough detail to improve your understanding and enable you to use these functionalities in both your implementations and day-to-day activities.

7.1   Interrogating SAP ERP Tables with the Data Browser (Transaction SE16)

You can think of your SAP ERP database as a large number of interlinked tables that store information. Each table has fields populated by entries made in the system. When data is loaded into the system, you can run reports that provide analysis of the information in that table, or, alternatively, you can simply view the contents. You can also use the tables to check the location of specific data in the system; this may be needed if you want to write a custom report pulling in data from different sources. Finally, you can use the core tables to look at posted documents when trying to reconcile data (this is sometimes easier than running query reports). As you can see, there are a number of possible reasons for you to want to use the Data Browser (Transaction SE16).

Consider a situation where you need to know where some specific data is stored, such as the asset description in the asset master record (Transaction AS03). From the display screen for the asset master record, find the DESCRIPTION field for an asset. Click that field, and then press F1 (Help). From the Help information that pops up, you can click the TECHNICAL INFO button and see the technical information, as shown in Figure 7.1.

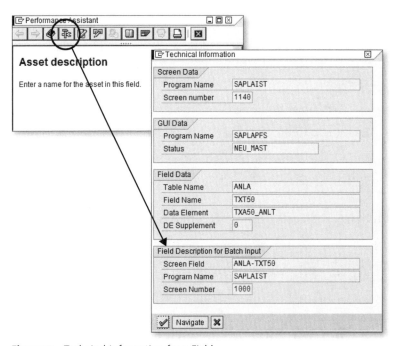

Figure 7.1 Technical Information for a Field

From the technical information provided, you can see that the asset description is contained in field TXT50, Table ANLA. SAP ERP provides the table browser tool for viewing data in a specific table. In our first special topic, we look at how you can use the table browser to see data stored in the asset Table ANLA.

> **Note**
>
> Table ANLA is just an example; there are many tables in SAP ERP that you may need to access as part of your day-to-day activities, and this process is applicable for all of them.
>
> Sometimes when you look at technical information, you will be directed to a structure. A structure is a combination of tables. In this situation, you will not be able to use Transaction SE16, and the system will display a message accordingly.

The table browser is located in the following area of the system: SAP EASY ACCESS • TOOLS • ABAP WORKBENCH • OVERVIEW • DATA BROWSER (Transaction SE16). The initial screen is shown in Figure 7.2.

> **Note**
>
> The screenshots in this section are all taken from Transaction SE16 in SAP ERP 6.0. You can also use Transaction SE16N, which is a more user-friendly way of accessing the data.

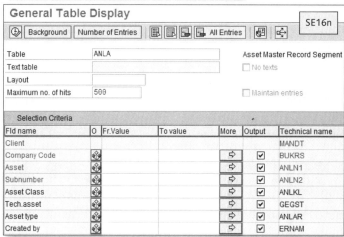

Figure 7.2 SAP Data Browser

Enter the table name in the TABLE NAME field, and press ⟨Enter⟩. In the resulting screen, you can select records in that table. If these parameters are not enough for you to see the contents, you can select the parameters you need.

Select SETTINGS from the menu, and then CHOOSE FIELDS FOR SELECTION. A window opens that lists all of the fields available in this table. Select the fields you want to search for in the contents of this table.

In our example, we want to see all of the asset master records for a specific company code. We enter the company code in the parameters and can also enter the asset number range (if we want to see specific assets details from this table). We also want to keep the field for MAXIMUM NO. OF HITS blank so that all of the assets are displayed in the output. Select the EXECUTE button, and the contents of Table ANLA are displayed in the next screen (Figure 7.3).

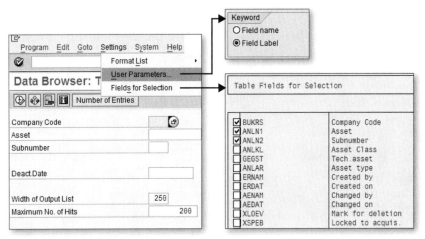

Figure 7.3 Additional Search

The NUMBER OF ENTRIES button shows you how many records are in the table for the criteria you have entered; this gives you an idea of the number of records you will bring back without running the full query.

When you click EXECUTE, you are shown the records in the table based on the selection criteria you specified. From this position, you can change the fields that you're shown because the table browser will show a default selection of fields. To do that, select the SETTINGS button from the menu, and then choose LIST FORMAT • CHOOSE FIELDS. A window similar to the one we used to select our parameters appears (Figure 7.4).

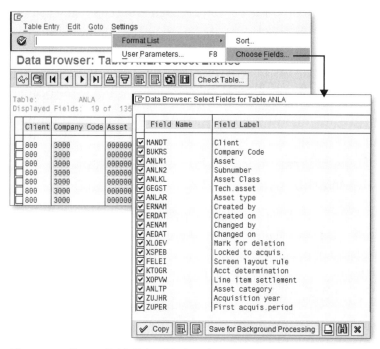

Figure 7.4 Change Fields Being Displayed

This screen displays all of the fields that are contained in this table for the asset master record, and all of them are selected as a default. You can deselect all of them by using the deselect option available on the screen. Select the fields you want to display, and then click the COPY button so that the output is restricted to your own set of fields.

After you have all of the right information on the screen, you do have other options, such as sorting the data in ascending and descending order, or refreshing the table to incorporate the newly created asset masters because this table will be updated with every new entry in the asset master record.

As you can see in the output, only fields that you selected in the previous step are displayed. This information can be used to review all of the assets created in your company code for further analysis. You can also download this into Excel by selecting SYSTEM • LIST • SAVE • LOCAL FILE. In the pop-up window titled SAVE LIST IN FILE, select the SPREADSHEET radio button, and click the green checkmark. In the next screen, enter the path where you want to save the file for further analysis, and click the GENERATE button. The file will be saved as specified, and you can work on it accordingly.

One of the other benefits of understanding different tables in SAP ERP is realized when creating queries. Although SAP ERP has provided many reports that fulfill most companies' requirements, knowledge of tables enables you to create customized reports for specific user requirements.

7.2 Easing Data Migration with the Legacy System Migration Workbench

Data migration is a significant activity that should not be underestimated. A large amount of time (and cost) is attributed to the process of defining load programs, and the Legacy System Migration Workbench (LSMW) represents a flexible, cost effective, and reliable tool for this purpose. In the process that follows, we explain the use of the tool in a way that anyone can follow. You can also use advanced processes, such as iDocs, but these require more technical knowledge, which is not the purpose of this discussion.

Although we focus here on the data migration usage, LSMW is frequently used for other reasons. As you get familiar with the tool, you'll realize that if you can create a batch recording of a process, then you can use LSMW. For example, you can use the creation of LSMWs for setting up annual accrual journals with more than 500 lines each, as well as for performing a large volume of reset and reversals. (The reset and reversal is particularly useful because the standard transaction only allows a mass reversal.)

The LSMW is essentially an ABAP program that can be configured to support all data objects in the system; it can be used to migrate your data into SAP ERP, as well as make mass changes to data already in the system. Your program first records the steps you define as being the process for the activity. You then create a spreadsheet that has the data you want to upload, and the LSMW program repeats the activity with all of the records you enter into the spreadsheet.

The import process is done via batch session; that is, a session that you can process in the foreground or in the background is created. This allows you to watch the data being imported, and, if there are any errors in the data, you can fix them at that point in time and reduce the disruption on the data load.

There are a number of benefits to using the LSMW:

▶ You can define a program without the need for ABAP programming and thus no need for a development key.

▶ You can change programs easily.

▶ You can create LSMWs directly in clients where needed, although we recommend creating them in development, testing them, and then using the import/export function to move through the required clients. .

▶ You can import and export programs between clients.

▶ You have access to a repeatable and reliable process in LSMW, and batch processing means that you control the data-entry process.

In addition to using the LSMW for creating master data, you can define LSMW programs to change data and even enter transactions in the system.

In this special topic, we explain the use of LSMW by walking through an example of an LSMW that you may want to create. The example we use is the creation of a general ledger account.

Note

The objective of this section is not to make you an LSWM expert but to explain how to define a simple LSWM. You should use this chapter and your own experience to create LSMWs that meet your organization's needs.

Before you start your definition of your LSMW program, you need to know the process that you want to record. In this situation, we are going to create a general ledger account with Transaction FS00.

As you may be aware, the general ledger account group configuration controls which fields are available for edits when creating a general ledger account. For this reason, when you create your screen recording, it is a good idea to create a general ledger account with an account group that has available all fields you would possibly need for all your scenarios (for example, you can create a group Group "Misc" with all fields optional for such scenario). For more information on configuring general ledger account groups, please consult our previous book, *SAP ERP Financials: Configuration and Design,* Section 3.2.3. Next, we explain the steps you should follow to create your LSMW.

7.2.1 Define the LSMW Parameters

You access LSMW by using Transaction LSMW. The system contains standard conversion programs, you can use; however, in our example, we are going to create the program from scratch to explain the full functionality.

Each LSMW program is seen as an object within a project and subproject; you must therefore define all three components. If you are unsure of how to structure this, then our suggestion for storing LSMWs within an SAP ERP implementation team is shown in Table 7.1.

Component	Description
Project	Enter your team names.
Subproject	Enter your master data object.
Object	Define whether the activity is the create or change program.

Table 7.1 Naming your LSMW

This needs to be done in stages in which you create the project, the subproject, and then finally the object. To begin, enter the name of the project, and click the CREATE button, followed by the subproject and the object.

When you click the EXECUTE button, you're taken to the LSMW (Figure 7.5). From here, you need to process the steps to configure the program correctly. We discuss this next.

7.2.2 Maintain Object Attributes

First, you must maintain your object's attributes by double-clicking on it from the task list (Figure 7.5). This takes you into the object. By clicking on the DISPLAY <–> CHANGE button, you can make changes.

From this screen, you want to make a batch input recording, so you should select this option and then enter Transaction "FS00". When you click the OVERVIEW button, the system shows you the existing recording for this transaction code (Figure 7.6).

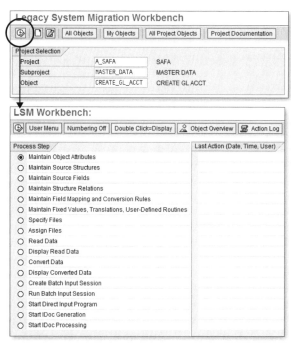

Figure 7.5 Task List to Create and Execute Your LSMW

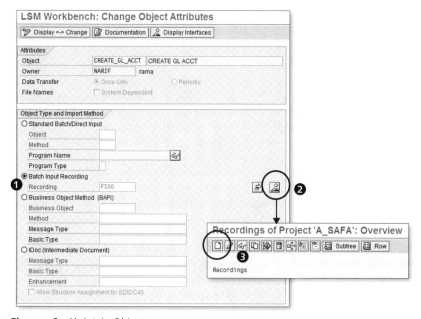

Figure 7.6 Maintain Object

From Figure 7.6, click the CREATE button to create your own recording, and give your recording a name, as shown in Figure 7.7.

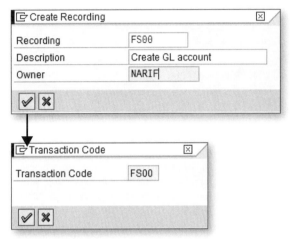

Figure 7.7 Create Object Recording

In our scenario, we only create a single recording, but you can create multiple recordings and link them to the same transaction code.

When you press ⌈Enter⌋, you are taken into the transaction that you are recording. From this point on, every action you perform is recorded, so do not click anything that you don't want to form as part of the recording. Also, make sure you click all of the fields in the correct order.

Our recording is concerned with the creation of a general ledger account, so at this point we need to complete the entire transaction related to creating a general ledger account. Every field and checkbox we want to include in our LSMW program needs to be included in our recording.

Thus, for our LSMW, we need to enter the general ledger account number ("60500"), and then click the CREATE button. After this, we follow all of the steps that should be included in our recording. You should think about this in advance, and make a list.

The steps marked with ** indicate fields that we want to include in the recording for some of our general ledger accounts. Enter a value in these fields so that the field is included in the recording.

Follow these steps; the screen is shown in Figure 7.8.

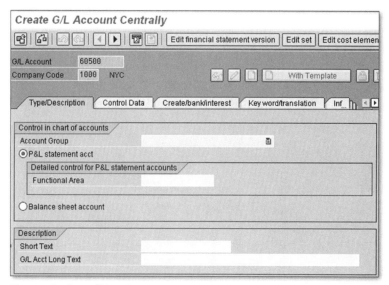

Figure 7.8 Record Your Process

1. Enter the account group in the Account Group field. (Select the account group with all fields optional to include the maximum number of fields in your recording.)

2. Select both P&L Statement Acct and Balance Sheet Account (you need both options to create both types of general ledger accounts).

3. Enter the short text.

4. Enter the long text.

5. Click the Control Data tab.

6. Enter the currency.

7. Enter a tax category. **

8. Click Posting Without Tax Allowed. **

9. Select a reconciliation account. **

10. Select Open Item Management.

11. Select Line Item Display.

12. Enter a sort key.

13. Click the Create/Bank/Interest tab.

14. Enter a field status group.

15. Click Post Automatically Only.

16. Click Recon Acct Ready for Input.

Now having included all of the fields and checkboxes in your recording, click the SAVE button. This returns you to the recording screen, shown in Figure 7.9. You have now successfully recorded the transaction and included all of the fields that you wanted to include.

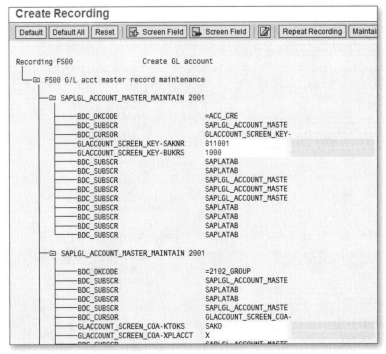

Figure 7.9 Activity Mapping for Your Recording

On this screen, you can see the fields in which you entered values, including that the general ledger account number is 60500 and that the company code is 1000. The next step is to name these fields, which you do by double-clicking the value. The screen shown in Figure 7.10 appears.

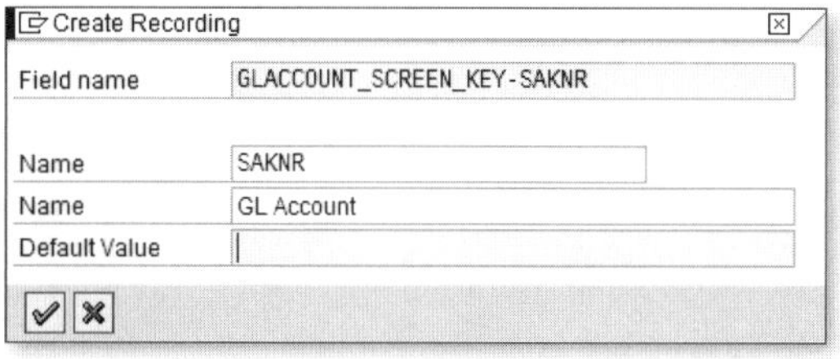

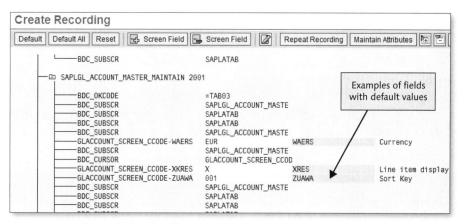

Figure 7.10 Assign Name to Activity

Begin by entering the Field Name; the first Name field is called SAKNR. In the second Name field, enter a description; here we used "GL Account." If you're dealing with a field that is to remain constant, you can enter a default value here. For example, you may want to define a default value for the sort key; in this case, enter "003" into the Default Value field. This activity needs to be completed for all fields. Figure 7.11 shows some examples of where we have assigned default values for fields.

Figure 7.11 Define Default Values for Activities

After all of the fields are defined, you can save the recording. A confirmation that your recording has been saved is displayed by the system. Use the green back arrow to return to the front. This completes the maintain object settings (Figure 7.12).

Figure 7.12 Completion of Maintenance of Object

You have now successfully defined your object, which is the target. Next you must maintain the source structure, which is the source of your data.

7.2.3 Maintain Source Structure

In this step (Figure 7.13), we define the source structure, which is simply identifying a placeholder for what will be your load file.

Click the CREATE button, and then enter the details of your source file. In our example (Figure 7.14), we named the source structure "LOAD_FILE" as it needs to be a single word.

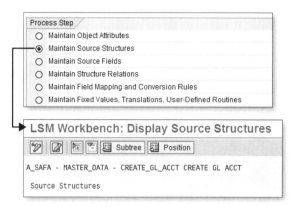

Figure 7.13 Change Source Structure

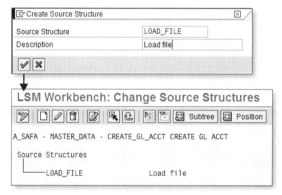

Figure 7.14 Link Source Structure to Load File

This is all we need to do for this step. Next, we maintain the source fields, which are the beginning of the source structure.

7.2.4 Maintain Source Fields

When you double-click this option from the task list, you're taken back into the source structure you defined in the previous step. From this screen, you go to the definition of the source fields, as shown in Figure 7.15.

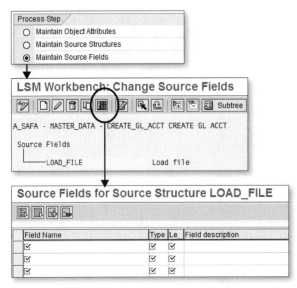

Figure 7.15 Define Source Fields

The source fields should be a list of the fields that are contained within the source structure (or source file) and should be the exact same list and order that was defined during the recording. You will eventually need to create a data load file (usually through Excel) and that load file needs to be in the same order and structure. We discuss this later in the chapter.

For each field (as shown in Figure 7.15), you need to assign the type of field (C), the field length, and a description. After you enter all this information, save your changes, and you can see the full list of fields that have been entered.

From the TYPE dropdown list, you can see different field types that you may choose to use (including N for numeric-only content). C works for most items, but you should always test out LSMW before you use it for a real load.

If you're creating a recording for uploading transactions, you may decide to use a different field type for some fields. When you have entered values for each field of the load file and saved the settings, you are finished with this step (see Figure 7.16).

With this step, you have completed the major aspects involved in configuring the program. As we mentioned at the start of this process, it's possible to link many recordings to a single transaction. In the next step, we link the recording to the load file.

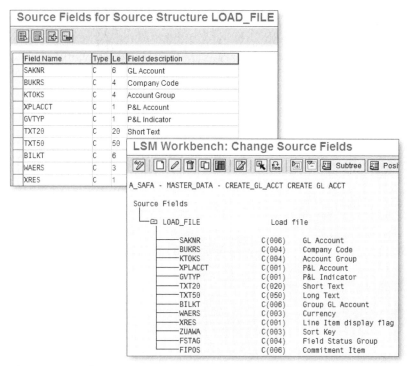

Figure 7.16 Finalize Source Fields

7.2.5 Maintain Structure Relations

In this step, we link the source structure to the load file by simply clicking the CRE-ATE RELATIONSHIP button. Because you only have a single source file and a single load file, this is simple to complete, as shown in Figure 7.17.

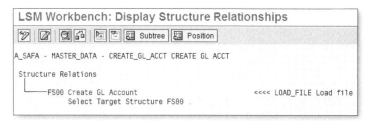

Figure 7.17 Change Structure Relationships

The next step is to map the fields between the load file and the upload program.

7.2.6 Maintain Field Mapping and Conversion Rules

This activity is where you link the information in the load file to the appropriate field on the general ledger master record. Although one-to-one mapping is available, the LSMW program can automatically enter a conversion routine as part of the upload.

In our example (Figure 7.18), we are simply taking the value from the load file to the master record. To do this, select the field in the source system that you have previously defined, click CREATE SOURCE FIELD, and then select the field to which it is mapped. If you've followed the steps so far, you have used the same naming conventions for the source fields as the load file fields.

When this is done, you'll additional information for each line. The default rule being applied to each field is a transfer (move), which means that the value is simply taken from one location to another. It is possible here to define conversions based on simple logic and code. For our purposes, we only need to do a simple mapping without any conversion.

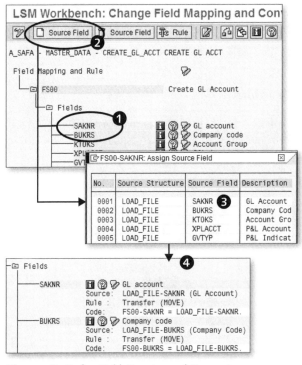

Figure 7.18 Define Field Mapping and Conversions

This mapping needs to be completed for all fields. After this is complete, you can save and move onto the next stage.

7.2.7 Maintain Fixed Values, Translations, and User-Defined Routines

We can skip over this step because we do not need to define any fixed values. If you did need a fixed value or translation, then you add these here (see Figure 7.19).

LSM Workbench:Fixed Values,Translations
Subtree
Reusable Rules
A_SAFA
SAFA
Fixed Values
Translations
User-Defined Routines

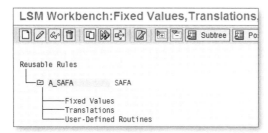

Figure 7.19 Define Fixed Values, Translations, and Routines

7.2.8 Specify Files

In this activity, you specify the file locations for the LSMW program. There are two sets of files needed here. First, you need to define files internal to the program, which are used during the processing of data. For this, you define files for imported data and for the conversion of data. The program provides default files for these based on the project and subproject name, which you should accept (see Figure 7.20).

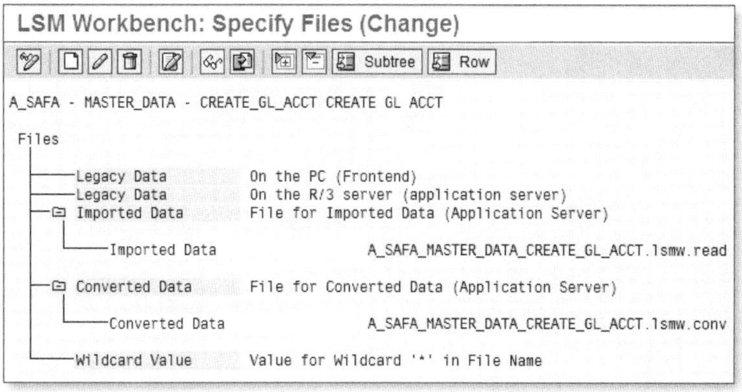

LSM Workbench: Specify Files (Change)
Subtree
Row
A_SAFA - MASTER_DATA - CREATE_GL_ACCT CREATE GL ACCT
Files
Legacy Data
On the PC (Frontend)
Legacy Data
On the R/3 server (application server)
Imported Data
File for Imported Data (Application Server)
Imported Data
A_SAFA_MASTER_DATA_CREATE_GL_ACCT.lsmw.read
Converted Data
File for Converted Data (Application Server)
Converted Data
A_SAFA_MASTER_DATA_CREATE_GL_ACCT.lsmw.conv
Wildcard Value
Value for Wildcard '*' in File Name

Figure 7.20 Specify Files

The next file you need to specify is the location of the load file. There are two available options here: You either upload the data from your PC (which could be a local drive or a network drive), or you upload from the application server (not recommended for our purposes). You can make changes to this file location at a later stage; the easiest approach here is to create a folder on your PC's directory structure where you will usually place the load files.

To do this, double-click the LEGACY DATA box, which relates to the PC (frontend). Next, click in the dropdown menu to search for the file location. When you locate the folder you want to use, enter a filename that you will also use; in our example, we use a file called GL1.txt (this is the location and filename from where we will upload our data, and we prefer to use the txt format even though we use Excel to create the data — this is explained later). This process is shown in Figure 7.21, as can the other settings that need to be made.

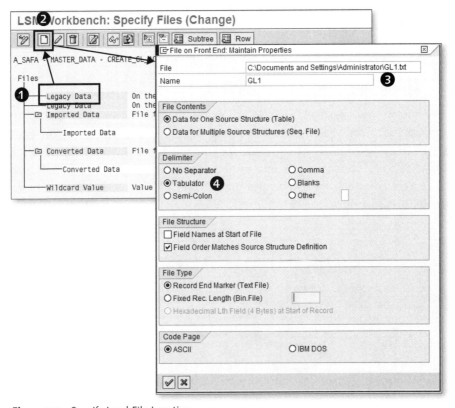

Figure 7.21 Specify Load File Location

You must define the file in the text format and as a tabulator delimited file because this is the upload format we will use.

Save these options, and return to the Workbench screen. When you go into the next activity, Assign Files, you will see that the file you specified in the previous step has already been assigned (Figure 7.22).

Figure 7.22 Assign Files

You have now completed the configuration of your LSMW program. Let's now look at the steps involved in running the program to upload data.

7.2.9   Create Load File

You should now look at the creation of your load file because this needs to be created in line with the specifications you made in the program (see the order defined in the source structure). For certain fields where you are required to check a box (in our example, we selected Line Item Display, P&L Type, etc.), you need to enter an (uppercase) "X" in that cell. As you can see from Figure 7.23, we have created this data in Excel format. Then, when we save the data, we convert it into a text file format.

Complete all of the information as correct in the system. If you leave any header information in your load file, be aware of it because you don't want to upload it. When you are happy that your load data is correct, you should first save the file as the correct spreadsheet format, and then as a text (tab-delimited) format. You should also be saving this in the same location and with the filename you entered previously in the LSMW *specify file* configuration step.

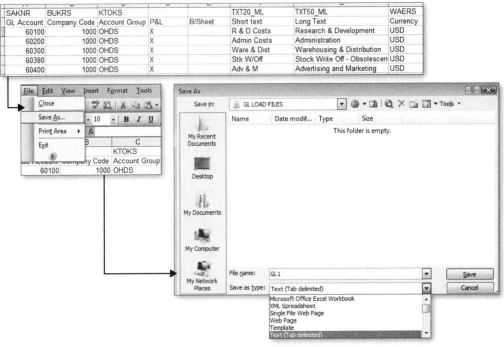

Figure 7.23 Create Load File as Tab Delimited

When your load file is ready, you can start the loading process. The loading process happens in three stages: First, you upload the data into the LSMW, then you transfer that data into a batch session, and, finally, you run the batch session (which performs the actual creation steps).

7.2.10 Upload Load File Data

To begin, go into the READ DATA activity (Figure 7.24). You have already specified the load file, so now when you go into this activity, the program upload from that specified location.

The program asks you which records should be uploaded. If you have left two rows of header information in the load file, remember to exclude them here. So, if your total number of records in the load file is 500, plus the 2 header records, you should import transactions 3 to 502. (The easiest thing to do is to not save any header rows in the load file. In that scenario, you can leave the transaction numbers blank, and the program will upload all of the records.)

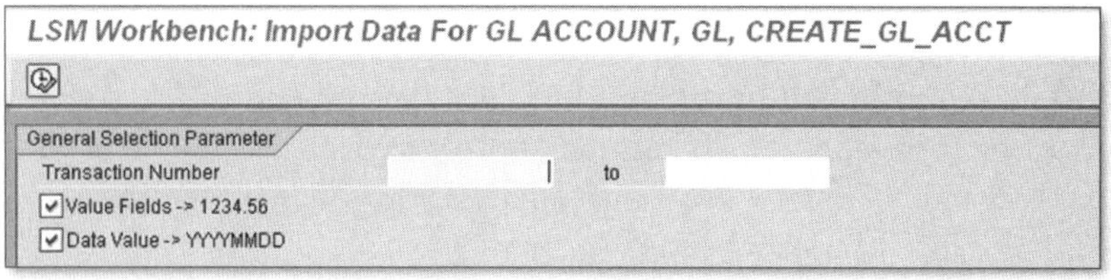

LSM Workbench: Import Data For GL ACCOUNT, GL, CREATE_GL_ACCT

General Selection Parameter

Transaction Number | to

☑ Value Fields -> 1234.56
☑ Data Value -> YYYYMMDD

Figure 7.24   Import Data

You will receive a confirmation message saying the number of records that have been uploaded upon completion (Figure 7.25).

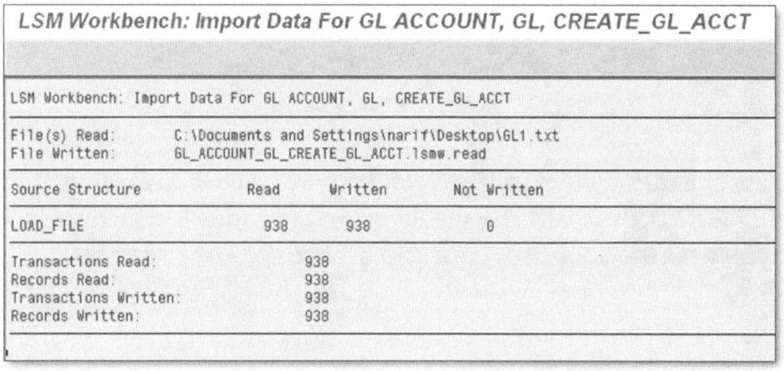

LSM Workbench: Import Data For GL ACCOUNT, GL, CREATE_GL_ACCT

```
LSM Workbench: Import Data For GL ACCOUNT, GL, CREATE_GL_ACCT

File(s) Read:        C:\Documents and Settings\narif\Desktop\GL1.txt
File Written:        GL_ACCOUNT_GL_CREATE_GL_ACCT.lsmw.read

Source Structure          Read       Written        Not Written

LOAD_FILE                  938         938              0

Transactions Read:         938
Records Read:              938
Transactions Written:      938
Records Written:           938
```

Figure 7.25   Import Data Confirmation

If you return to the LSM WORKBENCH screen, you can now display read data, which allows you to check the data that has been imported.

The next step is to convert data, which is when any conversions you defined are applied to the load data. Although we have not specified any conversions in our example, this step still needs to be completed. On both the import step and the conversion step, the program stores the information in temporary file locations. After the conversion step, you can display the converted data. At a minimum, you should check the first record, a record in the middle, and the last record against your original load file.

When you are satisfied that the correct data has been imported and converted, you should proceed to the create batch input session step.

7.2.11 Create Batch Input Session

This step transfers the information that was produced at the end of the convert data step into a batch session, which includes both the data and the steps you defined in your recording (Figure 7.26). This batch session will be processed using Transaction SM35, which you may be familiar with.

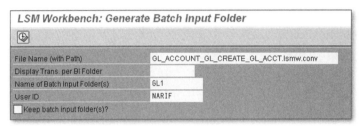

Figure 7.26 Generate Batch File

Here you should specify the name of the batch folder (you can use any convention that suits your purpose). The user ID is available, so you can sort the batch folders by user ID. Click the KEEP BATCH INPUT FOLDERS? checkbox to keep a record of the session that was run.

7.2.12 Run Batch Session

You can run the batch input session from this activity (see Figure 7.27), or you can go directly to Transaction SM35. Here, you can see your session, as shown in Figure 7.27.

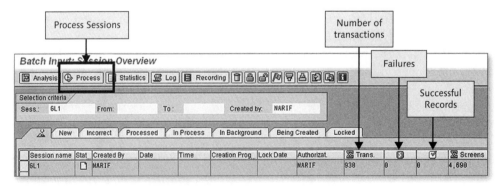

Figure 7.27 Process Batch Session

Select your session, and click the PROCESS button. Your processing options are as follows:

▶ FOREGROUND

With this option, actions are performed live on the screen. You must press Enter on each screen to move forward.

▶ DISPLAY ERRORS ONLY

With this option, the batch session keeps running and only stops when there is an error. You can then fix the error and press Enter, and the program will continue to run until it hits its next error.

▶ BACKGROUND

With this option, the session is run in the background and does not show errors. When the session is complete, you can look in the error log to retrieve the error messages, and then decide what to do to correct the error records.

In our experience, the DISPLAY ERRORS ONLY option is the most effective because you can fix the errors immediately and ensure your file is loaded. If you run a large file in the background, it's a bit messy trying to understand the errors and then fix them manually.

7.3 Making Your Vendor/Customer Line Item Reports Work for You

In this special topic, we explain how to make changes to the line item display reports in Financial Accounting (FI) to enhance the information available to you. We specifically focus on the customer and vendor line item reports because these reports are where you'll use this functionality most often, although the same changes are applicable to the general ledger line item report (FBL3N or FAGLL03).

We show examples from both the customer line item display (Transaction FBL5N) and vendor line item display (Transaction FBL1N) because this topic is applicable to both. SAP ERP has provided this standard functionality, which is very useful when you want to see more details about the vendors in that screen. To make the changes in the header data, use the following menu path: SAP EASY ACCESS • ACCOUNTING • FINANCIAL ACCOUNTING • VENDORS • ACCOUNT • DISPLAY/CHANGE LINE ITEMS (Transaction FBL1N).

In the vendor line item display screen, enter the vendor number or range of vendor numbers and other relevant details to display the open items, cleared items, or all items. Then click the EXECUTE button. In the next screen, select SETTINGS • LAYOUT • CURRENT HEADER ROWS (Figure 7.28).

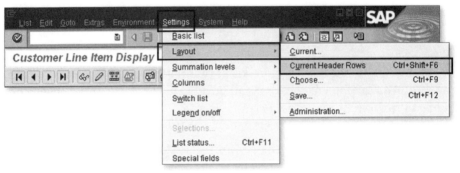

Figure 7.28 Change Current Header Rows for Vendor Line Item Display

Let's consider a scenario where you want to add a vendor's telephone number to the header. First, put the cursor at the place where you want to define the telephone number, and type in the description of the information you want to display. At the end of the description — that is, where you want to display the telephone number — place the cursor, and then click the GEN. VARIABLES button (Figure 7.29).

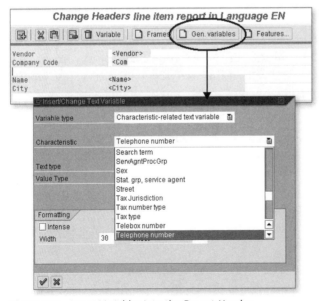

Figure 7.29 Insert Variables into the Report Header

From this screen, you can find the vendor telephone number, and the system will return this information from the vendor master record. For each variable you select, you can define whether you return the value or the description. For example, you may want to show the vendor's default payment terms as part of the header. You can decide here whether to see the short code (e.g., PAYMENT TERM = Z014) or the short text (14 days). This is a simple way of bringing in those fields that are useful for reporting. Think about which pieces of information need to be on this screen to enable your purchase ledger clerk or credit controller to do their jobs. With this in mind, let's look at an example of the customer line item report.

Figure 7.30 shows an example of a complex layout for customer line item display. In this particular case, users found that having this layout, which showed all of the customer information on the same screen, was a huge benefit when dealing with customer phone calls.

| Change Headers Customer line item report in Language EN | | | | | | |

Customer		\<Customer\> \<Com	No of items	\<Numbe
			Payment terms	\<Payme
Name		\<Name\>	Alt Payee	\<Alternati / \<Alternati
		\<Street\>	Contact No	\<Telephone number\> / \<Acct.clerks tel
		\<City\>	Fax no	\<Fax Number\>
		\<Postal Co	Contact Person	\<User at custom
			Email	\<Clrk's internet add.\>
Reconciliation Account		\<Reconciliation acct[Long text]\>		

Figure 7.30 Example of a Customer Line Item Layout

As explained previously, you can bring information into the header from either vendor/customer master records or from the selection parameters.

In the next section, we discuss additional settings that can be made to line item reports.

7.3.1 Changing Line Item Layout in Reports

Here we'll explain how to change the format of the screen layout when a report is run. We'll use the same transaction code to explain these settings. From the application tool bar, click the CHANGE LAYOUT button (Figure 7.31).

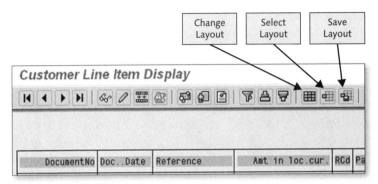

Figure 7.31 Changing the Line Item Display

As you can see, there are fields on both the left and right side. The fields on the left side of this window show the layout as it stands at present, and the fields on the right side show the total list of fields available for us to include in the layout.

On this same menu bar, you can see other settings, including filter and sort, both which maybe useful when wanting to analyze a customer's account. These settings can also be saved into the layout. For example, if you want to run the line item report for a specific document type only, you can include this in the filter option and save the layout.

When you're happy with the selection of the correct fields in your layout, you can save the layout. You can make it a personal setting, so only you can see it, or you can save it so everyone can see it.

7.3.2 Defaulting Layouts into a User's Profile

If you want to default this layout into any user's profile so that it automatically appears when the user runs the report, execute Transaction FB00 (Figure 7.32). The ACCOUNTING EDITING OPTIONS screen appears with multiple tabs. Select the LINE ITEMS tab, and, in the VENDOR LAYOUT section, enter the layout you saved in the previous step. Save your settings. The next time the user uses the line item display screen, the saved layout will automatically appear on the screen.

You can also make this a default setting through a parameter ID into user IDs, which is useful if you want to set up default layouts and ensure all your users use them. Your user administration team would make this type of change for you. For SAP General Ledger, FI line items report the parameter ID as FIT_ALV_FAGL_GL. Your security and authorizations team would create a full list of IDs.

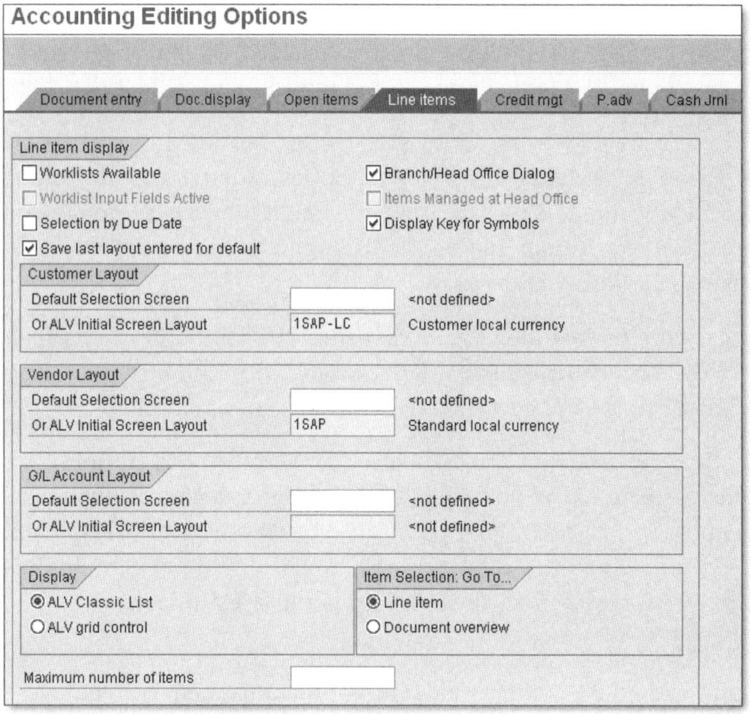

Accounting Editing Options

| Document entry | Doc.display | Open items | Line items | Credit mgt | P.adv | Cash Jrnl |

Line item display

☐ Worklists Available   ☑ Branch/Head Office Dialog

☐ Worklist Input Fields Active   ☐ Items Managed at Head Office

☐ Selection by Due Date   ☑ Display Key for Symbols

☑ Save last layout entered for default

Customer Layout

| Default Selection Screen | | <not defined> |
| Or ALV Initial Screen Layout | 1SAP-LC | Customer local currency |

Vendor Layout

| Default Selection Screen | | <not defined> |
| Or ALV Initial Screen Layout | 1SAP | Standard local currency |

G/L Account Layout

| Default Selection Screen | | <not defined> |
| Or ALV Initial Screen Layout | | <not defined> |

Display

◉ ALV Classic List   Item Selection: Go To...

○ ALV grid control   ◉ Line item

                      ○ Document overview

Maximum number of items

Figure 7.32   Defaulting Layouts in User IDs

7.4   Enforcing Additional Organization Checks by Configuring Your Own Validations

In this special topic, we explain the concept of defining validations in SAP ERP systems. *Validations* are additional controls that you may want to put into place to control something specific to your own organizational design. These validations are specific to your organization, and as a result, SAP ERP does not deliver these as part of the standard solution set but instead provides you the tools you need to build your own.

In this topic, we define a very simplistic validation. When you are comfortable with defining a validation, you can define anything that can be expressed in a logical statement. You can also make use of Z-tables (custom SAP ERP tables) to store variables, which you can include in your validation logic statements.

A validation is triggered when defined conditions are met, so they are additional checks over and above what SAP ERP has already provided. A validation checks settings according to certain predefined criteria and returns a message if the check condition is fulfilled.

In the following example, we define an FI validation that requires an entry in the TEXT field whenever a document is posted using document type SA. Although you could have done this same setting in the standard configuration, we used the validation method to explain how this works.

To define the validation, use the following menu path: IMG • FINANCIAL ACCOUNTING (NEW) • FINANCIAL ACCOUNTING GLOBAL SETTINGS (NEW) • TOOLS • VALIDATION/ SUBSTITUTIONS • VALIDATION IN ACCOUNTING DOCUMENTS (Transaction OB28).

In the initial screen of Transaction OB28, select the NEW ENTRIES button. This takes you to the next screen, where you enter the company code and call-up point. Double-click the entry, which takes take you to the CHANGE VALIDATION screen. Call-up points determine when the validation is run, and different call-up points are available for different areas. In FI, three call-up points are available:

▶ **0001: Document Header**
This call-up point is used for setting validations at the document header level.

▶ **0002: Line Items**
This call-up point is used for setting validations at the line item level.

▶ **0003: Complete Documents**
This call-up point validates the whole document and is triggered after the document is completed (or saved).

In Figure 7.33, you can see that we decided to create our validation at the line item level (because the TEXT field is on the line item).

Click the VALIDATION button available on the screen (Figure 7.33), and enter the validation name and its brief description on the right-hand side of the screen. A new folder appears under the LINE ITEM section. Select that folder, and click the STEP button to enter the logic of the check that will be carried out as part of this validation. You can choose to enter numerous steps within a single validation, which could each represent many business rules. Alternatively, you can set up a new validation for each business rule.

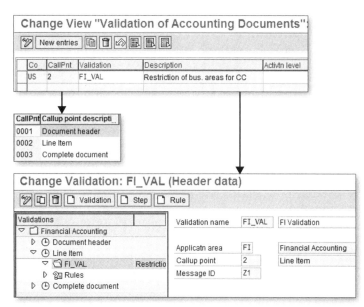

Figure 7.33 Create Validation (Header)

Within a step, you'll notice that you now have three activities:

▶ PREREQUISITE
Here you define what the system needs to look for before a validation check can be run (i.e., the trigger).

▶ CHECK
This is the check logic itself, where we say that if the prerequisite meets the criteria, then this particular check should be carried out.

▶ MESSAGE
This is where we tell the system what type of message should be returned if the check is unsuccessful.

We explain each activity next.

7.4.1 Define Prerequisites

To define prerequisites, see Figure 7.34, which shows the steps you need to follow. First we select PREREQUISITE, and then double-click the accounting document header because we want to set this validation on the document type SA for the TEXT field. This brings up all of the available fields for the accounting document header, one of which is DOCUMENT TYPE. When you select the DOCUMENT TYPE field, it appears on the upper portion of the screen, which means that the first part of the prerequisite is selected. You know that the validation check is for a constant value, so click the = button on the screen, and then select the constant value of SA in the pop-up window. This completes your setting for the prerequisite.

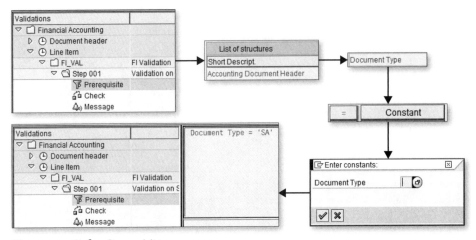

Figure 7.34 Define Prerequisite

After the prerequisite condition is met, this triggers the check (or the validation).

7.4.2 Define Checks

Now let's discuss the validation check. Select CHECK, and then select the accounting document header to find the field for TEXT because we want that field to be entered every time the document type SA is used. Double-click the document header text, and it appears on the upper portion of the screen. Select the arrow buttons (< >) to reflect that the TEXT field should be filled, and not left blank. Then click the Constant button. When the pop-up box appears, press ⌊Enter⌋ (Figure 7.35). This establishes that the field for the document header text should not be left blank. After this change, the green signal appears on the status, which shows that the check has been defined successfully. After completing the check in the validation, you can set the message that will be returned if the TEXT field is not supplied.

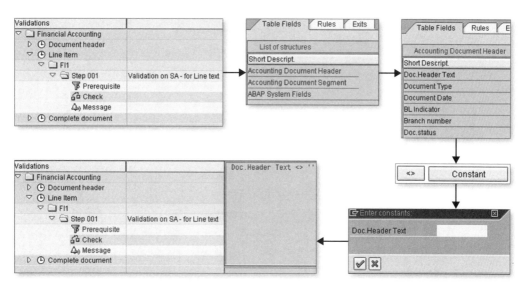

Figure 7.35 Define Check (Validation) Step

Now that you've defined the check, you can define what action needs to take place if the check is unsuccessful, that is, in this example, if the header text is not supplied.

7.4.3 Define the Message

You now need to define the message settings, where you first decide what type of message the user receives if the validation check is unsuccessful. First of all, decide what type of message you want to issue: an error message, a warning message, or an information message. In our case, we want an error message that can't be bypassed so you have to correct the error before you continue. Neither a warning nor an information message will stop a transaction from proceeding.

When choosing your message, you can select a standard message from the system-defined messages. Alternatively, you may want to define your own message, which is done by selecting the CHANGE MESSAGE CLASS option (Figure 7.36).

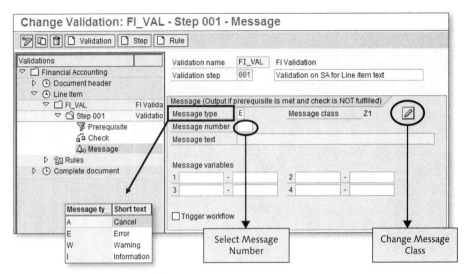

Figure 7.36 Define Message Class Settings

Figure 7.37 gives an example of a user-defined message.

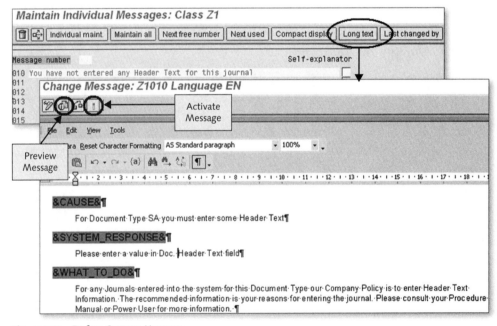

Figure 7.37 Define Custom Message

This completes our configuration of the validation. As you exit out of the validation, you need to ensure that at the header level, the validation is activated. When you do this (as per Figure 7.38), make sure to save because this needs to be included in the transport request. Note that you need to save to a customizing request (normal transport request) as well as a workbench request (as per Figure 7.38) — both need to be transported to successfully move the validation between clients.

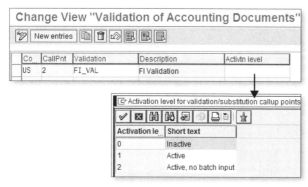

Figure 7.38 Activation of Validation

Next we look at the configuration of a substitution, which is similar to a validation.

7.5   Using Substitutions to Allocate Default Account Assignment Objects

In this special topic, we explain the concept of defining substitutions in an SAP ERP system. The definition of substitutions is very similar to validations; the only difference is the availability of fields that can be validated in these areas. Substitutions are used to replace values if a certain criterion is met, based on your definition of the logic.

In this example, we are going to define a substitution in FI that looks for a specific general ledger account and replaces the value of the cost center entered with a different, constant cost center as defined in this substitution. To define the substitution, use the following menu path: IMG • FINANCIAL ACCOUNTING (NEW) • FINAN-

CIAL ACCOUNTING GLOBAL SETTINGS (NEW) • TOOLS • VALIDATION/SUBSTITUTIONS • SUBSTITUTION IN ACCOUNTING DOCUMENTS (TRANSACTION OBBH).

In the initial screen, select the NEW ENTRIES button, and it takes you to the next screen, where you enter the company code and call-up point. Double-click that entry, and it takes you to the CHANGE SUBSTITUTION OVERVIEW screen. Call-up points determine when the substitution is run, and there are different call-up points available for different areas. In FI, three call-up points are available:

▶ **0001: Document Header**
This call-up point is used for setting substitutions at the document header level.

▶ **0002: Line Items**
This call-up point is used for setting substitutions at the line items level.

▶ **0003: Complete Documents**
This call-up point checks the whole document.

Figure 7.39 shows that we are setting up this substitution at the line item level. Click the SUBSTITUTION button, and enter the substitution name and its brief description on the right-hand side of the screen.

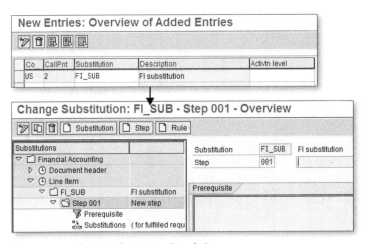

Figure 7.39 Change Substitution (Header)

A new folder appears under the LINE ITEM section. Select that folder, and click the STEP button to enter the logic of the check that is carried out as part of this substitution. A window appears with substitutable fields. As per our example, we select the cost center field and want it to be substituted with a constant value (Figure 7.40).

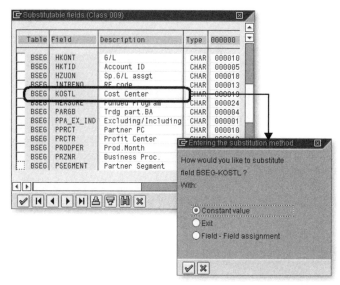

Figure 7.40 Select Field for Substitution

Within that step, notice that you now have two levels:

▶ PREREQUISITE
Define what the system needs to look for before a substitution can be performed.

▶ SUBSTITUTION
Define which value should replace the entered value.

7.5.1 Prerequisite

Select PREREQUISITE, and then double-click the ACCOUNTING DOCUMENT SEGMENT section to set this substitution on a specific general ledger account. This brings up all of the available fields on the accounting document segment, one of which is a general ledger account. You can also use the search option available on this screen to find the general ledger field more quickly. When you double-click the field, it appears on the upper portion of the screen, which means that the first part of the prerequisite is selected. You know that the substitution check is for a constant value, so click the = button on the screen, and then select the constant value of the general ledger account from the pop-up window (Figure 7.41). This completes our setting for the prerequisite.

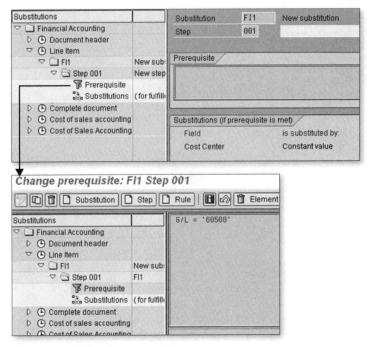

Figure 7.41 Define the Prerequisite

7.5.2 Substitution

In the next step (Figure 7.42), we introduce the substitution value. Select SUBSTI-TUTION, and you see that the COST CENTER field is available with a blank constant value field. Set the flag for the cost center, and enter the constant value of the cost center that you want to substitute when the specific general ledger account mentioned previously is entered in the system.

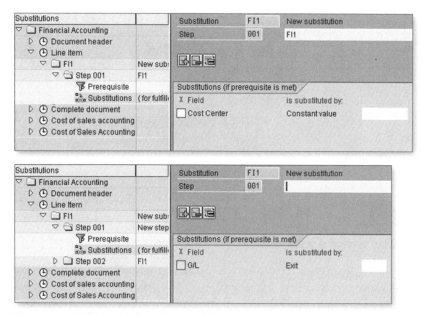

Figure 7.42 Substitution by a Constant Value or a User Exit

In our example in Figure 7.42, we substituted a fixed value, but as you saw earlier, you can also trigger a user exit. A user exit is a piece of ABAP code that you define.

Now that you have completed the definition of your substitution, you need to save it and save its assignment to the company code. When you save, make sure it's saved with an ACTIVE status in your transport request. Again, you need to save to both a customizing transport and a workbench transport (Figure 7.43). Both need to be transported to enable this to work.

With this, we complete our review of the validation and substitution tools, which are additional controls you can bring into your SAP ERP system to meet some specific local requirements. You can also define validations in other areas of the system; in the next section, we look at another place where you can make use of validations and substitutions.

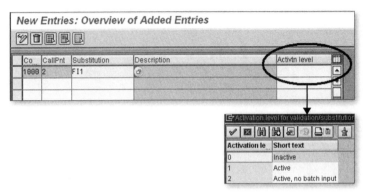

Figure 7.43 Activation of Your Substitution

7.5.3 Validations and Substitutions in Asset Accounting

The validations and substitutions we have seen so far work for Financials postings. You can also set these up elsewhere in the system — for instance, in Asset Accounting (AA), you may want to define rules about the creation of master data. We have found this particularly useful because AA is a complex area where it is important to maintain controls. It is sufficient to say here that these controls are managed in the IMG, as shown in Figure 7.44. The actual configuration of the controls is the same as discussed in the previous sections.

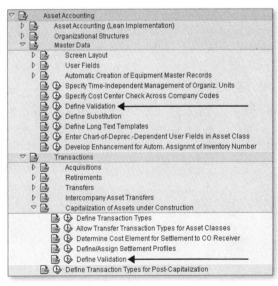

Figure 7.44 Validations and Substitutions in Asset Accounting

7.6   Summary

This special topics chapter is a bonus chapter that gives a selection of additional topics that will help you deliver additional benefit to your SAP ERP implementation. We included a small selection of topics that we thought would be most useful and would give you more advanced skills to supplement your configuration knowledge.

The Authors

 **Naeem Arif** worked on his first SAP project, on 3.0h, in 1995. Since then he has progressed through a variety of roles, completing 14 end-to-end implementations for some of the biggest organizations in the world. In addition, he has an MBA, a post graduate degree in Technology Management, and is certified in Prince2 (Practitioner), making him a well-respected subject matter expert in the SAP industry. Naeem has spent the last four years with Service Birmingham, where he currently manages the delivery of SAP ERP Financials service to more than 10,000 users, covering the FI, CO, MM, SD, and PLM modules.

 **Tauseef Sheikh Muhammad** is a highly experienced SAP consultant who has been involved in more than a dozen international SAP projects across North America, Europe, and Asia. He is experienced in all of the core components and subcomponents of Financial Accounting and Controlling, going back to the early 4.x releases of R/3. During his more than 10 years of SAP experience, Tauseef has enjoyed working in many different roles, including functional consultant, lead consultant, SAP Academy trainer, and subject matter expert. Tauseef, who is also a chartered accountant, is currently working with Smith & Nephew, Inc. as a senior FICO analyst on the company's global SAP implementation team.

Index

Interested in reading more?

Please visit our Web site for all
new book releases from SAP PRESS.

www.sap-press.com